CLAYTN-HQS STACKS
31012000479988
347.
The

W9-BZW-469

/ -3

CLAYTON COUNTY LIBRARY
865 Battlecreek Road
Jonesboro, Ga 30236

DISCARDED

The Rehnquist Court

The Rehnquist Court

JUDICIAL ACTIVISM ON THE RIGHT

Edited by Herman Schwartz

CLAYTON COUNTY LIBRARY
865 Battlecreek Road
Jonesboro, Ga 30236

HILL AND WANG

A DIVISION OF FARRAR, STRAUS AND GIROUX

NEW YORK

Hill and Wang
A division of Farrar, Straus and Giroux
19 Union Square West, New York 10003

Copyright © 2002 by Herman Schwartz
All rights reserved
Distributed in Canada by Douglas & McIntyre Ltd.
Printed in the United States of America
First edition, 2002

Library of Congress Cataloging-in-Publication Data
The Rehnquist court : judicial activism on the right / edited by Herman Schwartz.
    p. cm.
    Includes index.
    ISBN 0-8090-8073-7 (hbk. : alk. paper)
    1. United States. Supreme Court.   2. Rehnquist, William H., 1924–   3. Conservatism—
United States.   4. Judicial process—Political aspects—United States.   I. Schwartz, Herman,
1931–

KF8742.A5 R44 2002
347.73'2635—dc21

              2002068670

Designed by Jonathan D. Lippincott

www.fsgbooks.com

10 9 8 7 6 5 4 3 2 1

To Justice William J. Brennan
who brought this nation a little closer to
"liberty and justice for all"

Contents

Acknowledgments

ı

It is always a pleasure to record acknowledgments, especially since this is usually done when the book is at long last completed. In this case, it is especially pleasurable because it provides an opportunity to thank the many contributors to this volume. These hardy souls had to endure editing that was at times overly enthusiastic, had to meet pressing deadlines despite heavy schedules of their own, and even had to put up with my computer crashing. All who wrote for this book showed a remarkable patience, for which I am very grateful.

I would also like to express my appreciation to my initial editor, Elisabeth Sifton, whose encouragement and support got the book off the ground. Those who know Elisabeth are familiar with the way she provides her authors not only with the benefits of her professional experience and wisdom but also with the great pleasure of working with someone uniquely delightful and intellectually stimulating.

My second editor, Thomas LeBien, who came into the project toward its end, was also very helpful. His familiarity with the material from his previous work enabled him to take on the project without skipping a beat. His guidance in the endgame of putting the book together was invaluable.

I also want to acknowledge the support and personal friendship of Katrina vanden Heuvel, editor of *The Nation*, where shorter versions of some of these essays first appeared. Her willingness to devote virtually an entire issue of *The Nation* to those earlier pieces got the project started, and her enthusiastic backing for this book enabled it to go forward expeditiously.

As in almost every one of my publishing ventures, my agent, Milly Marmur, has been a treasure. For some fifteen years she has been not only a wise counselor, guiding me through the labyrinth of book publishing—this time through the special maze of putting together a book written mostly by others—but also a dear friend and confidante. I am deeply grateful that she has been willing to labor so tirelessly for someone who could add so little to her balance sheet.

I would also like to express my profound gratitude to my dean and dear friend, Claudio Grossman. He has been ever supportive, not just with financial support for summer grants and other assistance but with encouragement and creative suggestions whenever opportunities or problems have developed.

And finally, as always, to Mary, my wife of over four decades, who makes it all possible.

The Rehnquist Court

Foreword:

Reflections of a Court Watcher

TOM WICKER

The Supreme Court of the United States, a uniquely elitist institution in a democratic nation, is such an accepted part of American life that in the 2000 election it was able without much protest to force the choice of a president who had lost the popular vote. If the justices can choose the president, it's hard to imagine what future decision they might make that would call forth effective resistance, much less political or constitutional retribution. And if *that's* the case, might it not be fair to say that virtually anything the Supreme Court does—short of ordering surrender in a time of war—is now acceptable to the American people? Maybe not. Many traumatic decisions likely await the Court's attention—on abortion, on affirmative action, on civil liberties, which are newly threatened by the war on terrorism. And the makeup of the Court—no longer "nine old men" but seven suits and two skirts—could change in such a way as to be less palatable to the public. Still, in the wake of the Supreme Court's unprecedented—some would say unwarranted, but certainly unchallenged—crowning of George W. Bush as president, this proposition seems justified.

Americans now accept the authority of the Supreme Court's nine unelected, life-tenured justices as readily as they accept the laws passed by their chosen representatives in Congress and signed by the president. Perhaps more readily, because a law can be repealed more easily and rapidly than practically any Supreme Court constitutional decision can be overturned.

If the Court, therefore, ever was in practice something less than decreed by the Constitution, it is now in fact a coequal branch of the government, right up there with Congress and the executive. Indeed, its perch might be just a tad higher, for it is even better able to make its judgments stick.

Two examples from history of disputed but ultimately effective Court rulings provide a context within which to judge contemporary concerns:

In 1830, a time when conflict between Indians and whites still flamed on the American frontier, the state of Georgia prohibited white men from entering "Indian country" without a license. The law, as usual in those days, was designed not to protect Indians but to answer the complaints of whites; they wanted the "racial agitators" of that day to be prevented from inciting the Cherokees to resist state laws. Two white violators, sentenced to four years at hard labor, took an appeal all the way to the Supreme Court of the United States. On March 1, 1832, Chief Justice John Marshall and his Court declared unconstitutional, "void and of no effect" *all* the laws of Georgia dealing with the Cherokee nation and ordered the two appellants freed.[1]

President Andrew Jackson, who favored the Georgia laws and was planning to deport the Eastern Indian tribes to reservations west of the Mississippi, is supposed to have replied: "Well, John Marshall has made his decision. Now let him enforce it."

Echoing down the decades, that story has exemplified Jackson's imperious style and, not too many years ago, was quoted by any number of Southern diehards to justify their resistance to court-ordered school desegregation. Unfortunately for them, Jackson said no such thing—though his biographer, Robert V. Remini, concedes that the statement *sounds* like Old Hickory and may even reflect his thoughts.

Jackson was already in conflict with South Carolina over tariff nullification, however, and eager to avoid a controversy in another state. So he quietly pulled a few strings, privately nudged Georgia officials, and within the year the imprisoned men were freed. The Supreme

Court was "upheld"—at least its ruling was made effective, however belatedly.

More than a century later, Chief Justice Earl Warren and his Court delivered a ruling confounding a large share of public opinion and overturning what had been understood as established law, and again it did so without support from the White House. In 1954, the Court unanimously declared in *Brown v. Board of Education of Topeka, Kansas* that racial segregation of the public schools, as then practiced in seventeen states and in certain school districts of four others, was unconstitutional.[2]

In those states, mostly Southern, the decision caused an uproar. President Dwight D. Eisenhower, who personally disapproved of the ruling, told a news conference only that he was duty bound to support a decision that he conceded had become "the law of the land." For the rest of his first term, however, and for all of his second, he failed to do so. He simply stood silent on the issue, not even acting behind the scenes to produce compliance as Jackson had done in 1832. Quite the opposite: according to Warren's memoirs, Eisenhower at a private dinner party took ex parte action to head off what became the *Brown* ruling.

The ruling nevertheless was issued, and despite all outcry, progress in desegregation proceeded—though at less than a snail's pace and despite various forms of defiance. Not until 1957 did that defiance become flagrant enough to require the president to enforce the Court's ruling.

Governor Orval Faubus of Arkansas had called out his state's National Guard to prevent the court-ordered admission of nine black children to Little Rock Central High School. Even after a personal meeting with Eisenhower, Faubus refused to back down; worse, he called off his National Guard, creating a real potential for violence and loss of life as crowds of angry citizens converged on the school. Only then did the president finally send in *his* troops, the 101st Airborne Division. He also federalized the Arkansas guardsmen so they were no longer under Faubus's control. The admission of the nine black youngsters finally was achieved.

In his memoirs, Attorney General Herbert Brownell said he believed that the president's "decisive action" meant that "eventual enforcement of *Brown* was assured." Depending on what the meaning of the word *eventual* is, that was true; on opening day in 1970, thirteen years later, the South's old dual school system, predicated on the "separate but equal" doctrine, had mostly disappeared, at least legally. De facto school segregation remains a virulent fact today, particularly in large cities across the nation and particularly in the South.

The stories of these two decisions vividly illustrate, in their different ways, the strengths of the Supreme Court rather than any supposed weakness. They establish the fact that the Court's unelected, life-term justices define what the Constitution means and thereby establish principles of law that most elected bodies would not be willing to consider or propound. Just as the white legislature of Georgia was obeying the mandate of that state's voters in 1832, most legislative bodies are usually too well aware of the next election to defy public opinion; and just as the Marshall Court of 1832 did not have to fear being voted out of office, the Warren Court of 1954 was able—as its successors have been—to act on constitutional "principle" rather than out of fear of vox populi.

Not, of course, that the Court always does so. A well-established conventional wisdom is that the Supreme Court follows the election returns. Which is to say, it does not too often or too egregiously defy the demonstrated will of the people—not for fear of being voted off the bench but for the less immediate, less tangible, less definable fear of a damaging loss of institutional power or influence, owing to a Congress or a population, or both, too often confounded.

It may be time to question the validity of this fear. Even after the Warren Court added controversial rulings on criminal justice to the "earthquake" of its *Brown* decision, decades of public fulmination and "Impeach Earl Warren" campaigns brought no literal change or damage to the Court or its ruling—no constitutional amendment to curtail its powers, certainly no real move to impeach Warren, no long-term revival of legally enforced school segregation. Of course, all that agitation might have influenced, and probably did, the actions of subsequent Courts. Nevertheless, *Brown* stood and in the largest sense has prevailed for half a century.

Another, more direct effort at retaliation against the Court ended in somewhat similar ambiguity, though ostensibly in a bloodied political nose for one of the most popular and effective presidents of the twentieth century. Following his landslide reelection in 1936, Franklin D. Roosevelt moved to expand membership of the Supreme Court and to force the retirement of the conservative elderly justices he held responsible for striking down some of his New Deal innovations. Unexpectedly—to FDR, at least—Congress and the public rose up in political wrath at what was seen as a power grab by the executive branch and an unwarranted rearrangement of the powers of government.

In one of Roosevelt's most resounding defeats, his "packing plan" was rejected by Congress. Ironically, the Supreme Court of the thirties seemed nevertheless to have got the president's message; from then on, it was more receptive to New Deal legislation, upholding the Wagner Act and the minimum-wage law, for instance. The congressional outcome of Roosevelt's packing plan remains a warning note for politicians, even presidents, who would try to discipline or even change an unpopular, undemocratic Supreme Court, apparently respected, after all, as the third equal branch of government.

The Court's ability to survive not just outside attack but actions of its own that seem to reflect dubious political influence was demonstrated again when the public rather quickly accepted its unprecedented decision that the deadlocked 2000 presidential election had been fairly won by the Republican candidate, Governor George W. Bush of Texas, over the Democrat, Vice President Al Gore.[3] After many decisions in which various courts had refused to get involved in the "political thicket," even the jurisdiction of the Rehnquist Court was unclear. The Court was authorized to rule on the constitutional aspects of Florida election and recount law, not—to the public's knowledge—to definitively decide the outcome of the national election. That controversial role it took upon itself. Its 5–4 decision broke along its own internal conservative/liberal partisan lines, all five justices in the majority having been nominated by Republican presidents, including Justice Clarence Thomas, who was nominated by Bush's father, George H. W. Bush.

The election of 2000 had been hard fought, Florida's vote was marred by charges of racial and other irregularities, and few expected the Supreme Court to do more than settle disputed points. Certainly, few expected it to assume a responsibility no Court had taken on before—choosing a president. The Court's chosen victor, moreover, clearly had lost the popular vote cast in the forty-nine other states, maybe in all fifty states, and although the "minority president" was not unknown in American history, the victory of the popular-vote loser was still an oddity. What is more, Bush's Court majority appeared, at the least, to be more partisan than judicial.

Yet, though smoldering controversy remains, Bush's Court-ordered victory was all but immediately conceded—by Al Gore, by leading Democrats, by the general public. Not a credible voice was raised to suggest that the Court or any of its members be impeached, or that Bush's inaugural be stopped, or that some other method of settling the election be found. For all practical purposes, the Court's ruling—actually, its selection of a president—was accepted by the public. Some judicial and legal experts, their image of the Supreme Court's lofty virtues tarnished, and a few "yellow dog" Democrats did join in a faint, continuing rumble of dissent, but Bush proceeded to select a cabinet, take the oath, and settle unchallenged into the White House.

Despite these dramatic episodes, the Supreme Court has not always been prominently in the public bull's-eye. For most of its history, however coequal constitutionally with Congress and the presidency, the Court, compared with those branches, has stayed relatively in the background. In the eighteenth and nineteenth centuries, it was rarely even heard from and its major decisions were of more historical than headline significance.

It was not until 1803, fourteen years after George Washington's election as the first president, that the Court even asserted the power for which it is best known and which gives it its most celebrated and controversial function—that of reviewing congressional actions and sometimes declaring them unconstitutional.[4]

Even after that, the early Court waited another half century, until 1857 and the eve of the Civil War, to act again on its review power, declaring in its famous *Dred Scott* decision the Missouri Compromise to be unconstitutional and holding that Negro slaves could never be citizens of the United States and that they had no rights that anyone was bound to respect.[5] Abolitionists, of course, were outraged at a decision that, in effect, upheld slavery. As a means of averting a national crisis, however, the decision was a failure. For a number of reasons, including but not limited to *Dred Scott*, the Civil War followed. But as an institution, the Court managed to survive.

Even after the Thirteenth and Fourteenth Amendments seemed to have settled the question of *slavery*, the question of *race* lingered. *Plessy v. Ferguson* in 1896 was essentially another sectional compromise: North and South believed that if blacks would only be satisfied with the "separate but equal" status the Court had approved, the nation could imagine that the problem had been solved.[6] But a half century later, blacks weren't satisfied and the problem remained. *Brown* in 1954 not only reversed *Plessy* but forced the nation to face its failure to establish racial equality—a democratic value implicit if not specified in both the Declaration of Independence and the Constitution.

The Supreme Court has seldom performed such lofty service—and sometimes, as in choosing George W. Bush to be president, the justices have seemed mostly to reflect the political views of the presidents who nominated them. Presidents, in fact, exercise so much control over the makeup of the Court that its independence sometimes has been questioned. Not always, however. On occasion, the reverse happens. In 1952, during the Korean War, for instance, President Harry Truman, ostensibly acting to head off a threatened strike, seized the steel industry. In *Youngstown Sheet and Tube Company v. Sawyer*, the Court promptly ruled that he had no authority for such a drastic step and the president as promptly returned the steel mills to their private owners.[7] That Truman had appointed Fred M. Vinson, a poker-game crony from their Senate days, chief justice apparently did not sway the Court in the president's favor.

President Eisenhower chose several outstanding justices—among them John M. Harlan, William J. Brennan, Potter Stewart, and, perhaps most important, to succeed Vinson, Earl Warren—but failed to advance the Warren Court's most significant achievement, the unanimous *Brown* ruling. And despite his original high opinion of Warren, the president later told friends that nominating Warren was "the biggest damn fool mistake" he had ever made.

The Johnson administration was notable for its part in several Supreme Court developments: Johnson nominated Thurgood Marshall, the lead attorney in the *Brown* case, to be the first black member of the Supreme Court and talked President Kennedy's appointee, Arthur Goldberg, *off* the Court and into the ambassadorship to the United Nations—during the Vietnam War, theoretically a more important post. Johnson also named Earl Warren, while chief justice, to serve as chairman of the commission that investigated Kennedy's murder. The precedent of outside service had been set for the Court when Justice Robert H. Jackson served on the Nuremberg war crimes tribunal. Nevertheless, perhaps as a measure of growing public esteem for the Court's independence, the Warren appointment was criticized as establishing an improper role for a chief justice.

Two Republican presidents, however—Richard Nixon and Ronald Reagan—have most directly influenced today's Supreme Court, and their actions reach ahead to affect its future. Nixon had the distinction of nominating *two* chief justices—Warren E. Burger directly and William H. Rehnquist as an associate justice later named chief by Reagan. Nixon stumbled badly and twice in succession, however, when a first choice, Clement Haynsworth, and then a second, G. Harrold Carswell, were rejected by the Senate. Continuing to seek a Southerner for the Court, Nixon later nominated Lewis F. Powell, Jr., of Virginia, who was easily confirmed. Ironically, it was this Court that in effect forced Nixon to resign the presidency by ordering him to surrender what the press termed the "smoking gun" tape, which fixed his guilt in the Watergate coverup. An important distinction should be drawn, however. Nixon chose to resign. The Court was not seen as having directly forced him out, as later it was considered to have "chosen" Bush over Gore.

That Nixon in one and a half terms had six opportunities to nominate justices, four of whom were confirmed by the Senate, illustrates the erratic nature of Supreme Court nominations, as well as the unpredictable makeup of the Court itself. In ordinary circumstances, after all, such nominations can be made, and that makeup changed, only

after the death or resignation of someone on the bench, a relatively in-
frequent occurrence. Nixon's successor, the "accidental president" Ger-
ald Ford, had only one chance to nominate a justice—John Paul
Stevens. Jimmy Carter, the first Democrat in the White House after
eight years of Nixon and Ford, had none. Carter did nominate many
blacks and women to the lower courts, an indication of what he might
have done in regard to the Supreme Court. Had Carter been given the
opportunity to appoint a Supreme Court justice, it's not unreasonable
to suppose that Al Gore rather than George Bush would be president
today.

During his two terms, Ronald Reagan nominated and saw confirmed three justices who remain on today's Court—the so-called
Rehnquist Court because he also named William H. Rehnquist, a sitting associate justice for fourteen years, as chief justice. The first
woman justice, Sandra Day O'Connor, joined the Court under Reagan's patronage. Reagan also put forward perhaps the most controversial nomination of modern times, perhaps ever—that of Robert Bork,
a well-known conservative with views on civil rights and abortion that
almost guaranteed opposition. Bork failed to win confirmation in a vi-
cious Senate battle, and after Nixon's two failed nominations and
Bork's defeat, judicial nominations became highly political actions.
President Bush I and Bill Clinton seemed careful to choose moderates
unlikely to evoke the fierce opposition Bork aroused. Bush's first choice,
David Souter, though ostensibly a conservative, has compiled a reasonably liberal record and was not among the majority five that put
Bush II in the White House; Bush's other choice, Clarence Thomas,
has turned out to be probably the Court's most conservative member.
Clinton nominated Ruth Bader Ginsburg, the second woman to join
the Court, and Stephen Breyer, and both won fairly easy confirmation.

Clinton's nominations notwithstanding, Republican occupation of
the White House in twenty of the last thirty-two years has resulted in
at least nominal Republican dominance of the Supreme Court as
measured by the party affiliations of the presidents who appointed the
justices. Suffice it to say, today's Court is entirely a product of these
thirty-two years. During that period, the Republicans won five presidential elections and the Democrats three. But during that same period, four Republican presidents (Nixon, Ford, Reagan, and Bush I)

chose ten confirmed Supreme Court justices, including two chiefs (Burger and Rehnquist), while one Democratic president, Clinton, appointed only two justices and no chiefs. As a not entirely predictable result, the Rehnquist Court has a relatively stable but not fixed conservative majority of five: Rehnquist, Scalia, Thomas, Kennedy, and O'Connor. But since Justices Kennedy and O'Connor are sometimes "swing votes," the usual liberal four—Stevens, Souter, Ginsburg, and Breyer—are not invariably in the minority.

This philosophical lineup seems unlikely to change anytime soon, though the faces and names might. Rehnquist, O'Connor, and Stevens, owing to age, health, and length of service, might be among the earliest to leave the Court; if they do so within the next two years, however, their seats would be filled by Bush II, a Republican and a conservative. Of course, death is always unpredictable and so, sometimes, are resignations, and it's at least conceivable that a Democrat or a more liberal Republican (or, less likely, an Independent) could become president in 2004. The makeup of the Senate that must confirm any presidential nomination is also a variable. Further, the records of David Souter and, say, Byron White (President Kennedy's first appointee) are ample proof that justices do not always reflect the views and politics of the presidents who nominate them. For all these reasons, at least, it's impossible to predict the future makeup of the Supreme Court, much less its conservative/liberal division. On the evidence available, however, it can be predicted that whatever changes in the Court may occur in the future, and whatever rulings a Court at any given moment may render, the public is likely to accept both the Court and its decisions—with screams of agony, perhaps, as after *Brown* in the fifties, but without challenging a decision or causing effective political reprisal against the institution or the justices.

In fact, the Supreme Court—unelected and lofty as it is—seems to have reached a position that, if not untouchable, is at least as authoritative and accepted as that of any institution in the nation. The Court is not only peculiarly American, as often noted, but also peculiarly powerful.

Introduction

HERMAN SCHWARTZ

In the introduction to *The Burger Years* (1987), I wrote that the appointment of Associate Supreme Court Justice William H. Rehnquist as the sixteenth chief justice of the United States and the elevation of Court of Appeals Judge Antonin Scalia to the high court mark "the beginning of a reshaping of the Supreme Court, the contours of which are still unknown." Fifteen years later, we know those contours. The Rehnquist Court is the most conservative Supreme Court since before the New Deal. Ronald Reagan's efforts to reshape the American judiciary have succeeded.

For a half century, from 1937 until as late as 1987, the Court could be characterized as moderate to liberal, for even the Burger Court, the Rehnquist Court's predecessor, turned out to be far less conservative than had been anticipated after Nixon appointed four justices. But in 1988, Anthony Kennedy succeeded Justice Lewis F. Powell, Jr., who, though fundamentally conservative, had often voted with the Court's liberals on such issues as affirmative action and church-state separation. Kennedy has been more consistently conservative, which has produced a fairly firm five-justice majority. This majority has persistently used its one-vote margin to move the constitutional and legal clock back toward the 1920s and early 1930s. It has not been able to do so completely, and probably has not even wanted to in all respects. Indeed, in some areas, such as women's rights and to some extent the rights of gays and lesbians, the Court has consolidated earlier gains and even moved beyond them, though usually over the objections of Rehnquist, Scalia, Clarence Thomas, and either Kennedy or Sandra Day O'Connor. Nevertheless, the conservative bloc has moved as aggressively as its slim margin has allowed to undermine or restrict many of the gains for social justice and civil rights that the Court consolidated over the preceding fifty years.

Two events dominate this period, both coming at its end and within a year of each other: *Bush v. Gore* and the terrorist attacks on September 11, 2001.[1] Their long-term consequences for the future of the Supreme Court and the nation are still unclear, despite their immense immediate impact. There may not even be any real long-term consequences to *Bush v. Gore*, and the Court will probably not be harmed or even affected by the outrage that decision produced. Soon after the decision, most Americans appeared willing to forget and forgive whatever the Court did that was wrong. Moreover, impartial studies of the contested balloting indicate that although Vice President Al Gore would have won by a very narrow margin if all the votes cast in Florida had been recounted, the limited recount that the Court blocked—the only matter at issue before it—would not have changed the outcome.[2] This, of course, does not change the fact that in its handling of that case, the Court's conservative majority displayed blatant partisanship and judicial unscrupulousness, as John P. MacKenzie's essay in this collection demonstrates. But those studies make it less likely that the Court's public standing will be seriously undermined by its behavior.

In part, this is because the conventional wisdom that the Supreme Court has been hurt by a series of self-inflicted wounds (*Dred Scott* is the most frequently cited example) is wrong. The Court hasn't really suffered all that much from these "wounds." It has become so "peculiarly powerful," as Tom Wicker puts it, that it is less affected by public reaction than the other two branches of government. The Court's decisions since *Bush v. Gore* certainly show no tendency on its part to pull in its horns.

As to the consequences of September 11, it is certain that there will be important ones. At least some of the many intrusive security measures adopted by the Bush administration on its own and by Congress at its behest—surveillance of lawyer-client conversations of prisoners in custody, secret military commissions with the power of life and death over all noncitizens in deliberately hasty proceedings under rules made up by the secretary of defense, military detention of American citizens without access to counsel or a judicial hearing, expanded surveillance powers—will come before the Court.[3] And if history is any guide, these measures will almost always be upheld. The Supreme Court's record in defending our liberties at a time of foreign threat is not reassuring. If anything, the Court as a body and some justices individually have made things worse. From the Alien and Sedition Acts during the Napoleonic Wars through the Court-sanctioned punishment of dissent in World War I and the Palmer Raids in 1919–20, through World War II, the internment of the Japanese Americans (even after any danger of a West Coast invasion—the ostensible justification—was past), and the trial of General Yamashita, and on through the McCarthy years, the Court has rarely prevented or even criticized flagrant violations of fundamental rights.

Even when we haven't had a national emergency, the Supreme Court has not generally been in the forefront of the fight for liberty and equality. Because the Warren and Burger Courts were in the vanguard of this fight (with some backsliding by the Burger Court), many of us have come to think that the Court was always like that. But for most of its history the Supreme Court has been concerned more with protecting the interests of the haves and maintaining the status quo than with protecting the have-nots by advancing social justice and human freedom. As Wicker's brief historical survey notes, the Bill of Rights under which we live today is a largely modern creation, dating mostly from the 1930s. The first case in which the First Amendment's freedom of speech and press provisions were enforced against official action came in 1931 and the first decision protecting freedom of religion in 1940.[4] The Equal Protection Clause, the first constitutional effort to make a reality of the Declaration of Independence proclamation that "all men are created equal," was not fully enforced until the *Brown v. Board of Education* school desegregation cases in 1954.[5]

It is thus not unusual to find that the current Supreme Court majority is not interested in, and is even sometimes hostile to, promoting civil rights and civil liberties. And in light of the Court's treatment of blacks in America before 1938, it seems altogether fitting that one of the areas where it has done the most damage to progressive hopes is in the many decisions and settings where race is at issue—discrimination, affirmative action for racial minorities, criminal justice (including especially capital punishment) and the rights of prisoners. As William L. Taylor's contribution to this volume shows, in almost every area where progress in racial and other kinds of justice—education, employment, voting—was made, the five-member majority that currently dominates the Supreme Court, aided and abetted by conservative lower-court judges picked by Presidents Reagan and George H. W. Bush, has begun to implement William Rehnquist's original agenda: to undo the gains of the last fifty years by making it ever more difficult for racial and ethnic minorities, battered women, the disabled, the elderly, and the otherwise unfairly treated to achieve justice through the courts.

Stephen B. Bright's essay shows, in saddening detail, how the conservative justices have used their slim majority to allow the representation of people charged with capital offenses, a disproportionate number of whom are black, to be so minimal that it amounts to no representation at all. At the same time, they have shut off almost every avenue by which prisoners condemned to death can challenge their death sentences for constitutional defects. Yet it is becoming ever clearer that, as Justice Harry A. Blackmun said after hearing scores of capital cases, "the death penalty experiment has failed. . . . No combination of procedural rules or substantive regulations ever can save the death penalty from its constitutional deficiencies."[6]

Charles Ogletree's contribution broadens the picture to include other areas of criminal procedure in which the Supreme Court has narrowed the rights of the accused. The war on drugs has produced an especially large volume of Fourth Amendment search-and-seizure cases, where, because of the flagrant racial and ethnic discrimination endemic to the enforcement of drug laws, the impact of the Court's decisions falls most heavily on African Americans. Ogletree explains how the Court, without expressly overruling the most significant decisions of the Warren Court, such as *Miranda v. Arizona*, has whittled them down.[7] Recent decisions have also facilitated widespread use of racial profiling by allowing searches in connection with trivial traffic and other offenses. Some recent decisions, as Ogletree notes, do enhance the defendant's rights, but such decisions are few and far between.

Just as most of the capital punishment and criminal defense cases appear not to be race cases but are, so too for the prisoners' rights cases. In the late 1960s and early 1970s, the national conscience was shaken by the appalling conditions of our prisons, and although the criminal justice reform movement effectively ended in 1968, the prisoners' rights movement went into high gear almost immediately thereafter. Following some scattered rulings in 1964 and in 1968 on religion and on racial segregation in prison, in 1969 the Supreme Court issued a series of decisions that promised to improve living conditions, discipline, and medical care, to permit access to reading matter and to courts and legal services, and to rein in the near-total power of prison officials over the lives of prisoners. In 1972, however, Rehnquist and Powell joined the Court. By 1974, decisions favorable to prisoners dwindled and conditions dramatically worsened. The war on drugs produced a huge rise in the prisoner population, composed of a disproportionate number of racial and ethnic minorities, and terrible overcrowding. The Court began to turn away prisoner petitions with increasing regularity so that today, as William E. Hellerstein shows in his essay, almost all the decisions favorable to prisoners have been either overturned or substantially narrowed. A prisoner is again at the mercy of prison officials.

Speech, abortion, gay rights, and religion enjoyed greater solicitude from the Rehnquist Court. In such controversial areas as pornography on the Internet, flag burning, and political satire, the Supreme Court, as Jamin B. Raskin concedes, blocked efforts to interfere with someone's speech because of what was said. But when major public institutions like public television, schools, and the federal government have tried to control who uses their facilities or public money and how, this Court has given them virtual carte blanche. And the Court's apparent special concern for maintaining the two-party system, for which there is no constitutional basis, has worked to the detriment of minor parties.

Abortion issues also received a mixed reception from the Court. On the one hand, as Susan Estrich observes, *Roe v. Wade* was affirmed, and the ban on criminalizing abortion was kept in place.[8] And Estrich does not think this will change, since only justices appointed by a Republican president would be inclined to overrule *Roe*, and the Republican Party understands that the political damage of such a decision would be prohibitive. As *Bush v. Gore* showed, Republican judges can be very solicitous of Republican Party interests. But the chief beneficiaries of *Roe* are middle-class women, for violence by so-called prolife groups and other pressures have made it difficult for poor women to find doctors willing to perform abortions. Moreover, the Court's delphic utterances in the *Casey* case describing what restrictions may be imposed on abortions, have encouraged states and localities to create numerous obstacles to terminating a pregnancy.[9] Not surprisingly, the resulting burdens have fallen most heavily on the poor.

Gay rights is the one area where this Court has realized some, albeit halting, progress. We are indeed a long way from the open hostility toward gays reflected in the 5–4 majority in *Bowers v. Hardwick*, when the Supreme Court allowed states to criminalize consensual homosexual activity. Now, Chai R. Feldblum finds, the Court is showing greater respect for gay people's rights, evident not only in the 1996 decision striking down a Colorado constitutional amendment that denied gay people almost all legal protection against discrimination but even in decisions like *Boy Scouts v. Dale* and the Boston St. Patrick's Day parade case, both of which went against the gay litigants.[10] The essential question, according to Feldblum, is whether a majority of the Court and the country will come to believe that homosexual conduct is morally equivalent to heterosexual conduct, for judicial decisions are and always have been influenced by judges' moral perceptions.

A more confusing pattern is disclosed in Norman Redlich's comprehensive essay on church-state separation and the free exercise of religion. The decisions of the Warren and Burger Courts made it quite difficult to provide financial support for religious education or to allow official prayers in schools. (Voluntary student prayer that has no state involvement has always been permitted.) Demands for financing and officially sanctioned school prayer have continued, and the Rehnquist

Court has responded sympathetically to the first but not to the second. A major question is whether the Court's decision allowing publicly financed vouchers to be used for religious school attendance will extend to permitting public financing of other religious activities. Also, the Court's attitude toward school prayer is not unambiguous. The Court has treated prayer as speech and has viewed schools as public forums; consequently, public schools and colleges must provide religious groups with a place to pray or other school resources, including money, if the schools provide equivalent benefits to nonreligious groups.

Perhaps the most contentious area of the Rehnquist Court's jurisprudence has been its federalism decisions. In an astonishing display of judicial activism not seen since the 1930s, the Court's five conservatives have struck at the power of the federal government by annulling more federal statutes than any court in recent memory, almost always by 5–4 majorities and over outraged dissents. The claim that this has been done in the name of states' rights and federalism is a facade, one casually abandoned whenever federalism conflicts with more material interests like race, money, and power. Part of the conservative attack on federally created social programs, these decisions reflect the Reagan-Bush agenda that still animates the Republican Party. It is no coincidence that the losing litigants in these decisions are the disabled, the elderly, and working people. The nation and indeed much of Congress do not share the Court's Reaganite philosophy, but the fortuity of Supreme Court departures and appointments has allowed Republican presidents disproportionate opportunities to nominate justices, so that regardless of popular opinion, today's Supreme Court majority is able to further the Reagan social agenda. As Wicker's essay points out, this Supreme Court was put together during a period that covers eight presidential elections, of which the Republicans won five and the Democrats three. But during that same period, Republican presidents put all but two of the present justices on the Court, with Reagan appointing three, including Scalia, one of the most doctrinaire members of the Court, and with Nixon appointing the equally conservative Rehnquist in 1972.

The resulting hostility to social legislation is illustrated in Andrew J. Imparato's essay, which traces this Court's undermining of the Americans with Disabilities Act, the landmark statute that gave hope to so many who suffer from the indifference usually shown the disabled. Disability law is, however, developing swiftly, and since disability law is largely statutory, Congress may correct some of the Court's misinterpretations.

The disability cases are, however, but one group among many. The five conservatives on this Court are hostile not just to the welfare state but to the use of the courts by private citizens to enforce any of their constitutional and legal rights, as David C. Vladeck and Alan B. Morrison demonstrate and as the federalism cases illustrate. For example, the Freedom of Information Act is now riddled with judicially sanctioned exceptions; judicial review of regulatory action, except with respect to suits by business, is curtailed; and the majority has consistently overridden state regulatory laws that are tougher on business than on their federal counterparts.

The resistance to citizen suits also appears in the environmental context, as James Salzman documents. Although the Court's record on construing and applying substantive environmental laws does not show a consistent pattern, it has used environmental law cases to raise the barriers to citizen suits in general and to environmental suits in particular.

The tilt toward business interests is especially pronounced in the antitrust cases. Eleanor M. Fox shows how the Court has adopted the teaching of the Chicago School of Economics. This doctrine, the shortcomings of which are more and more apparent, presupposes that markets work efficiently and governmental intervention is harmful. It is totally indifferent to concentrations of economic power, even though it was the fear of such conglomerations of economic muscle that produced the Sherman, Clayton, and antimerger antitrust laws. As a result of the current Court's rulings, antitrust law today is largely probusiness and giant corporations like Microsoft are left largely unregulated.

The last essay, by Lawrence E. Mitchell, shows how the Court has cut back on the protective aspects of the securities laws, leaving the field to the courts of the state of Delaware. This is bad news for investors, for these courts are notoriously tender toward management. The need for federal supervision has recently been brought home with special force with the collapse of the giant Enron Corporation and the many other revelations of big business corruption, in which executives have walked off with millions, while investors lost huge amounts of money and many employees lost their life savings.

During the Rehnquist era, the Supreme Court has been hostile to minority aspirations and has cut back on the rights of the accused and the imprisoned; it has opened the doors of the execution chamber and shut the doors of the courthouse; it has chipped away at abortion rights, lowered the barrier between church and state, and undermined the free exercise of minority religions; it has allowed public institutions to discriminate; it has restricted the opportunities of students, minority candidates, federal fund recipients, and others to make their views known; it has shrunk federal power and narrowly interpreted federal social legislation by misreading congressional intent; and it has promoted business interests. On the positive side, it has kept alive efforts to fight discrimination against homosexuals, has maintained the ban on officially sanctioned school prayer, and has protected traditional speech.

By and large, these actions mirror the Reagan agenda for the courts. A 1984 study of the performance of Reagan appointees noted with satisfaction that these judges had dismissed suits by Medicare patients whose funding was terminated without a hearing, had prevented union members from suing their union, and had rejected claims by public assistance recipients, refugees, American Indians, handicapped children, the elderly, victims of Securities Act violations, public housing tenants, antitrust plaintiffs, and, of course, prisoners and others suing under any of the various civil rights acts.[11] Things haven't changed.

One of the more curious aspects of the Rehnquist era is the current Court's sharp cutback in its caseload. In 1985–86, the year before Rehnquist became chief justice, the Court decided 172 cases, with 159 opinions. During the 2001–2 term, it decided 76 with opinions. This drastic cutback will continue in part because of the Republican dominance of the lower courts established during the twelve Reagan-Bush years. Senate Republicans' obstruction during the Clinton presidency

ensured that this imbalance was not offset by liberal Clinton appointees, and so the lower courts' rulings are largely in line with the
high court's. Not surprisingly, it finds there is no need to review them.

During the 2001–04 presidential term, one or more Supreme
Court vacancies are virtually certain, for several of the justices are elderly and have served for many years. The next presidential term is
likely to see even more vacancies. The enormous role that the Supreme
Court now plays in American life guarantees that these nominations
will be controversial. Nevertheless, whoever survives the confirmation
process will almost certainly be moderately to very conservative.
Republicans have vowed there will be "no more Souters," and unless
Democrats decide to be far more confrontational on judicial appointments than they have been, nominees who are not glaringly far from
the mainstream will easily get through, especially if President Bush is
reelected. In her essay in this collection, Susan Estrich reports that
President Bill Clinton told her that he thought Bush was much more
conservative than people assumed. Judging by the Bush nominations
to the circuit courts as of this writing and other evidence, Clinton was
correct. The bizarre quirks of the 2000 presidential election may prove
to have long-term consequences little appreciated now, producing a
Court that for years to come will do what the Supreme Court has all
too often done in the past—helping the powers that be to comfort the
comfortable and afflict the afflicted.

Equal Protection for One Lucky Guy

JOHN P. MacKENZIE

"Our consideration is limited to the present circumstances, for the problem of equal protection in election processes generally presents many complexities."

That quiet sentence, in the unsigned opinion that stopped the recount and hastened to hand the presidency to George W. Bush, is very likely the most scandalous feature of the amazing case of *Bush v. Gore*.[1] More outlandish than the conservative majority's trashing of federalism principles and all the rules of restraint it usually lays claim to, this one-sentence disclaimer of legal principle was the linchpin of the majority's selective, inappropriate application of equal protection doctrine in favor of a presidential candidate whose claim would have been dismissed under the rules that apply to everyone else.

The Court was saying that this decision, purporting to enforce the Constitution's guarantee of equal protection of the laws, set no precedent. The statement was itself unprecedented. Before December 12, 2000, such a bald remark was unknown in Supreme Court annals; indeed, it was unthinkable. *Of course* a high court pronouncement on law or the Constitution sets a precedent for future cases. Not this time—at least not if the five-justice majority could help it. This decision, itself a legal orphan lacking a respectable precedent, is designed for one and only one beneficiary: George W. Bush.

That little sentence betrayed a Rehnquist Court self-portrait that is both ominous and damning. A court that will not be bound by its own decisions is a court that refuses, when it thinks necessary, to be a court at all—a tribunal that claims the right, when it thinks necessary, to be a law unto itself.

Although the nonprecedential statement has no precedent, it decidedly creates a dangerous one that points toward a lawless future. The majority of five gives every outward sign that it stands ready to repeat this performance if asked by the right parties. "When contending parties invoke the process of the courts," said the five, "it becomes our unsought responsibility to resolve the federal and constitutional issues the judicial system has been forced to confront." That grandiose assertion of power and right brings to mind the lament of Justice Robert Jackson, in the 1944 case that upheld the confinement of Americans with Japanese faces, that the Court had invested government with power that "then lies about like a loaded weapon ready for the hand of any authority that can bring forth a plausible claim of an urgent need."[2]

It does not redeem the five that Bush has turned out to be the "winner" in the news media ballot studies. What matters is what the justices knew and valued when they ruled. A consortium of large news organizations studied the ballots for many months and reached judgments about the probable outcome if certain ballots were recounted. But the Court did not allow the recounting. Nor does it matter that the political process of congressional counting of electoral votes probably would have elected Bush. It matters far more that the Supreme Court's lawless five prevented the constitutional, regular political process from operating. The survey results in late 2001 took some of the sting out of arguments that the Court stole the election for Bush, and President Bush's subsequent conduct in the White House has enhanced his personal claim to legitimacy, but that leaves the Supreme Court as the major institution whose legitimacy is deeply questioned. Far from vindicating the Court's actions, the ballot surveys emphasize how extreme was the Court's abuse of its discretion to intervene on Bush's behalf, since Bush was not the injured party in the case. People who wanted to vote for Gore, notably minorities, had thousands of ballots nullified, yet the Court assumed without justification that Bush had suffered the injury and thus had legal standing to complain.

Unique though it may be, this way of executing justice bears an ugly family resemblance to other aspects of the Court's regular business since 1991, when Clarence Thomas replaced Thurgood Marshall, creating a hard-core majority bent on radically altering the legal landscape with a series of increasingly high-handed, injudicious rulings. The five—Chief Justice William Rehnquist and Justices Sandra Day O'Connor, Antonin Scalia, Anthony Kennedy, and Thomas—have used their razor-thin majority to drive American jurisprudence far to the right of the centrist, moderate understandings of most Americans.

The decision ranks with history's worst. No, *Bush v. Gore* is not *Dred Scott* and it's not *Plessy v. Ferguson.*[3] It didn't consign black Americans to unendable slavery or render the Fourteenth Amendment moot by sanctioning racial apartheid in America. But it shares a salient characteristic with the *Dred Scott* decision of 1857. In reaching these decisions, both Courts decided matters beyond those necessary to resolving the case, cloaking themselves in the mantle of statesmanship, national savior, and crisis averter. The *Dred Scott* justices, seeking a politically smooth settlement of slavery issues, spoke well beyond the needs of the case and inflamed the nation, announcing not only that Dred Scott could not sue for his freedom but that he and other blacks in his situation could *never* win it. Another candidate for worst decision, *Plessy v. Ferguson*, the 1896 separate-but-equal ruling, was also tragically wrong. But at least in *Plessy* the Supreme Court was the proper decision maker. The Supreme Court never had any business in the cases that became *Bush I* and *Bush II.*

The Court had no business in *Bush I* for relatively technical, prosaic, but important reasons, even apart from its flimsy merits. Chiefly, the case was moot, legally dead. On November 24, when the Court agreed to review the Florida Supreme Court's extension of the election protest period, that extension had two days to run, and by the time the Court heard oral argument on December 1, that extended deadline had passed, ending the extension issue in favor of Bush, the plaintiff and Supreme Court petitioner who, despite the court-ordered extension, emerged from the protest period with a certified lead of 537 votes. The state system already had moved into the election law's court-administered contest period. When a controversy is over, the lack of a live case or controversy puts the dispute beyond the Court's power, a barrier the Court takes seriously most of the time. Not here. Instead the Court sent the case back to Florida for clarification.

As for *Bush II*, the review of Florida's Supreme Court order for a statewide manual recount, the larger reason why the highest court had no business there was that the Constitution and governing federal law assign it no role. Congress has a role: it counts electoral votes and, when necessary, decides between competing slates of electors. States have a role: their legislatures make the state rules and their courts, in Florida as in many other states, are assigned to interpret them and manage postelection judicial contests. As a nation we probably could have enlisted the Supreme Court for these tasks when we structured our government, but we never did.

The November 7 election was a tie, a phenomenon that apologists for the Court have used as a starting point in an argument that the Court heroically served as tiebreaker. Al Gore had half a million more votes nationwide than Bush, but both candidates needed Florida's 25 electoral votes and Bush led initially, it was said, by 1,784 votes, out of nearly 6 million recognized as cast. When the vote appears to be a tie, it's always possible that at some stage in a recount the lead will shift. From the initial mandatory recount through the protest period and the court contest period, an important and realistic goal for Gore, aside from ultimate victory, was to pull ahead if only temporarily, to show that Florida was still a jump ball and to make Bush abandon his stance that the election was over and the votes all counted. For Bush the name of the game was the reverse: stop the counting even when it appeared he led by as few as 154 votes. For Gore that meant to accelerate recounts, for Bush it meant to stall and run out the clock.

To understand the enormity of the Court's errors and their shock effect it is necessary to recognize how the law and federal litigation work normally. In our system a state's high court is the authoritative interpreter of that state's law so far as the United States Supreme Court is concerned. The U.S. high court does not interpret a state's law but takes it as expounded by the state's highest legal authority and only then decides whether that law squares with the U.S. Constitution or federal law. State supreme courts may interpret their state laws in ways that a justice in Washington would consider bizarre, yet that interpretation is binding. Even when a state high court seems to violate equal protection doctrine, the U.S. high court regularly ignores the case unless it is brought by a complaining party who has legal standing to complain, which usually means the party has been legally hurt.

These are not liberal inventions. They are the bedrock of the federal legal system. They help to explain why a broad consensus of legal specialists and experienced Court observers thought the justices would never hear Bush's claims, much less rule in his favor, and why literally hundreds of law professors protested the Court's actions. Liberal bias does not explain this reaction, notwithstanding apologists for Bush.

Hence the hostile reception of many outsiders to Bush's first petition and wonderment that the Supreme Court agreed to hear the case. The petition made three claims. First, that the Florida Supreme Court changed its state law, extending the protest period deadline so as to "violate" the governing 1887 Electoral Count Act. The act, said the petition, "requires that a state resolve controversies relating to the appointment of electors under 'laws enacted prior to' election day." Second, that the state court's decisions had so changed the duly enacted state election law that it violated the Constitution's Article II, Section 1, which provides that each state appoint its electors "in such manner as the Legislature thereof may direct." And third, that the court-ordered "arbitrary, standardless and selective manual recounts that threaten to overturn the results of the election" violated equal protection and due process rights.

"Court observers"—constitutional law teachers and practitioners, talking heads on television and the journalists who specialize in court coverage—mostly gave the petition no chance of winning Supreme Court review. First, courts don't "violate" that 1887 law and the law "requires" nothing; the worst a court can do is make it harder for a state to gain the law's so-called safe harbor—certain approval by Congress of electors chosen pursuant to laws enacted before the election. Second, the notion that Florida's high court had changed the state's law, as opposed to interpreting it, seemed loony; even legal neophytes knew full well that state high courts are the authentic interpreters of their states' laws. The United States Supreme Court may strike down a state law but will not second-guess the state court as to what that law says. The constitutional provision that the state's "Legislature" sets the state's election rules surely did not mean that there was no court review or interpretation permitted of the election code the legislature enacted. Or did it? Third, the equal protection argument seemed to take the Supreme Court into uncharted territory and at least the five most conservative justices had long been loath to expand those rights.

But Court observers were wrong. While the justices declined to consider the equal protection claim, on November 24 they did grant review on the first two questions and set a breakneck course for briefing and oral argument, scheduled for December 1. At the oral argument, what had seemed loony became surreal. The notion that Florida's highest court had changed rather than interpreted its state law struck some justices as compelling. Justice Scalia and Chief Justice Rehnquist were vocal about it, while the quiet Justice Thomas probably was a third vote. At times Justices O'Connor and Kennedy seemed challenged by the argument as well. Justices John Paul Stevens, David Souter, Ruth Bader Ginsburg, and Stephen Breyer seemed solidly of the traditional view that, ordinarily at least, a state high court's rulings on its state laws were authoritative.

Only Justice Breyer suggested the obvious, saying he guessed the case was moot since the secretary of state had already certified Bush the winner on November 26 so it didn't matter whether delaying the certification until that date had been proper. But no justice pressed the parties to explain why there might still be a live controversy.

Late in the argument Justice Ginsburg, perhaps sensing that Justice Scalia's reading of the Florida Supreme Court opinion was attracting votes, suggested remanding the case so the state justices could clarify their opinion. Three days later that is what the Court did in an unsigned opinion setting aside the Florida ruling and sending the case back to the state's high court.[4] It was now up to the Florida justices to say whether they had impermissibly changed state law and had failed to consider adequately the state's interest in reaching that safe harbor where its presidential electors could be counted by Congress without challenge.

When the protest period ended with the certification of Bush as winner by 537 votes and the court contest period began on November 27, Gore now sought court review of ballots allegedly legal but not tallied. Circuit Judge N. Sanders Sauls in Tallahassee repeatedly refused to look at the ballots. A week later, on December 4, Judge Sauls ruled that Gore had failed to carry the burden of proving that there were enough uncounted legal votes to *change* the election. The trouble was, as the state supreme court said on review of Sauls's decision on Friday, December 8, Sauls had misstated the legal test for deciding when to review the ballots, since the law required Gore to prove only that the number of legal disputed ballots was "sufficient to change *or place in doubt* the result of the election."[5] Judge Sauls's misreading of the statute was elementary, judicially substandard, and costly to the Gore forces in terms of time. If Judge Sauls had ordered ballot examinations on December 4, the job would have seemed much more doable before December 12 than it appeared with each passing day. Six of Florida's seven supreme court justices agreed that Sauls had erred, but the ultimate vote to order an immediate recount was 4–3.

The recount order was broader than Gore's requested four large counties. All the so-called undervotes—ballots that showed no vote for president for whatever reason—were to be examined. Amid complaints from Bush that the proposed recounting was standardless and vague, the state justices avoided decreeing a standard any more specific than state statutes mentioned: counters and a circuit judge must determine the intent of the voter. The state justices were very likely spooked by the arguments in the U.S. Supreme Court over the effect of court-induced changes in the state law. The demand for more specificity seemed a trap that the Bush forces would spring if the case got back to Washington, arguing that the state court had again "changed" the law.

Just as the manual recounting was getting under way on Saturday, December 9, came the Supreme Court's order to stop. The Court granted a Bush stay application and permitted review once again. The stay application in *Bush II* offered basically the same issues as *Bush I*, including the equal protection argument the Court had ignored in the earlier review. Under Supreme Court practice, such a stay would be granted only when a majority thought Bush would succeed and that he would be irreparably harmed if the ballot review continued while the case was being heard. The stay, carrying those implications, stunned many but the 5–4 lineup did not. Justice Stevens, joined by Justices Souter, Ginsburg, and Breyer, filed a pointed dissent that showed how issues and attitudes had hardened. The dissenters said the majority had already displayed disrespect for a state high court on questions of state law and abandoned traditional judicial caution on a matter that was ultimately for Congress to decide.

In caustic reply, Justice Scalia filed a concurring opinion warning that the stay did indeed indicate that five justices thought Bush would probably win. As for irreparable harm, that would flow from "the counting of votes that are of questionable legality," which would harm Bush "and the country by casting a cloud upon what he claims to be the legitimacy of his election." And Scalia flagged the equal protection issue: "the propriety, indeed the constitutionality, of letting the standard for determination of voters' intent—dimpled chads, hanging chads, etc.—vary from county to county."[6]

The oral arguments two days later, on December 11, showed no sign of a change in the now familiar lineup. If anything, Justices Souter and Breyer explored the equal protection issue in a way that pointed even further to a reversal of the Florida Supreme Court's December 8 judgment, though their questions envisioned fashioning a standard and proceeding with the ballot review. Justice Ginsburg questioned whether imposing a standard not set forth in preexisting state statutes wouldn't prompt the Bush forces to redouble their complaint that new law was being made in conflict with the safe harbor federal law.

Justice O'Connor expressed annoyance that the Florida court had not yet responded to the remand order calling for clarification of its November 21 opinion. That opinion was filed that evening.[7] It took the form of a substitute opinion that reiterated its basis in conventional statutory construction, the reconciling of conflicting provisions of the election code. This time it avoided mentioning the state constitution, apparently to appease any United States Supreme Court justice who thought it was making new law by using the state charter in interpreting the state statutes. The Florida justices indicated that they had been too swamped with election cases to respond earlier. There was a single, rather odd dissent by Chief Justice Charles Wells, who had been part of the unanimous court in the November 21 decision but who had dissented on December 8. "I dissent from issuing a new decision while the United States Supreme Court has under consideration *Bush v. Gore*," he said. In light of Justice O'Connor's expression of annoyance that this response had not yet been made, what was the problem with issuing it now? That was never explained. It is unclear whether the new Florida opinion changed any votes in Washington, for the Washington justices never discussed its significance.

Just before 10 p.m. on December 12, two hours before the safe harbor period would end, the Court came down with its judgment: no more counting, 5–4. That ended the 2000 election, unless the stay issued three days earlier had already dealt the death blow. Five justices, and you know who they are, accepted the equal-protection argument that varying counting procedures and too broad a definition of a valid ballot deprived someone—it was never clear exactly whom—of the right to equal treatment of his, her, or their ballot or ballots. Then, observing the lateness of the hour, the Court said the counting had to stop because Florida's legislature had expressed the desire to make the safe harbor and avoid any possible contest between competing slates in Congress. There wasn't time, they said, for Florida to arrange uniform ballot review standards.

Somewhere in the middle of the unsigned opinion they said, "Our consideration is limited to the present circumstances, for the problem of equal protection in election processes generally presents many complexities." Awkwardly out of place, this comment served to disengage the majority from their assigned duty to expound the Constitution and federal law and divert it to their present mission of breaking the national election tie at the behest of the only candidate who contended that the mission was legitimate.

Three of the five—Chief Justice Rehnquist and Justices Antonin Scalia and Clarence Thomas—accepted the argument that Florida's highest court had changed the state's laws in the guise of interpretation, "impermissibly distorted them beyond what is a fair reading," violating the directive of Article II, Section 1, of the Constitution that each state choose its presidential electors "in such manner as the Legislature thereof may direct."

Of the four dissenters, Justices David Souter and Stephen Breyer saw merit in the equal protection argument but dissented heartily from the decision to halt the counting. They said it was for Florida to decide if time was lacking and whether to seek greater accuracy even at the risk of losing the safe harbor of indisputable acceptance by Congress of its results. Like Justices John Paul Stevens and Ruth Bader Ginsburg, they contended the Court never should have taken *Bush II* or, for that matter, *Bush I*. They roasted the concurring three justices for disrespecting the Florida Supreme Court's interpretation of state law.

Three months later, Justices Kennedy and Thomas were before a House appropriations subcommittee on the Court's budget. As sometimes happens, subcommittee members like to talk about decisions. Representative José Serrano of the Bronx told the witnesses that he and his constituents were hurt and baffled by *Bush v. Gore*. Justice Kennedy said that he understood but that the Court had no choice but to hear the case. "Sometimes it is easy to enhance your prestige by not exercising your responsibility," he said, "but that has not been the tradition of our Court." He went on: "Ultimately, the power and the prestige and the respect of the Court depend on trust. My colleagues and I want to be the most trusted people in America." Justice Thomas said he, too, would have ducked "if there was a way," but there wasn't.

There was. It might have taken more courage, but the Court could have and should have sat idly by while the presidential election worked its political course. Florida had a messy decentralized system governed by sometimes confusing statutes, but its courts were working at their assigned duty. The state supreme court justices, while not steeped in the nuances of United States Supreme Court review, were diligently focused on the state's own law. In *Bush I* they construed reasonably the mosaic of state laws, and in their opinion they threw in the state's constitution and its high value on the right of the people to govern. That should not have fueled the federal justices' suspicions that they were "changing" the law. They were doing "what judges do," as Justice Stevens argued. If they got their state law wrong, the Supreme Court was supposed nevertheless to take the law as state-interpreted and not reinterpret it. Again, this norm is not some liberal invention. It is one of the building blocks of federalism.

By contrast, as the history of the 1887 federal electoral count law demonstrated, there was no assignment for the federal courts. The federal law with its safe harbor provision was a set of rules for Congress, created by Congress to guide its acceptance or rejection of sometimes competing electoral slates submitted from the states. Those rules were enacted more than a decade after the seismic battle over the Hayes-Tilden deadlock of 1876. To ease the task of deciding between conflicting slates, Congress sought to discourage maneuvers to change state laws during the postelection contests. The law gave conclusive status to slates of electors chosen six days before the Electoral College's votes were tallied in accordance with laws enacted before the election itself. A state having trouble deciding who won its vote for president might pass up the safe harbor provision if it wished, devoting the time to achieving a more accurate result.

Some have asked what a Supreme Court is for if not to settle national questions of this magnitude. The answer is plain: unless there is a major question of constitutional or federal law raised by someone with legal standing to raise it, the Supreme Court's duty is to do nothing. Some have said we mustn't have Congress mucking around in these matters, and the answer to that is: that's our system. Even if Congress wanted the system to be different, if it passed a law, for example, assigning the Supreme Court as the arbiter of disputed electoral slates, the Court probably would have to decline the task on the constitutional ground that it was a nonjudicial chore. But the Court showed distrust of our political arrangements and of the fitness of Congress to judge electoral disputes. It was not the first time this Court so dismissed Congress. Much of the Rehnquist Court's reputed emphasis on federalism is a retreat from generations of opinions that trusted Congress to regulate interstate commerce and to enforce the Fourteenth Amendment, as that amendment provides, "by appropriate legislation."

The Court's claim that it could decide this case without setting a precedent for others is of a piece with its refusal of late to give adequate leeway to Congress in matters of commerce and civil rights. It's a clumsy assertion of supremacy beyond the restraints the judiciary is supposed to observe. It's beyond activism—a refusal to be bound by the contours of the job of judging even at the high court's lofty level, indeed especially at that level, for the Supreme Court sits not as a court of high correction but as an agency of high legal policy. Precedents are the stuff of that job—setting them, recognizing them, even breaking with them on rare occasions. Justices O'Connor, Kennedy, and Souter paid their dues to precedent in their controlling 1992 opinion refusing to overrule *Roe v. Wade*, saying, "the very concept of the rule of law underlying our own Constitution requires such continuity over time that a respect for precedent is, by definition, indispensable," but of the three, only Souter did not join the unsigned "no precedent" opinion.[8]

Perhaps the most outspoken justice on the virtue of precedent as limiting judicial excess is Scalia. He has noted that a Court that recognizes the consequences of a decision on future cases is more likely to take care not to decide too much in the case at hand. His statement in his 1996 dissent from the decision desegregating the Virginia Military Institute was correct (the dissent itself was not): "The Supreme Court of the United States does not sit to announce 'unique' dispositions. Its principal function is to establish precedent."[9] That statement alone should have given Justice Scalia pause when joining the *Bush v. Gore* majority in disavowing the setting of precedent—if the justice considered his own statements binding. Yet again, this is not a liberal or conservative position. It is quite common for justices of any philosophy to point out to lawyers that a victory for their clients might set a precedent that may prove regrettable in cases down the road. That's what it means to say, "Hard cases make bad law," that is, sympathetic cases cause bad precedents.

It's also the significance of the quip that a Court decision of no lasting principle is like a ticket "good for this day and train only." Dissenters often use such barbs to charge that a majority's decision is one of those without a respectable lasting principle and is doomed to an early death, but until *Bush v. Gore*, majority justices had never so plainly said that their own decision had no legs. True, some justices have a greater tendency than others to stress the facts of a case in ways that limit the future utility of the legal holding. I can think of a 1972 case, *Wisconsin v. Yoder*, in which the majority was moved to uphold the religious free-exercise claims of Amish parents to keep their children out of the public high schools.[10] The justices feared, with some reason, that too broad a ruling would invite all kinds of claims that they were not ready to recognize, like conscientious objection to paying taxes that help pay for war. So the Court laid out the facts in full array and observed that few could match the religious claims of the Amish in this regard. But there, by contrast to *Bush v. Gore*, the assumption was that the *Yoder* decision inescapably created a precedent.

The claim of power to deny precedential effect to a court's own opinion is a dangerous claim indeed. As it happens, lower federal courts are asserting it thousands of times a year, in the alleged superior interest of judicial economy. Many appellate court rules provide that a panel of judges may order that their opinions be neither published nor cited, which deprives many parties of the benefit of precedent. It will be interesting to see if the Supreme Court justices someday pass on the constitutionality of this practice and whether they will recognize it as kindred to their own audacious assertion in *Bush v. Gore*. Judge Richard Arnold of the Eighth U.S. Circuit Court of Appeals has written that the practice goes unconstitutionally beyond the judicial power, but his decision was vacated when the Internal Revenue Service rendered the controversy moot by changing the policy that was at issue in the case—insisting as it did so that it was not setting a precedent.[11]

Any one of a number of factors that counseled caution could have spared the majority justices such a flagrant assertion of power. They could have honored their own principle of deference to state courts about state law. They could have applied their traditionally conservative views of equal protection and long-standing neutral rules about legal standing—especially since George W. Bush had totally failed to demonstrate injury, irreparable or reparable, from the recounting. Or they could have shown awareness of the bad looks of it all: candidate Bush had praised Scalia and Thomas as his kind of justices, giving them every incentive to rule for the candidate more sympathetic to their kind of justice. Or they could have avoided the distrust springing from appearances: Scalia's son in a law firm representing Bush, Thomas's wife recruiting job candidates for a Bush administration. Or they could have averted the obvious perception that they would never have stretched their own rules for the candidate not named Bush. Did the four dissenters suffer from comparable appearance of bias? Even assuming they did, their opinions showed that they voted and reasoned without violating so many valued principles.

The kindest comment about *Bush v. Gore* was that of Richard Posner, a sitting federal judge, who said that the sloppy job had the "pragmatic" effect of averting a "crisis." But that alleged crisis was merely the prospect that the regular machinery would operate so that Congress, the constitutionally chosen instrument for counting electoral votes, could count them notwithstanding the Rehnquist Court's pathological distrust of that coordinate branch.

A number of law professors say that regardless of the Court's disclaimer, *Bush v. Gore* inevitably will spawn more equal protection rulings and potentially a new era for that right, especially in voting cases. Paul Freund used to tell his Harvard Law students that equal protection was "like a little boy who knew how to spell *banana* but didn't know when to stop." It may well develop that equal protection is not so casually limited. If so, it won't be the doing of the five, most of whom are not expansionist about equal protection except, perversely, in certain civil rights cases. (The five are often found recognizing the rights of white men, who were not the intended beneficiaries of the Fourteenth Amendment, to equal treatment when some rules are bent to diversify the workforce.)

The hope that *Bush v. Gore* has a silver lining is based not only on principle but also on an attitude that is respectful to the point of being patronizing. Will lower courts start enforcing equal protection based on emanations from *Bush v. Gore*, and if they do, will the five sit by and let it happen? Don't count on it. Anyone who was shocked by *Bush v. Gore* but expects the five to reform themselves into recognizable judges is better advised to prepare for more shock. Indeed, the five may look at the public's relatively tepid reaction to *Bush v. Gore* and perceive not condemnation but rather encouragement, while Bush's approval ratings, especially after September 11 and the findings of the press consortium on the news media ballot studies, may serve to mask the Court's performance and the election controversy itself. Will the justices reform and refrain from issuing decisions good for this day and train only? Don't count on that, either. This gang uses real bullets and they pack Justice Jackson's loaded weapon, ready to fire whenever they feel the need.

RACE AND

CRIMINAL JUSTICE

Racial Equality:
The World According to Rehnquist

WILLIAM L. TAYLOR

During the sixteen years Earl Warren presided over the Supreme
Court, from 1953 to 1969, constitutional rights and liberties flourished
as never before in the nation's history. With its unanimous 1954 decision in *Brown v. Board of Education* striking down racial segregation laws
in public education, the Court became a catalyst for a largely peaceful
revolution in civil rights.[1] Resistance by Southern leaders to the Court's
decree led to a peaceful protest movement. Violent repression of that
movement brought about a national consensus in favor of equality of
opportunity that found expression in the civil rights laws of the 1960s.

Toward the end of the Warren years, the Supreme Court, finally
supported by the legislative and executive branches, felt able to provide
effective desegregation remedies, to give new life to Reconstruction
laws eviscerated by the Court in the nineteenth century, and to extend
equal protection to other groups suffering discrimination. By 1969, we
were a different nation. The formal racial caste system in the South
was eliminated and new opportunities for black Americans and other
people of color had opened in the North as well.

Between 1969 and 1986, during which Chief Justice Warren Burger presided, the Court was a study in contradictions. On the one
hand, the Court sanctioned remedies for public school racial segregation that had been long deferred and that provided new opportunities

for black youngsters throughout the South. The Court also extended protections against intentional racial segregation of students in the North and West in states that did not have segregation laws in 1954. And for the most part the Burger Court interpreted the new federal civil rights laws so as to enable them to achieve their purposes, notably in the *Griggs* case, in which it struck down practices that served as a barrier to the employment of black applicants where those practices could not be shown to be necessary to the operation of the business.[2]

On the other hand, in two major decisions, *San Antonio v. Rodriguez* in 1973 and *Milliken v. Bradley* in 1974, a narrow 5–4 majority of the Burger Court sanctioned the retention of major barriers to the educational progress of minority and poor students.[3] *Milliken*, by treating local school district lines as almost impermeable barriers, locked urban children of color and poor children out of the better opportunities provided in suburban schools. *Rodriguez*, by justifying state systems of financing public schools largely through property taxes, denied many poor urban students improvement of their segregated schools.

In addition, during the Burger years, the Court placed new emphasis on the need for proof of intent to sustain claims of constitutional violations in employment, housing, and voting, relegating remedies in these areas to liberal interpretation of civil rights statutes.[4]

In both the pro– and anti–civil rights decisions, the Burger majority paradoxically may have been drawing lessons from *Brown v. Board of Education*. In its desegregation remedy decisions, the Court majority may have been motivated in part by a perceived need to protect the Court as an institution from giving in to the body blows it received from so many sources in the years following the *Brown* decision. If after that stormy time a practical desegregation remedy was not available, what had the struggle been all about?

At the same time, some justices in the majority in *Rodriguez* and *Milliken*, notably Potter Stewart, who was the pivotal vote in each case, may have been motivated by another lesson drawn from *Brown*—that the Court encounters trouble whenever it ventures into areas that have large social consequences without some solid core of public support. In *Milliken*, the Court was being asked to call for urban-suburban school desegregation in the very state where George Wallace had made a strong showing in a presidential primary held less than two years earlier and in a national climate far less hospitable to the protection of civil rights than in the early 1960s. In *Rodriguez*, the Court was being asked to invalidate a state school financing system in ways that would have called for a major redistribution of public resources. As Justice Thurgood Marshall said of *Milliken*, the decision was "more a reflection of a perceived public mood that we have gone far enough in enforcing the Constitution than it is the product of neutral principles of law."[5] The same could be said of *Rodriguez*.

If there is ambivalence and conflict in the record of the Burger Court on civil rights, there is no such uncertainty in the record of the Rehnquist Court. Chief Justice William H. Rehnquist has led a working majority hostile to civil rights from almost the day of his ascent to that office in October 1986. Ever since Justice Clarence Thomas (succeeding Thurgood Marshall in 1991) joined the Court, a bloc of five justices (Rehnquist, Antonin Scalia, Sandra Day O'Connor, Anthony Kennedy, and Thomas) has worked assiduously to chip away at both the scope of the civil rights laws and the remedies for their violation. The most affected areas have been fair employment, equal educational opportunity, voting rights, and affirmative action.

Interestingly, to some extent, the damage done by the Court to the opportunities offered to African Americans and other people of color has been mitigated by Congress's willingness to correct some of the Court's restrictive readings. Also, other major institutions in society—among them major employers, colleges, and universities that had stood mute or in opposition to the holdings of the Warren Court—have come to embrace affirmative action policies to extend opportunities to minorities. That the progress has proved durable through the decades of Nixon, Reagan, and the two Bushes is testimony to the work of the civil rights movement and the Warren Court, to the claim of equal justice on the American conscience, and to the changing demography of the nation, which has resulted in a changing calculus for both our political and economic systems.

Nevertheless, civil rights progress has been stymied, particularly for the worst off in society. Moreover, the Rehnquist majority has recently grown bolder. No longer restricting itself to crabbed interpretations of civil rights statutes, it is inventing whole new doctrines under the Commerce Clause, the Eleventh Amendment, and Section 5 of the Fourteenth Amendment that severely constrict the other branches of the federal government in their capacity to act on behalf of minorities and the poor. Whether this latest trend will abate or intensify will depend on the next appointments to the Court. Although hard to predict, it could ultimately result in a clash with the Congress or the executive branch, as occurred during the New Deal. One thing does appear fairly certain: if the current trend continues, racial and socioeconomic isolation in the nation and the gap between haves and have-nots will increase, with a great potential for division and conflict.

The previous career of William Rehnquist unambiguously foreshadowed the imprint he would make as chief justice. As a law clerk to Robert Jackson, Rehnquist wrote a memorandum to the justice during the 1952 term of the Court to assist him in deciding the pending *Brown* case. In it he said:

> If this Court, because its members individually are liberals and dislike segregation, now chooses to strike it down, it differs from the McReynolds Court only in the kinds of litigants it favors and the kinds of special claims it protects.
>
> I realize that is an unpopular and unhumanitarian position . . . but I think *Plessy v. Ferguson* was right and should be reaffirmed.[6]

When Rehnquist returned to Arizona to practice law, his political activities included running "ballot security" programs for the Republican Party and, according to the testimony of several witnesses, challenging the literacy of black citizens at the polls.[7]

Once on the Court, Justice Rehnquist quickly staked out positions that he would follow throughout his judicial career. Much of the early work was summarized by Harvard professor David Shapiro in an incisive analysis of Rehnquist's opinions from March 1972 to July 1976. Among the characteristics noted by Shapiro are the following:

Too often, unyielding insistence on a particular result appears to have contributed to a wide discrepancy between theory and practice in matters of constitutional interpretation, to unwarranted relinquishment of federal responsibilities and deference to state law and institutions, to tacit abandonment of evolving protections of liberty and property, to sacrifice of craftsmanship, and to distortion of precedent.[8]

One example of these traits (not cited in Shapiro) is Justice Rehnquist's position on school desegregation. In 1973, he was the lone dissenter when the Court decided in *Keyes v. School District No. 1 of Denver* that the *Brown* decision could be applied to school districts in the North and West even absent formal statutes commanding segregation.[9] Four years later, Justice Rehnquist wrote for the Court in remanding a Dayton school desegregation case for further proceedings because of a failure of the lower courts to make proper findings. The decision was not controversial, but Justice Rehnquist could not resist a bit of extra verbiage:

If [school segregation] violations are found, the District Court in the first instance . . . must determine how much incremental segregative effect these violations had on the racial distribution of the Dayton school population as presently constituted when their distribution is compared to what it would have been in the absence of such constitutional violations.[10]

Justice Rehnquist was asking the impossible. Assuming that some segregation would likely exist in public schools even if the government had never decreed it, there is no known method for extracting the effect of that segregation from the immeasurable consequences of a public order that had segregated and stigmatized black people for more than two centuries. Unless such a method is discovered, Justice Rehnquist's quest for the "incremental segregative effect" is an exercise in fiction.

In the film *It's a Wonderful Life*, the protagonist (played by James Stewart) considers his life a failure and is on the verge of suicide when a guardian angel intervenes. The angel (Clarence by name) is able to re-create the distressed circumstances of the hero's town, friends, and family as they would have been if the hero had never lived and thus demonstrates to him that he has not been a failure but has made a real contribution to the well-being and prosperity of all. The movie ends happily. Lacking such divine intervention, judges and lawyers in school segregation cases cannot re-create the situation that would have existed if the officially created segregation had never occurred. The party bearing the legal burden of persuasion—a burden that Rehnquist would place on the minority students—would always lose. Justice Rehnquist conveniently omitted any mention of the *Keyes* decision in which Justice William J. Brennan, writing for the majority, held that once a substantial violation is proved, the burden of justifying a limited remedy falls on school officials.

When the *Dayton* case came back to the Supreme Court in 1979 with proper findings made by the lower court, the majority rejected the Rehnquist view, saying that once deliberate practices of discrimination are proved, it is the defendant's burden to demonstrate that any segregation that is not to be subject to the court-ordered remedy was innocently caused.[11] But as will be seen below, as chief justice, Rehnquist has had what may be the last word, not just in erecting barriers to remedy in education but also in employment, affirmative action, and voting.

The first sustained application of the Rehnquist treatment of civil rights came in a series of fair-employment cases decided in 1989 and 1990. The most important of these decisions was *Wards Cove Packing Company v. Atonio.*[12] In *Griggs v. Duke Power Company*, a unanimous Court, in an opinion written by Chief Justice Warren Burger, had decided in 1971 that Title VII of the Civil Rights Act of 1964 could bar employment practices that had an adverse impact on minorities or women. Once plaintiffs proved that the practice adversely affected them as a group, the burden shifted to the employer to show that the practice was required by business necessity.

The *Griggs* decision was undergirded by a practical understanding of the barriers that had long faced people of color. The Court said:

Absence of discriminatory intent does not redeem employment procedures or testing mechanisms that operate as "built-in headwinds" for minority groups and are unrelated to measuring job capacity.

Two years later, the Court observed in another case:

Griggs was rightly concerned that childhood deficiencies in the education and background of minority citizens resulting from forces beyond their control not be allowed to work a cumulative and invidious burden on such citizens for the remainder of their lives.[13]

Griggs brought about many new opportunities for minorities. Once paper-and-pencil tests and other qualifications that could not be shown to be related to job performance were dropped or reversed, minority applicants gained access to jobs as police officers, firefighters, over-the-road truckers, and a multiplicity of white-collar occupations.

Congress had been presented with a real opportunity to change the *Griggs* interpretation when it made major revisions to Title VII in 1972. Yet Congress left the law intact amid strong indications that many supported its approach. But this did not deter a bare 5–4 majority in *Wards Cove* from undermining *Griggs*. First, the Court said that, even after the establishment of adverse impact, the burden of persuasion with regard to the legitimacy of the business practice still resided with the plaintiff. Second, the majority said that business necessity did not mean that the practice must "be 'essential' or 'indispensable' to the employer's business for it to pass muster."[14] Thus the rule of *Griggs* was changed from business necessity to business convenience.

A second decision in 1989, *Patterson v. McClean Credit Union*, did much to rescind the promise of enforcing a post–Civil War statute that gave minorities the same right as white persons to make and enforce contracts.[15] While the statute had been eviscerated by post-Reconstruction decisions that refused to apply it to private discriminators, the Warren and Burger Courts had restored it to its original purpose by finding violations against realtors and private schools that engaged in discrimination.

In the *Patterson* case, Mrs. Patterson claimed she was verbally abused at her job as a bank teller because of her race. Justice Kennedy, writing for a 5–4 majority, rejected the claim, saying that on its face the statute covered only the making and enforcement of contracts and not their terms and conditions. In his dissent Justice Brennan pointed to legislative history that included concerns about freed slaves who were being whipped on the job. He also noted that if Mrs. Patterson had been explicitly advised that she could have the job but would be racially abused, she would not have the same rights as whites.

In 1991, after a two-year struggle, Congress revised the Court's interpretations of the law in *Wards Cove* and *Patterson*. In the process, Congress also reversed five other 1989 Court decisions that erected barriers to enforcement of federal fair employment.[16] President George H. W. Bush had threatened to veto the bill as favoring "quotas" but backed down when Republican senators said they might not vote to sustain his veto. They were concerned about both the growing influence of African Americans in elections and the danger of being viewed as outside the consensus favoring equality of opportunity.

This rebuke by Congress in the 1991 Civil Rights Act had little impact on the Rehnquist Court's determination to curb the application of civil rights laws. In the *Bakke* case in 1978, the Burger Court had left broad scope for race-conscious affirmative action policies as long as they were carefully crafted for remedial purposes or to further goals of achieving diversity.[17] But in striking down in 1995 the application of a federal program designed to promote affirmative action, the Rehnquist 5–4 majority in *Adarand Contractors v. Pena* held that, in order to pass constitutional muster, race-conscious programs designed for a remedial purpose must meet the same exacting standards of judicial review as those designed to subjugate minorities.[18] In the aftermath of *Adarand*, the Court left in place lower-court decisions aggressively attacking affirmative action, including a Fifth Circuit decision holding that Justice Powell's opinion in *Bakke* was "not binding precedent" and that discrimination lower down in the University of Texas's public education system was no justification for affirmative action at the university's law school.[19]

The *Hopwood* decision not only sought to divorce "societal" discrimination from government discrimination but to so compartmentalize government discrimination that one department or agency could not be held accountable for remedying wrongs committed by another. This approach was clearly inconsistent with the Warren Court's historic decision in the Little Rock case treating the state of Arkansas as a single entity in order to effectuate *Brown*.[20] It was also in direct conflict with the pragmatic philosophy of *Griggs* and its progeny that practices that disadvantaged children should "not be allowed to work a cumulative and invidious burden" on them for the rest of their lives.

But this new approach fit neatly with Rehnquist's view that private and public discrimination could be separated by a bright line and that the latter could and should be compartmentalized, sliced, and diced so as to limit government's duty to afford a remedy.[21]

With enactment of the Voting Rights Act of 1965, Congress and the Johnson administration took effective action to end century-old devices that disenfranchised black people in the South. Thereafter the major challenge became finding ways to deal with the myriad electoral practices that diluted the influence of newly enfranchised black voters. One classic device was electing candidates for office at large rather than through districts in which black voters would have the ability to elect one or more candidates of their choice.

When a 1980 decision of the Burger Court required proof that the dilution was intentional, it seemed that many such practices would survive judicial challenge.[22] To overcome the effects of that decision, when Congress in 1982 enacted an extension of the Voting Rights Act, it dispensed with the need to prove intent, stating that it was enough to show that the practice at issue had the effect of diluting minority votes.

In a series of cases beginning in 1993, however, the Rehnquist majority has whittled down the protections of the act. The key decision came in 1993 in *Shaw v. Reno*, in which white voters challenged a North Carolina reapportionment plan that, for the first time since Reconstruction, included two majority black congressional districts.[23] In the past, the Rehnquist majority had applied increasingly rigorous rules of standing to bar minorities from access to federal courts. In *Shaw*, however, the majority ignored those rules and allowed the white plaintiffs to pursue their case even though they did not claim that their ability to participate had been impaired or their votes diluted. Having decided that such claims would be heard by the federal courts, the majority insisted (and continues to insist) that race (i.e., the aggregation of black voters to elect a black candidate) not be the "predominant concern" over political and other factors traditionally used in the drawing of lines.

Districting cases like *Shaw v. Reno* are not free from complexity. The ultimate objective of the Voting Rights Act is to deal with practices that dilute the influence of minority voters. While districting that distributes black citizens among many districts may have a dilutive effect, so may practices that pack many black voters into a single district. The latter practices may ensure the election of a black candidate in a particular district, but they may rob voters of potential significant influence in surrounding areas. It is important that a fair balance be struck.

The influence of minority voters has indeed increased significantly since the 1982 extension of the Voting Rights Act, but the 2000 election—where many African-American and Latino voters were faced with inferior voting equipment, long lines at the polls, improper purges, and other problems—demonstrates the long distance that remains to be traveled to reach equal voting opportunity. For more than six decades during the last century, the Court, even during its years of countenancing segregation, was the strongest proponent of enforcing the Fourteenth and Fifteenth Amendments to eliminate discrimination in the electoral process. Now, as long as a Rehnquist majority prevails, the Court is more likely to be an impediment than an ally in overcoming remaining obstacles.

In the 1990s the Rehnquist Court turned its attention to the question of when federal court orders for school desegregation should be terminated, releasing states of the obligation to assist the desegregation process and leaving school districts free to pursue their own systems of student assignment.

During the Burger years, the Court had indicated that the test for government officials claiming to have eliminated their racially dual systems and reached "unitary" status would be rigorous. They would have to demonstrate that they had abolished both the trappings of segregation, such as one-race schools, and the vestiges of the segregated system. What were those vestiges? In the 1971 *Swann* case, the Court had found that planned segregation of schools led to segregated housing, with families clustering in residential patterns around schools that accepted their children.[24] And in *Milliken II* in 1977, a unanimous Court reinforced the findings of *Brown* concerning the damage done by segregation and concluded:

> Pupil assignment [for desegregation] alone does not automatically remedy the impact of previous, unlawful educational isolation; the consequences linger and can be dealt with only by independent measures.[25]

The language of *Swann* suggests that as long as substantial housing segregation persists and a return to "neighborhood schools" would mean a return to racial segregation, the vestiges of the old order remain and unitary status has not been attained. The language of *Milliken II* suggests that time is needed for both desegregation and state-financed school improvement measures to narrow the gap between black and white student achievement.

But in three cases in the 1990s, the Rehnquist majority gave short shrift to such considerations, indicating an impatience to return schools to local control.[26] In a 1992 case, *Freeman v. Pitts*, Justice Kennedy wrote for the majority that residential segregation might be a product more of differing preferences by blacks and whites on the racial composition of neighborhoods where they seek to locate than of state-fostered segregation. In the 1995 *Missouri v. Jenkins* case, the Rehnquist majority reached out to take on unitary issues that had not been litigated in the lower courts. Again, Chief Justice Rehnquist sounded his familiar theme of "incremental effect." Conceding that the district court had previously found that "segregation has caused a systemwide reduction in achievement in the schools [of Kansas City]," he replied that the lower court "never has identified the incremental effect that segregation has had on minority student achievement or the specific goals of the quality education programs."

In the Rehnquist worldview racial inequality is the "natural condition" and efforts to ameliorate it through government remedies demand strict proof that government created the inequality.

In his dissent in the 1991 *Dowell* case, Justice Marshall said that "a

desegregation decree cannot be lifted so long as conditions likely to in-
flict the stigmatic injury in *Brown I* persist and there remain feasible
methods of eliminating such conditions." For Rehnquist, however, it is
clear that the stigma is gone (if it ever existed) and that we live in a
color-blind society in which no special efforts are needed to redress
past racial wrongs.

Beginning in 2000, the Rehnquist majority grew bolder both in its
assault on congressional powers and in its efforts to curb judicial authority to provide civil rights remedies.

Until recently, the constitutional power of Congress to regulate
commerce under Article I, Section 8 (a power whose broad reach had
been affirmed in many New Deal–era cases), seemed a sturdy basis for
dealing with many forms of discrimination by private institutions. In
1964, the Commerce Clause was a major predicate for those sections
of the Civil Rights Act that barred discrimination in places of public
accommodation and by private employers.

But in May 2000, a 5–4 majority informed the nation in *United
States v. Morrison* that the clause did not allow Congress to provide a
remedy to protect women against domestic violence because it did not
extend to matters that are "non-economic in nature."[27] In doing so, the
five justices spurned the traditional deference the Court gives to Congress, which had made extensive findings about the tangible effects of
violence against women, calculating costs of about $3 billion in one
year alone. Nor was the majority impressed by the fact that thirty-six
states supported the Violence against Women Act before the Court.

Similarly, while the Eleventh Amendment affords states a "sovereign immunity" defense in some situations, students of the Constitution long had considered that these situations were very limited and
did not preclude suits against states to enforce obligations imposed by
federal statutes. Yet in *Kimel v. Florida Board of Regents*, the same five-
member majority ruled that Congress could not invoke its explicit constitutional power to enforce the Fourteenth Amendment and override
sovereign immunity so that state employees who had been victims of
age discrimination could seek damages from their own state for the violation of federal law.[28] Age discrimination, the majority opined, is not
as serious a matter as race and gender discrimination. Consequently,

the Age Discrimination in Employment Act failed a test of "congruence and proportionality," a newly invented construct of the Rehnquist majority. Later the same majority used sovereign immunity to bar suits based on violation of the rights of persons with disabilities.[29] It remains to be seen whether the Spending Clause, which has provided a basis for suits against state agencies that receive federal money, will also be narrowed.

Finally, in April 2001, the Rehnquist majority renewed its war against discrimination cases that were based on disproportionate racial impact rather than intent. In 1964, Congress passed Title VI of the Civil Rights Act requiring nondiscrimination in programs and activities receiving federal funds. While the Supreme Court subsequently ruled that Title VI itself reached only acts of deliberate discrimination, it also allowed federal departments and agencies to go further in implementing regulations. In the very first regulation issued after enactment, the Justice Department in 1964 forbade fund recipients from utilizing "criteria or methods of administration which have the effect of subjecting individuals to discrimination."

Since the Court had explicitly ruled that individuals suffering discrimination under Title VI could seek redress in the federal courts, it was widely assumed that private individuals could also bring actions for violations of the regulations that simply implemented Title VI. But in April 2001, the Rehnquist majority ruled otherwise, rejecting a suit brought by a Latino resident of Alabama who was denied the opportunity to take an exam for a driver's license in Spanish.[30] While the Title VI regulations can still be enforced by federal agencies, there is no realistic prospect that the many violations that occur can be redressed even by federal officials more committed to civil rights than the Bush administration.

The consequences of this ruling are sweeping. Title VI regulations have been employed to help minorities gain more equal access to public transportation, to ensure that they are not relegated to dead-end classes for the mentally retarded based on faulty tests, and to deal with myriad other discriminatory practices. All are now in jeopardy.

Since discriminatory practices these days are rarely accompanied by neon signs advertising their invidious intent, the Court has made the struggle for equal opportunity more difficult for hundreds of thousands of people.

In writing the Court's opinion in *Brown*, Earl Warren forsook conventional constitutional analysis in a plea for public understanding of the flesh-and-blood realities facing the Court. "Look," he appeared to be saying to people in the South, "we know we are disturbing a set of mores and traditions that are deeply embedded in your life, but we must do so because segregation is damaging the lives and opportunities of little children."[31]

When William Brennan became a dominant force on the Court in the late 1960s and the 1970s, perhaps in response to attacks on the *Brown* opinion, he made more use of traditional legal principles in his decisions. So, in *Keyes*, he relied on rebuttable presumptions to derive the need for a systemwide desegregation remedy from a proven violation that affected only part of a district. But Brennan's presumptions were "common sense" and he explained why it was reasonable to infer that school authorities who deliberately segregated some schools should be held responsible for curing segregation that existed at others. He also was acutely aware of a judge's role in balancing competing interests and insisted that in examining challenges to affirmative action policies to benefit minorities, the court must determine whether the interests of whites are "unduly trammeled."

In contrast, a concern for flesh-and-blood realities, for common-sense analysis, and for weighing competing interests is what is absent from the arid legalisms of the Rehnquist approach. An analysis grounded in common sense and reality would not sustain Rehnquist's fanciful notion that it is possible to separate out with neat precision the consequences of persistent, unconstitutional state practices from conditions of inequity that would have existed without the unlawful practices. Sometimes the legal analysis borders on the absurd. For example, it has become accepted doctrine that racial practices that disadvantage minorities are subjected to the strictest judicial scrutiny because they are invidious and can be justified rarely, if ever. The Rehnquist Court has now extended that doctrine to hold that race-conscious efforts to *remedy* such invidious racial practices must also be subjected to strict scrutiny. So in the Rehnquist lexicon, the more severe the discrimination, the less one can do to remedy it.

Nor can the work of the Rehnquist majority be justified in the conventional parlance still used to praise conservative judges. It is not "strict constructionist," as witness the radical departure in *Kimel* from both the text and history of the Eleventh Amendment to erect new state sovereignty barriers to remedies for discrimination. It is not "respectful of precedent," as witness the readiness of the Court to overturn years of expansive interpretation of the Commerce Clause. And it most certainly does not exhibit "judicial restraint," as is apparent in the Court's willingness to disregard congressional findings and to exalt its own wisdom over that of any other branch of government.

Most of all, the Rehnquist majority seems willfully ignorant of the realities of life for many poor and struggling people. That was evident in a 5–4 decision of the Court in March 2002 in the case of *Hoffman Plastics Compounds v. National Labor Relations Board.*[32] The issue was whether to uphold an award of back pay by the NLRB to an unauthorized alien who had been illegally discharged by his employer for engaging in union activity. There was no specific provision in either the labor laws or the immigration laws prohibiting such awards and it appeared uncontested that back pay awards were one of the most effective ways of deterring illegal labor practices.

But Chief Justice Rehnquist, writing for the majority, said that "awarding back pay in a case like this not only trivializes the immigration laws, it also condones and encourages future violations." In dissent, Justice Stephen Breyer, with a firmer grasp on the real world where employers hire people they know or suspect are illegal aliens to secure cheap labor, wrote that "to *deny* the Board the power to award back pay" might increase the strength of "the magnetic force" that pulls illegal immigrants to the United States by lowering the cost to the employer of labor law violations (emphasis in original).

The decision stands in stark contrast to *Plyler v. Doe* two decades earlier, in which the Court struck down a Texas law barring the children of undocumented aliens from public schools.[33] Against similar claims that providing a free public education would encourage illegal immigration, Justice Brennan wrote that the law

> imposes a lifetime hardship on a discrete class of children not accountable for their disability status. The stigma of illiteracy will mark them for the rest of their lives. By denying these children a basic education, we deny them the ability to live within the structure of our civic institutions, and foreclose any realistic possibility that they will contribute in even the smallest way to the progress of our Nation.

While public officials of all political persuasions struggle with the issues surrounding illegal immigration, few outside the Rehnquist majority believe that large numbers of illegal aliens already here will leave, and that others will be deterred from coming, because of draconian measures affecting their employment or the education of their children.

In the new millennium the nation faces important challenges: how to avert racial and ethnic tensions in an increasingly diverse society, how to provide economic opportunity in a postindustrial age to those who have faced deprivation and discrimination, and how to encourage participating citizenship for all. In its policies fostering a renewal of racial isolation in our schools and public life, and in squelching efforts of other branches of government and private institutions to offer a helping hand to those worst off, the current Court majority has become one of the "built-in headwinds" that its predecessors recognized and deplored.[34] If the Rehnquist majority (or its successor) continues on its current course, the Court will have virtually abandoned its historic role of affording remedies for "discrete and insular minorities" who cannot rely on the ordinary political processes for their protection.

The Rehnquist Revolution in Criminal Procedure

CHARLES J. OGLETREE, JR.

The Rehnquist Court has had a tremendous impact on criminal justice issues, significantly rolling back the procedural rights of criminal defendants. This result owes much to the leadership of Chief Justice William H. Rehnquist, as can be seen in the way many of the Court's recent decisions on matters of criminal procedure were foreshadowed by his dissenting opinions prior to 1986, as associate justice. However, it would be an overgeneralization to assert that all the decisions of the Rehnquist Court have restricted the rights of criminal defendants. Rather, the current era can be seen as one of ideological tension between competing and fluid understandings of the scope of constitutional protections of a criminal defendant's procedural rights. While a criminal defendant today would certainly enjoy narrower procedural protections than sixteen years ago, there has been a certain amount of ideological back-and-forth in the Court's decisions over that period. One example of how this ideological tension has played out is in the issue of racial profiling, and the same tension will no doubt inform the Court's approach to the challenging and pressing questions of constitutional criminal procedure that arose in the aftermath of the September 11, 2001, terrorist attacks in Washington and New York.

What does it mean to talk about the jurisprudence of the Rehnquist Court? What responsibility can we attribute to the chief justice for the decisions of "his" Court? Normally, when we talk about the decisions of a particular Court, invoking the name of the presiding chief justice simply sets historical limits on the decisions we are considering. We may, in addition, attempt to discern the dominant legal philosophy characterizing the Court's decisions during his tenure. This practice has its uses: it provides neat comparisons for different periods of legal history and focuses analysis on the opinions, dissents, and concurrences in each case, rather than purely on the holding.

But the Court is, after all, composed of nine individual justices, each with his or her own legal philosophy. Furthermore, the Rehnquist Court is an extremely fractured one, reaching consistent and relatively predictable 5–4 votes along many issues, which makes it all the more difficult to talk in terms of a unitary, dominant judicial philosophy. It is with these caveats, then, that we can analyze the decisions of the Rehnquist Court as creating an identifiable corpus of criminal procedure law.

To better understand the criminal jurisprudence of the Rehnquist Court, we might consider that there are two models of criminal justice for the Court to draw upon: the *crime-control* model, which promotes deterrence and punishment of crime as the most important end of the criminal justice system, and the *due process* model, which is concerned with vindicating constitutional rights and maximizing individual freedom from government control.[1] The crime-control model permits government agents considerable discretion in pursuing criminals, requires them to submit only to a relatively formal, uniform set of rules to control that discretion, and exhibits significant confidence in the government's identification of suspects as guilty of the crime with which they are charged. By contrast, the due process model requires stricter adherence to constitutional guarantees when the government is surveilling, detaining, and searching individuals; protects those constitutional guarantees through early judicial oversight of the police to ensure that the investigative process is free from bias or error; and emphasizes the presumption of innocence and the burden of proof in determining the guilt or innocence of a suspect.

While these models are neither exhaustive nor particularly sophisticated, they are useful as a framework for understanding different approaches to constitutional criminal procedure. To appreciate how these models apply in practice, it is worth considering the general features of a police investigation and arrest. The investigation typically begins with police observation of an individual's behavior. The Fourth Amendment's prohibition of unreasonable searches and seizures ensures that the police may not arrest people without good reason—what is commonly called "probable cause." A somewhat ambiguous and loosely defined concept, probable cause generally requires that the police have a "substantial basis" for believing that a search will provide evidence that the individual is guilty of an offense. A lesser standard is imposed when the search is likely to be less than ordinarily intrusive. For example, when an officer simply wishes to stop and perhaps frisk an individual at a roadblock or an airport security checkpoint, the less onerous "reasonable suspicion" standard is used. Reasonable suspicion requires no more than some articulable reason to believe that a crime has been or will be committed.[2]

Let us imagine that an officer has reasonable suspicion to stop and search you—she has information that someone driving the same make of car as you is planning to rob a department store, and you have driven slowly past that department store five times in the last half hour. With such evidence, the officer may detain you for a brief time, ask you questions, require you to exit your car, frisk you, and look around your car for weapons. You have a limited right to walk away, and at this stage of the investigation, anything you say to the police will be voluntary. If that investigation turns up sufficient information for the officer to establish that she has probable cause to believe that you plan to rob the store—for example, she sees a fake gun and a mask on the back-seat—she may arrest you, impound your car, and take the mask and gun into police custody. To conduct a further search, including a search of your home, she must obtain a warrant from a magistrate, again based on probable cause.

Once she has decided to arrest you, the officer may continue to question you only after delivering a warning of your rights. This so-called *Miranda* warning—familiar to all viewers of TV cop shows—informs you of your Fifth Amendment right to avoid self-incrimination and the right to obtain the assistance of an attorney during any questioning that takes place. These rights, however, can be waived. If you continue to talk after the warning and without your attorney—perhaps to tell the police that the mask and gun are your son's Halloween costume and that you were only looking at a particular pair of shoes in the store window—the police can use anything you say as evidence against you in a criminal trial.

The checks on the power of the police to search and seize are of relatively recent vintage. Although they are based upon, and arguably required by, the Fourth, Fifth, and Sixth Amendments, the three cases that created these protections—*Miranda v. Arizona, Massiah v. United States,* and *Mapp v. Ohio*—were decided by the Warren Court in the 1960s.[3] They all reflected a marked shift in the Court's attitude toward the powers of the police vis-à-vis the rights of individual citizens and attempted to give some teeth to the elements of the due process model present in the Constitution. It is in contrast to the Warren Court in particular, with its emphasis on vindicating the individual constitutional rights of criminal defendants, that the Rehnquist Court is usually presented.

There is little doubt that the Rehnquist Court is particularly conservative in the field of criminal law and has strongly endorsed the crime-control model of criminal justice. In contrast to the Warren Court, with its due process leanings, the Rehnquist Court has, as Stanley H. Friedelbaum observes, "moved decisively to rework a wide array of judicially devised components of the criminal law by directly overturning or materially eroding their value as precedents."[4]

No Court has been perfectly consistent in its application of jurisprudential models or in its ideological approach, mainly because of the fact-specific nature of many adjudications as well as shifts in majorities based on where along the ideological spectrum a particular case falls. For example, consider *Terry v. Ohio,* ironically a Warren Court decision and one of the most important contributors to the conservative erosion of the Warren Court's legacy.[5] The facts presented in *Terry* are rather like the circumstances in the typical police investigation described above. An officer noticed Terry and another man on a street corner and observed an unusual pattern of behavior, in which they "pace[d] alternately along an identical route, pausing to stare in the same store window roughly twenty-four times; . . . followed immediately by a conference between the two men on the corner" and a discussion with a third man several blocks away. Based on these observations, the police officer stopped the three men and conducted a limited search for weapons. Guns were found, which formed the basis for Terry's conviction on charges of carrying a concealed weapon. The Court found that the police officer had acted reasonably in stopping the suspects, in part because the officer conducted not a full-blown search and seizure but only a "stop and frisk" for weapons. Although the Court limited the original rationale of *Terry* to a search for weapons and required some objective justification for the stop, subsequent decisions have substantially broadened its effect. The *Terry* decision has ultimately been used to authorize pretextual stops and has resulted in an increase in racial profiling.

In fact, this use of Warren-era precedent to erode Warren-era doctrine is a feature of the Rehnquist Court's conservative jurisprudence. Instead of disputing the content of the constitutional rights available to a citizen when stopped and questioned by the police, the Rehnquist Court has simply removed the adverse procedural consequences of police breaches of those rights.

For example, in *Caplin & Drysdale, Chartered v. United States*, a criminal defendant challenged a criminal forfeiture statute because, in taking his possessions, the state had left him without the means to retain the counsel of his choice.[6] He claimed that this violated his Sixth Amendment right to counsel. The Court disagreed, noting ,that he could retain an attorney—if one would work for free—and that the Sixth Amendment did not entitle him to the attorney of his choice, only to representation by counsel. The Court did not narrow the constitutional right to counsel—it simply adopted a rule that collaterally removed the defendant's meaningful enjoyment of the right.

The use of such judge-created procedural rules to limit the meaningfulness of constitutional rights is Chief Justice Rehnquist's own contribution to the jurisprudence of the Supreme Court. Three areas of law particularly demonstrate this impact: searches and seizures under the Fourth Amendment, the Fifth Amendment's right to avoid compelled self-incrimination, and the Eighth Amendment's prohibition on cruel and unusual punishment. In each area, Rehnquist's opinions during his tenure as an associate justice, often in dissent, foreshadowed the future direction of the Court.

The Warren Court determined that the only way to prevent police officers from violating the Fourth Amendment was to adopt a rule precluding the prosecution from using any evidence obtained in an unreasonable manner—in other words, without probable cause or without a validly issued warrant. That rule—called the exclusionary rule because such evidence was excluded from consideration at trial—is deeply unpopular with proponents of the crime-control model. Chief Justice Rehnquist has been extremely critical of the Fourth Amendment's exclusionary rule and has argued in dissent that *Mapp v. Ohio,* one of the principal Warren Court precedents developing this doctrine, be overruled.[7]

Of particular importance for the Fourth Amendment is the rule that searches and seizures may ordinarily be conducted only after obtaining a warrant from an impartial magistrate based on probable cause. The strictest application of the warrant requirement was given by the Warren Court, which held that "searches conducted outside the judicial process, without prior approval by judge or magistrate, are *per se* unreasonable under the Fourth Amendment—subject only to a few specifically established and well-delineated exceptions."[8] The contrary view, and one articulated strongly by Chief Justice Rehnquist, is that if the searches are "reasonable," the warrant requirement is redundant. Thus, if a suspect consents to a search, the officer may reasonably search anywhere he believes that consent would reach, including closed containers within the area to be searched.

The chief justice's adherence to the crime-control model of criminal justice and his disapproval of the due process model can be seen in his support for eliminating the exclusionary rule. His justification was based on a central element of the crime-control model: because admission of evidence from an unconstitutional search will injure only guilty defendants, not innocent ones, any evidence seized illegally should be permitted. In dissent, Rehnquist contended that "generally a warrant is not required to seize and search any movable property [such as "clothing, a briefcase or suitcase, packages, or a vehicle"] in the possession of a person properly arrested in a public place."[9] In *Delaware v. Prouse*, again contrary to the majority's view, he would also have allowed random stops of motorists in order to check driver's licenses and registration, finding that the state had an interest in preventing unlicensed, unsafe motorists from driving.[10] He has also argued that the police may execute an arrest warrant by searching the home of a third party even absent a search warrant, exigent circumstances, or consent and that police in carrying out a search warrant may frisk all patrons in a bar even without reasonable individualized suspicion that the patrons were armed.[11] In *Dunaway v. New York*, he argued in dissent that a defendant was not "seized" where he had "voluntarily accompanied the police to the station to answer their questions" and where the police behavior "was entirely free of physical force or show of authority."[12] Finally, he would have limited the circumstances in which courts may consider excluding evidence because of police misbehavior. In *Franks v. Delaware*, the central case entitling a defendant to a hearing to exclude or "suppress" illegally obtained police evidence, he would have held that probable cause could be based on a false statement and should not trigger an evidentiary hearing.[13]

The approach to criminal justice manifested in these dissenting opinions bore fruit in the majority opinions of the Court once Rehnquist became chief justice. For example, one way of getting around the warrant requirement is for the criminal suspect to waive those rights— so police often have an incentive to induce waiver or to "encourage consent." Many people do not realize that they have a right to refuse to consent to a search, or to limit the scope of a search, pending a warrant from a magistrate. So, in the example that began this chapter, if you were the car's driver, you could have refused to let the police officer search your car, particularly the trunk, without a warrant. However, if you mistakenly thought the officer was just being polite in asking and could search your car regardless of your consent, you might allow any search suggested by the officer. Chief Justice Rehnquist has not required that police inform suspects of their right to refuse consent: "The community has a real interest in encouraging consent, for the resulting search may yield necessary evidence for the solution and prosecution of crime, evidence that may ensure that a wholly innocent person is not wrongly charged with a criminal offense." So the chief justice's argument, which is now the law, is that "if [a suspect's] consent would reasonably be understood to extend to a particular [area or thing], the Fourth Amendment provides no grounds for requiring a more explicit authorization."[14] The scope of a search is determined not by where you would have drawn the line but by where a reasonable police officer would have done so. What matters is the officer's interpretation—given police priorities in searching—of your consent.

The Rehnquist Court has extended this principle even further in the case of searches outside the home—it has crafted an "exception" to the Fourth Amendment's warrant requirement for packages in a car. In *California v. Acevedo*, the Court permitted the police to search a container located within an automobile if they have probable cause to believe it held contraband or evidence but don't have a warrant for the package or probable cause to search the vehicle as a whole.[15] This is a direct application of the crime-control model that Chief Justice Rehnquist often articulated in dissent as an associate justice.

This same conception of criminal justice informs Chief Justice Rehnquist's approach to the Fifth Amendment. As an associate justice, Rehnquist often argued in dissent that the Fifth Amendment's protection against self-incrimination was being applied too broadly. One of the fundamental aspects of the right not to incriminate oneself (the "right to silence" or "taking the Fifth") is that a jury may not draw any adverse inferences from a defendant's refusal to testify. The burden is on the government to prove its case, not on the defendant to establish his or her innocence. In his dissenting opinion in *Carter v. Kentucky*, then-Justice Rehnquist would have eliminated this presumption and have held that there is no constitutional obligation on state trial judges to give "no adverse inference" instructions to the jury.[16] And in *Doyle v. Ohio*, he would have affirmed the defendants' convictions even though the prosecutor attempted to use their post-*Miranda* silence against them at trial.[17]

Under Chief Justice Rehnquist, the Court has evinced a deep skepticism about the validity of the *Miranda* decision itself. It has, for example, virtually eliminated the requirement that the *Miranda* waiver be given knowingly and intelligently. Such a requirement ensures that a suspect knows the consequences of starting to talk—that the evidence may be used to convict him—and so embodies a standard concern of the due process model of criminal justice. In *Colorado v. Connelly*, the Court refused to find that the waiver of a suspect's *Miranda* rights and his subsequent confession were involuntary, even though the suspect suffered from hallucinations rendering him unable "to make free and rational choices" at the time of his confession.[18] Chief Justice Rehnquist's use of the crime-control model changed the scope of the inquiry; the previous standard, which inquired whether a waiver had been knowing, intelligent, and voluntary, was abandoned for an analysis of police coercion: so long as the confession was not a product of police coercion, there was neither a *Miranda* nor a voluntariness violation.

The constitutionality of *Miranda* finally came before the Court in 2000 in *Dickerson v. United States*. This case dealt with the question of whether *Miranda* was simply a set of prophylactic judge-made rules that could be overruled by an act of Congress or was instead a constitutional basis for the exclusion of evidence. For years, the Rehnquist Court had indicated that the *Miranda* warnings had no firm basis in the Constitution. Rather, the decision was often characterized as a judge-created procedural rule that could be repealed by appropriate legislation. Although Chief Justice Rehnquist had frequently characterized *Miranda* the same way, in *Dickerson*, writing for the Court, he ultimately conceded the constitutionality of the *Miranda* decision. *Dickerson* thus seems, at first glance, to be an entrenchment of the due process model and an anomaly in the general approach of the Rehnquist Court's jurisprudence.[19]

Behind the chief justice's concession, however, stands a simple fact: the Court did not need to overrule *Miranda*, because it had already eviscerated most of its protections. The Rehnquist Court has burdened the assertion of *Miranda* rights with a variety of procedural impediments. One of the most important has been the "harmless

error" rule—the legal equivalent of the phrase "no harm, no foul."
Originally, where the courts found that evidence had been entered er-
roneously, they would reverse the verdict; the result was many technical acquittals. To evade this rule, subsequent courts developed the
harmless-error doctrine: as long as a defendant's case is not substantially harmed by the introduction of tainted evidence, there is no reason for a court of appeals to reverse the conviction. The Supreme
Court initially applied the federal harmless-error rule only to nonconstitutional errors. Under the Rehnquist Court, however, it was extended to include constitutional errors, even those that had previously
been considered so fundamental as to require automatic reversal, such
as the introduction into evidence of a coerced confession.

Confession evidence is often vital to a trial. Prosecutors will often
not even go to trial without confession evidence because it establishes
the government's case so compellingly. Coerced confessions, however,
are unconstitutional—they have, by definition, been obtained in violation of the defendant's Fifth Amendment rights. And the confession
has usually been coerced in a situation in which only the police and the
defendant know the facts, and the defendant has just been discredited
as a reliable witness because he has effectively convicted himself. If he
retracts his testimony, he can be impeached because he must either be
lying to the jury now or have lied to the police when he gave his initial
testimony. How could such an error ever be harmless?

Chief Justice Rehnquist has argued that the answer to that question turns on the difference between "structural" and "trial" errors.
Structural errors are those that make the trial as a whole a sham, such
as a biased judge or the refusal to provide defense counsel. "Trial" errors do not render the trial qualitatively unjust, according to the chief
justice, and can be cured—or rendered harmless—in a variety of ways,
including permitting further cross-examination or by the judge's in-
structing the jury to ignore the error. There is thus no need for a per se
rule of reversal for trial errors. So long as the evidence does not taint
the jury's decision-making process, the error is in fact harmless and,
because no legal "foul" has been committed, the verdict will be allowed
to stand.

Given the inability of the defense to counter such evidence, the per
se rule must apply to coerced confessions as well. Trials in which the

verdict is premised upon unconstitutionally obtained evidence of the defendant that cannot effectively be challenged surely suffer from a structural defect every bit as damning as having a biased judge or being refused defense counsel. It is simply not true that "the admission of an involuntary confession is a 'trial error' similar both in degree and kind to the erroneous admission of other types of evidence," as Rehnquist claims. In most cases, the defense counsel must rely almost exclusively on procedural objections to the improper admission of the evidence. The trial becomes skewed, and appellate courts cannot meaningfully apply harmless-error analysis.[20]

Chief Justice Rehnquist's approach here is another example of the crime-control model applied through a jurisprudence of "procedural narrowing." The chief justice does not change the right of a defendant to have his involuntary confession declared unconstitutional, but he does significantly narrow the number of occasions upon which that unconstitutionality will matter in practice.

Rehnquist's dissenting opinions as an associate justice also demonstrate a focus on restricting the constitutional protections established by the Eighth Amendment prohibition of cruel and unusual punishment and on limiting the scope of federal habeas corpus rules establishing a defendant's right to challenge the legal basis of his or her imprisonment.

The Eighth Amendment is particularly important because it has been used to attack the constitutionality of capital punishment. During the brief period between 1972 and 1976 during which the administration of the death penalty was often declared to violate the Eighth Amendment, Rehnquist joined the dissent in *Roberts v. Louisiana*, which argued that mandatory imposition of the death penalty does not amount to cruel and unusual punishment.[21] He also would have upheld a state statute that eliminated a "guilty without capital punishment" verdict, the effect of which was a mandatory death sentence if the defendant was found guilty. Furthermore, he would have held that imposing the death penalty for rape, or for aiding and abetting a felony during the course of which a murder is committed, or on an insane prisoner, does not violate the Eighth Amendment.[22]

Federal habeas law provides another example of the limitation of the constitutional rights of criminal defendants. Often defendants are represented by court-appointed counsel who—due to the lack of an effective public defender program, underfunding, or inexperience—are unprepared to mount an adequate defense of their client. As a consequence, they fail to raise important issues at time of trial. The consequences of this failure can be significant. Prior to *Wainwright v. Sykes*, the failure to raise a legal issue waived that issue only if there was an intentional relinquishment or abandonment of a known right or privilege.[23] For example, if the failure to raise a claim was made for tactical reasons, the issue could not be presented on appeal or during habeas proceedings. If the issue was dropped inadvertently, however, it could still be raised on appeal. In *Wainwright*, Justice Rehnquist overturned this rule and instituted a new test for habeas claims, as a result of which a defendant can raise a new issue for the first time during a habeas proceeding only if he can establish some overriding reason why he did not do so before—which is extremely difficult to satisfy unless there has been a change in the law or the state has withheld facts—and that the failure to raise the claim actually prejudiced his case.

This restriction of access to collateral review has been extended even further during Rehnquist's tenure as chief justice. In *Teague v. Lane*, the justices decided an issue not briefed by the parties that drastically narrowed the scope of habeas relief.[24] The issue was, again, a procedural one: whether a new constitutional rule could be applied in a petition for habeas corpus. *Teague* held that when a habeas petitioner argued for the application of a newly established rule of constitutional criminal procedure, a federal court could not decide the matter unless the new rule was one that would be applied retroactively. Moreover, in *Teague* and subsequent decisions, the Rehnquist Court has read the retroactive application exception very narrowly. The dramatic restriction effected by *Teague* can be seen in Justice Brennan's dissenting opinion, which lists many rights that were recognized for the first time on habeas corpus review.[25] As James S. Liebman states, "If Warren Burger led 'The Counter-Revolution That Wasn't,' then *Teague* reveals William Rehnquist in the vanguard of the Thermidor that is."[26]

Despite the general focus of its decisions on restricting the procedural rights of criminal defendants, it bears reemphasizing that the Rehnquist Court is not a monolithic entity. In fact, some commentators contend that the Rehnquist Court's more recent decisions have "reflect[ed] [its] efforts to refine its established conservative criminal justice doctrine."[27] The Court has handed down a number of decisions that could be characterized as falling within the due process model of criminal procedure; in just the 1999–2000 term, for example, one observer notes, "the Rehnquist Court decided in favor of individuals in cases concerning such issues as Fourth Amendment searches and seizures, Sixth Amendment ineffective assistance of counsel, ex post facto laws, Miranda warnings, and the Fifth Amendment privilege against compelled self-incrimination."[28] In these cases, in which the Court upheld a criminal defendant's constitutional rights, Chief Justice Rehnquist, however, found himself with the dissenters.

One effect of the Court's criminal policy has been to enlarge the potential for the use of racial profiling by the police. Its decisions increase the power of the police to arrest and search individuals and their automobiles for baseless, pretextual offenses. Unfortunately, the temptation for the use of racially motivated arrests and stops has proven far too great, and minorities have suffered accordingly.

Two decisions of the Rehnquist Court in 1996 and 2000 have made it particularly easy for the police to engage in racial profiling. In the first, *Whren v. United States*, the Court allowed police to stop a car and arrest the occupants for a minor traffic violation, such as turning without signaling, in order to follow up a suspicion that the occupants were engaged in something more serious.[29] Since such minor violations are very common, the decision makes it very easy for the police to stop a car just because the occupants are black or Mexican. The lower courts, following the lead of the Supreme Court, have pushed the *Whren* case to its limits. In one case, they allowed police to arrest the driver of a truck with four black occupants for not signaling when changing lanes to avoid a police car deliberately driven close to the truck; in another case, a black driver was arrested for momentarily crossing a yellow line.

In the second case, *Illinois v. Wardlow*, a black man in "an area known for heavy narcotics trafficking"—a description of many African-American and Hispanic neighborhoods in the United States—looked in the direction of patrolling police officers and ran away.[30] That was all, but it was enough for a 5–4 majority of the Court, in an opinion by Chief Justice Rehnquist, to allow the police to stop and frisk the man. Rehnquist called the man's action "unprovoked flight." As the dissenters pointed out, however, "among some citizens, particularly minorities and those residing in high crime areas, there is also the possibility that the fleeing person is entirely innocent, but, with or without justification, believes that contact with the police can itself be dangerous, apart from any criminal activity associated with the officers' sudden presence. For such a person, unprovoked flight is neither 'aberrant' nor 'abnormal.' "

Data demonstrate that racial profiling is not an illusory concern. Racial profiling and pretextual traffic stops, enabled by the *Terry* decision and facilitated by *Whren* and *Wardlow*, have become so endemic in many cities and on many highways that the offense has been termed "Driving While Black." The ACLU recently reported that almost 73 percent of motorists stopped and searched on I-95 in Maryland in 1996 were black, even though black violators made up less than 17 percent of observed traffic violators.[31] A review of police videotapes of stops by a Florida drug squad showed that black and Hispanic motorists made up 70 percent of the stops and 80 percent of vehicle searches on the Florida Turnpike; only nine of the more than one thousand recorded stops resulted in traffic citations, despite a Florida Supreme Court decision that allows traffic stops only for legitimate traffic violations.[32]

Perhaps the most insidious application of racial profiling occurs when all members of a certain race are considered suspects for a crime committed by a person of color. In 1988, during a police hunt for a rapist known as the "Central City Stalker," described as an African-American man in his early twenties with a mustache, 5'6" to 5'8", weighing between 120 and 140 pounds, the police stopped and frisked several hundred men and arrested sixty more simply because they were African American.[33]

In 1992, Oneonta College in upstate New York gave the names of 125 black students, its entire black male student body, to police officers investigating the attempted rape of an elderly white woman who alleged her assailant was a young black man.[34] Thirty-seven of the students who were stopped and questioned by the police sued the city, and the lower courts denied their claims. Perhaps not surprisingly, the Supreme Court declined to review that decision.

After the September 11 terrorist attacks, many persons appearing to be of Arab descent or of the Muslim faith were treated as suspects by the government and by individual Americans. As of October 13, 2001, U.S. authorities had arrested or detained 698 people.[35] As of October 2, 2001, the Council on American-Islamic Relations had received 785 reports of anti-Muslim incidents.[36]

Laws have been proposed that would authorize the police and the federal government to restrict criminal procedure protections, beyond that which would normally be constitutional, in cases where a criminal investigation involves suspected terrorism. The Supreme Court's approach to the constitutionality of these proposed laws, as well as to the persistent and widespread practice of racial profiling of racial and ethnic minorities, will depend on whether it follows the dominant thread of the Rehnquist Court's decisions or some of the recent cases protecting constitutional rights.

No Rights of Prisoners

WILLIAM E. HELLERSTEIN

For much of America's history, prisoners had no rights to speak of. Even after slavery had been abolished, courts spoke of prisoners as slaves of the state, and well into the twentieth century courts adhered to a hands-off policy concerning prisoner complaints about their treatment. Between 1956 and 1969, however, the Warren Court produced a constitutional revolution in criminal procedure that extended to state criminal defendants almost all the procedural protections of the Bill of Rights. Although only a few of the Warren Court's decisions addressed the rights of prisoners as such, its concern with due process of law and equal protection created a much wider sensitivity to the rights of prisoners that was not easily cabined.[1] Thus, as the Warren Court era drew to a close, the lower federal courts began to display a considerable and expanding receptivity to inmate grievances, especially those arising due to the living conditions and disciplinary practices in some of the country's most notorious prison systems.[2] These developments were accompanied by prison disturbances and several bloody prison riots, including the one in September 1971 at New York's Attica State Prison that took the lives of forty-three people.

Keeping pace with these events, there emanated within a short period of time from the newly constituted Supreme Court, under Chief Justice Warren Earl Burger, a host of decisions involving prisoners' rights to freedom of religion, freedom of speech, procedural due process, and adequate medical care.[3] Although the Burger Court subsequently reined in the thrust of some of its earlier rulings, its first years remain the high-water mark for prisoners' rights.

The Rehnquist Court, in contrast, has had a unique two-pronged negative effect on prisoners' rights. First, through its own jurisprudence, it has cut back significantly on the progressive rulings of the Burger Court, with some exceptions. Second, and perhaps with greater lethal effect, its jurisprudence has carried an implicit message that prisoners' rights are fair game for further evisceration, a message that Congress was quick to embrace in the highly restrictive Prison Litigation Reform Act of 1996.[4] Although some Rehnquist Court decisions have been favorable to prisoners, in virtually every major segment of prisoners' rights jurisprudence the Court's impact has been devastating. Here I will deal with four of these areas: freedom of speech and religion, due process, access to the courts, and inhumane treatment.

Three of the Rehnquist Court's earliest prisoners' rights cases involved the First Amendment's free speech and free exercise of religion clauses, and the Court left little doubt as to its hostility to such claims. A Missouri prison regulation restricted the rights of inmates to correspond with inmates in other penal institutions. The lower courts, applying the strict scrutiny standard normally attendant upon free-speech cases and following Burger Court precedent, had declared the regulation unconstitutional because it was more restrictive than necessary to meet the prison's security concerns.

In the Rehnquist Court this traditional speech standard was abandoned. Writing for a 5–4 majority in *Turner v. Safley*, Justice Sandra Day O'Connor declared that "when a prison regulation impinges on inmates' constitutional rights, the regulation is valid if it is reasonably related to legitimate penological interests." She added, "In our view, such a standard is necessary if 'prison administrators, . . . and not the courts [are] to make the difficult judgments concerning institutional operations.' "[5]

Almost sixty years ago, in his dissent in the infamous Japanese internment case, Justice Robert H. Jackson warned that a principle as "elastic and deferential" as whether official conduct is reasonable can lie "about like a loaded weapon ready for the hand of any authority that can bring forth a plausible claim of an urgent need. Every repetition imbeds that principle more deeply into our law and thinking and expands to its new purposes."[6] The decision in *Turner* bears out Jackson's admonitions, for as Justice John Paul Stevens—joined in dissent by Justices William J. Brennan, Thurgood Marshall, and Harry Blackmun—pointed out, an "open-ended reasonableness standard makes it much too easy to uphold restrictions on prisoners' First Amendment rights on the basis of administrative concerns and speculation about possible security risks rather than on the basis of evidence that the restrictions are needed to further an important governmental interest."

Just two years later, in *Thornburgh v. Abbott*, Justice Stevens's fears were realized. Applying the *Turner* standard, the Court allowed prison officials to reject a publication sent to an inmate "if it is detrimental to the security, good order, or discipline of the institution or if it might facilitate criminal activity."[7] The feeble protection provided by the "reasonableness" standard applied by the Court in *Thornburgh* was apparent on the face of the trial record, for many of the rejected publications criticized prison conditions or presented points of view that prison administrators simply did not like. There was no evidence that the particular incoming publications, some of which had been delivered to inmates in other prisons, had ever caused a disciplinary or security problem.

With *Turner*'s highly deferential "reasonableness" standard firmly embedded in the Court's First Amendment prison jurisprudence, a prison inmate's assertion of a right to provide legal assistance to other inmates stood no chance of success. In *Shaw v. Murphy*, Justice Clarence Thomas, writing for a unanimous Court, framed the issue as "whether *Turner* permits an *increase* in constitutional protection whenever a prisoner's communication includes legal advice" (emphasis added). He concluded that it does not because the "*Turner* factors concern only the relationship between the asserted penological interests and the prison regulation," and affording "First Amendment protection for inmate legal advice would undermine prison officials' ability to address the 'complex and intractable' problems of prison administration."[8]

Religious freedom fared no better, and again the contrast with the Burger Court is marked. In 1972, in *Cruz v. Beto*, the Burger Court held that a Buddhist was entitled to a reasonable opportunity to pursue his Buddhist faith comparable to that offered prisoners who adhered to more conventional religious precepts.[9] A harbinger of what the future might hold was the lone dissent by the Court's new associate justice, William H. Rehnquist. He severely criticized the majority for being insufficiently deferential to the administrative discretion of prison officials and denounced the Court's liberal construction of *pro se* prisoner complaints, those filed by prisoners themselves. In his view, prisoners cared less about the merits of their case than they did about obtaining "a short sabbatical to the nearest federal courthouse."

Within a year of Rehnquist's confirmation as chief justice in 1986, a different approach to prisoners' rights became apparent. In *O'Lone v. Estate of Shabazz*, decided in 1987, a bitterly divided Court upheld prison policies that prevented Muslim prisoners on work detail from attending Jumu'ah, a weekly Muslim congregational service commanded by the Koran.[10] Rehnquist, writing for the five-member majority, conceded that the prisoners' sincerely held religious beliefs compelled attendance at Jumu'ah. Nonetheless, he found that the lower court had erred in placing the burden on prison officials to show that there existed no less restrictive ways to meet prison needs. In putting that burden on the prison officials, declared Rehnquist, the lower court had failed to show the respect and deference the Constitution allows for the judgment of prison administrators.

Following *O'Lone*, federal courts have allowed prison officials asserting debatable security concerns or merely administrative inconvenience to prohibit inmates from wearing head coverings required by their religions, to prohibit possession of rosaries, to deny religious dietary restrictions, and to require the cutting of hair or the shaving of beards in contravention of the legitimate precepts of the inmates' religions.[11]

Life in prison is hard, even if served without incident. But such uneventful prison time is rare, and there are many things that prison officials can do that make life in prison even harder. To prevent the arbitrary imposition of prison sanctions and other officially imposed hardships, the Burger Court gave a broad interpretation to the Due Process Clause of the Fourteenth Amendment that a state shall not "deprive any person of life, liberty, or property without due process of law." It focused on either the severity of the deprivation or whether state rules governing the imposition of the deprivation gave the prisoner certain rights.[12] In *Wolff v. McDonnell* (1974), for example, the Court held that inmates could not be punished without a fair hearing for infractions of prison rules that resulted in the deprivation of good time credit, including notice of the charges, an opportunity to be heard and to present evidence, and a written statement of reasons for the decision reached.[13] Later cases, which involved decisions to assign prisoners to harsher prisons or to administrative segregation units, focused on whether the state had established criteria or limited discretion in the matter. The result was to give prisoners some procedural protections even as to the denial of relatively small freedoms or privileges.

In 1995, in *Sandin v. Conner*, these gains were lost.[14] A five-member majority led by Chief Justice Rehnquist greatly reduced a prisoner's right to a fair decision-making process by holding that when a prisoner was sentenced to punitive segregation he or she did not have a "liberty interest," an interest worthy of protection by due process. This decision represented a sea change in the Court's jurisprudence. Prisoners, unlike everyone else seeking due process of law, must now plead and prove that they have suffered an "*atypical* and *significant* hardship . . . in relation to the ordinary incidents of prison life*" (emphasis added). Prison litigation is different from other due process litigation, argued Rehnquist. Prison administrators need freedom to run secure prisons, and permitting them to punish inmates in ways that are not "atypical" or do not constitute "significant hardships" allows them the necessary flexibility.

As the impact of *Sandin v. Conner* continues to unfold, two consequences already are known. Prisoners can be sent to punitive segregation units regardless of a state's statutory law or regulations, without justification and even vindictively, without recourse to federal court because they have not suffered an "atypical" or "significant hardship."

Second, the decision has produced substantial confusion as federal judges try to figure out the meaning of those terms. Judging by the plethora of cases that still abound, all that the Court seems to have achieved is simply a reduction in the quantum of due process to which a prisoner is entitled.

A core principle of both the Warren and Burger Courts was that a prisoner had a right of access to the courts. Building on the 1969 Warren Court decision in *Johnson v. Avery* that prison officials could not interfere with a prisoner's right to prepare legal documents, in 1977 the Burger Court ruled in *Bounds v. Smith* that this included an affirmative right either to an adequate law library or to legal services to prepare legal documents.[15] In *Lewis v. Casey* in 1996, however, the Rehnquist Court seized the occasion to level a broadside against a prisoner's right to litigate in federal court.[16]

In *Lewis*, twenty-two inmates from Arizona prisons complained that Arizona's prison law libraries were inadequate to afford them access to the courts to which they were entitled. Their complaints included the inadequate training of library staff, insufficiently updated materials, and lack of assistance for illiterate or non-English-speaking inmates. After a three-month trial, the district court accepted their claims and appointed a special master to hold a hearing and draft an injunction that set forth standards and procedures for Arizona's prison law libraries.

All nine Supreme Court justices agreed that the injunction issued by the district court was overly broad. Rather than remand the case, however, Justice Antonin Scalia, for a five-member majority, complained about overuse of federal equitable power and the excessive reliance by federal judges on special masters, and he underscored the need for federal judges to defer to prison administrators and to be attentive to principles of federalism and the separation of powers. In the course of his opinion, Justice Scalia declared that prisoners did not have an abstract, freestanding right to a law library or legal assistance. To establish a constitutional violation, he said, an inmate must demonstrate that he or she suffered an actual injury brought about by shortcomings in the prison library or legal assistance program that have hindered, or are presently hindering, his efforts to pursue a nonfrivolous legal claim.

The conservative majority did not stop there. It had to dispose of affirmative language in the *Bounds* case that prison authorities must also enable a prisoner to determine the legitimacy of his grievances and to litigate effectively in court. It accomplished this simply by asserting that those principles had no antecedents in the Court's pre-*Bounds* cases and therefore should now be disclaimed. And to round out its circumscription of a prisoner's right of access to the courts, Justice Scalia added that *Bounds* also does not guarantee inmates the wherewithal to file any and every type of legal claim but requires only that they be provided with the tools to attack their sentences, directly or collaterally, and to challenge the conditions of their confinement. Insofar as a prisoner might be rendered unable to research or receive legal assistance with respect to other matters of importance, such as his or her parental or marital status, this language effectively imposes a form of civil death on a prisoner, a throwback to the days when states enacted civil death statutes.

Given the Rehnquist Court's diminution of prisoners' speech and religious rights, due process, and access to the courts, the Eighth Amendment's Cruel and Unusual Punishment Clause has taken on increasing importance as a bar to inhumane treatment. With but a few exceptions, however, the Court has rendered it more difficult for prisoners to seek redress under that amendment as well.

In 1976, the Burger Court's decision in *Estelle v. Gamble* made it possible for prisoners to win damages or obtain injunctive relief if prison officials were "deliberately indifferent" to their medical needs.[17] In *Hutto v. Finney*, decided two years later, the Court held that extensive confinement in an Arkansas prison's isolation unit constituted cruel and unusual punishment in light of the brutal conditions in that unit.[18] Because the conditions were so inhumane, the meaning of "deliberate indifference" was not an issue. Both decisions were of cardinal importance because the principles they announced became the foundation for lower federal court rulings that required prison officials to provide prisoners with basic human needs such as adequate food, clothing, shelter, and physical safety, including suicide-prevention procedures.

In *Wilson v. Seiter* the Rehnquist Court, in a majority opinion by Justice Scalia, turned the silk purse victory by prisoners in *Estelle v. Gamble* into a sow's ear.[19] Deliberate indifference, which requires proof of culpable intent, may be appropriate for measuring a discrete instance of the denial of medical care, as was the case in *Estelle*, but it is not meaningful to talk of the intent of prison officials when overall prison conditions are at issue. In *Wilson*, the Court treated them the same.

Wilson, an Ohio prison inmate, invoked the Cruel and Unusual Punishment Clause to challenge overcrowding, excessive noise, inadequate ventilation, unsanitary dining facilities and food preparation, and housing with mentally and physically ill inmates. Ignoring prior decisions that it was the objective nature of the conditions that determined whether they amounted to cruel and unusual punishment, the Court ruled that the prisoner must show that prison officials deliberately intended to create these conditions or were "deliberately indifferent" to their existence. But intent is often impossible to prove, especially where prison conditions are involved, for as the dissenters pointed out, "inhumane prison conditions often are the result of cumulative actions and inactions by numerous officials inside and outside a prison, sometimes over a long period of time. In those circumstances, it is far from clear whose intent should be examined."

Three years later, in *Farmer v. Brennan*, the Court explained what "deliberate indifference" meant: the prisoner has to show that prison officials actually knew the prisoner faced a substantial risk of harm and disregarded that risk by failing to take reasonable measures.[20] The result is that, as Justice Blackmun bitterly observed, if the "legislature refused to fund a prison adequately, the resulting barbaric conditions should not be immune from constitutional scrutiny simply because no prison official acted culpably."

In two Eighth Amendment rulings, the Rehnquist Court did provide prisoners with some added protection. In *Hudson v. McMillian*, the Court held that the use of excessive physical force against a prisoner can constitute cruel and unusual punishment even though the prisoner does not suffer serious injury.[21] At his Senate confirmation hearings the year before, Justice Clarence Thomas had testified that from his court of appeals windows he used to gaze upon lines of handcuffed prisoners and think "there but for the grace of God go I." Nevertheless, in solitary dissent he complained that "today's expansion of the Cruel and Unusual Punishment Clause beyond all bounds of history and precedent is, I suspect, yet another manifestation of the pervasive view that the Federal Constitution must address all ills in our society." He again dissented the following year, this time with Justice Scalia, when the Court in *Helling v. McKinney* allowed a Nevada prisoner to try to prove his claim that prison officials, with deliberate indifference, had exposed him to levels of tobacco smoke from other prisoners that posed an unreasonable risk to his health in violation of the Eighth Amendment.[22]

In 1996, Congress passed the Prison Litigation Reform Act (PLRA), which drastically curtails a prisoner's right to improve his conditions of confinement. The act includes significant limitations on the ability of prisoners to proceed without paying fees and on the award of attorneys' fees, thereby reducing prison inmates' ability to interest lawyers in their cases. In addition, the PLRA bars prisoners from bringing damages lawsuits for mental or emotional injuries "without a prior showing of physical injury." As recently interpreted by the Rehnquist Court in *Booth v. Churner*, the act also requires prisoners to exhaust administrative remedies, even when they are suing only for damages, a remedy that prison officials have no authority to provide.[23]

Furthermore, the act significantly circumscribes a federal court's remedial powers. It provides that prospective relief with respect to prison conditions shall not be granted "unless the court finds that such relief is narrowly drawn, extends no further than necessary to correct the violations of the Federal right, and is the least intrusive means necessary to correct violation of the Federal right." Courts are instructed not to construe the act "to order the construction of prisons or the raising of taxes, or to repeal or detract from otherwise applicable limitations on the remedial powers of courts." The act also restricts severely the effects of consent judgments, a large number of which are the result of settlements agreed upon by the parties rather than fully litigated cases.

For many years, federal courts have ordered prisoners released in order to remedy severe overcrowding. The act now explicitly limits this authority to cases in which a court must have previously ordered less intrusive relief that failed to remedy the situation. Also, these orders can now be issued only by three-judge district courts after a finding by "clear and convincing" evidence—rather than merely a preponderance—that "crowding is the primary cause of the violation of a Federal right and no other relief will remedy the violation of the Federal right." Finally, the act makes it much easier for prison officials to terminate injunctive relief obtained by prisoners and to even obtain a stay of such relief by simply filing a motion to terminate.

Under our Constitution's structured separation of powers, each branch of government is normally deemed responsible for its own actions. But the question can be asked whether the Prison Litigation Reform Act, whose draconian effect on the rights of prisoners is still unfolding, would have become law had the Rehnquist Court stood more firmly in defense of principles laid down by decisions of the Warren and Burger Courts. The question suggests at least two possible answers. On the one hand, Congress has every right to attempt to override a decision or a line of decisions of the Court that it disagrees with, as it did unsuccessfully when it legislatively sought to supersede the Court's landmark ruling in *Miranda v. Arizona*, an effort that was rebuffed by the Court in *Dickerson v. United States*.[24] On the other hand, Congress can proceed not only in a direction that it believes fits comfortably within the Court's jurisprudence but also where there is room for it to move beyond where the Court has gone. With respect to prisoners' rights, proving the existence of a direct causal link between the Rehnquist Court's decisions and the enactment of the Prison Litigation Reform Act may be difficult. It seems very likely, however, that those decisions, and perhaps even more importantly their language, mostly in dicta, in which the Court either trivialized or minimized the claims of prisoners, contributed significantly to a climate in which Congress felt exceptionally secure in its own programmatic savaging of a prisoner's right to redress in the federal courts.

Speculation on the future direction of the Supreme Court's jurisprudence in a particular area can often be a fool's game. But such speculation with regard to the Rehnquist Court's prisoners' rights jurisprudence incurs but slight risk. Without any changes in its membership, the Court will continue to be grudging in its willingness to value prisoners' concerns over prison officials' ability to run their institutions without interference from federal courts. The Court will probably remain protective of inmates when they are subjected to physical harm, as several of the Eighth Amendment cases suggest. But in virtually all other aspects of prison life, new ground will not be broken on behalf of prisoners; rather, prisoners will have their hands full merely retaining whatever gains have been secured. The Prison Litigation Reform Act undoubtedly will prevent many types of cases from even being heard in federal courts, let alone the Supreme Court.

The prisoners' rights "revolution," if it can even be called that, has been over for some time. To the extent that society was led to believe that it was all about whether a prisoner had a constitutional right to "chunky" rather than "smooth" peanut butter, the revolution had no chance. One can only hope that we are not on our way back to the bread-and-water stage.

Capital Punishment:

Accelerating the Dance with Death

STEPHEN BRIGHT

Having virtually conceded that both fairness and rationality cannot be achieved in the administration of the death penalty, the Court has chosen to deregulate the entire enterprise, replacing, it would seem, substantive constitutional requirements with mere aesthetics, and abdicating its statutorily and constitutionally imposed duty to provide meaningful judicial oversight to the administration of death by the States. . . . The path the Court has chosen lessens us all.   —Justice Harry A. Blackmun[1]

The Rehnquist Court has made it easier for states to carry out executions no matter how incompetent the lawyer appointed to defend the accused, no matter how clear the racial discrimination in the infliction of the death penalty, and regardless of whether the condemned was a child at the time the crime was committed, mentally ill, or even innocent. A return to states' rights has taken precedence over the vindication of the Bill of Rights, and "finality"—bringing proceedings to an end and carrying out executions—has taken precedence over fairness.

William H. Rehnquist has always been a strong supporter of the widest application and most expeditious imposition of the death penalty. In his first year on the Court, he dissented from *Furman v. Georgia* (1972), which declared the death penalty unconstitutional because of the arbitrariness and discrimination in its infliction.[2] Four years later, he voted to uphold five death penalty statutes enacted by the states in response to *Furman*. These included laws that made the death penalty mandatory for certain crimes and that the majority struck down because the laws ignored the individual circumstances of the person facing execution.[3]

In 1981, Rehnquist expressed concern over the delay caused by appellate review of capital cases and suggested that the Supreme Court review every case in order to expedite executions.[4] Although that suggestion was rejected by the other members of the Court, Rehnquist led a campaign to erect what Justice Harry Blackmun described as a "byzantine morass of arbitrary, unnecessary, and unjustifiable impediments to the vindication of federal rights."[5] Rehnquist has nevertheless prevailed. In a series of decisions—with Rehnquist often writing the majority opinion—the Court has imposed numerous barriers to federal court review of capital cases and drastically restricted the scope of that review.

Those efforts have been so successful in shredding the safety net of constitutional protections that even supporters of capital punishment have expressed grave concern about the lack of fairness and the risk of executing the innocent. Justices Blackmun and Lewis Powell, who voted with Rehnquist to uphold the death penalty in *Furman v. Georgia* in 1972 and to uphold even the mandatory laws in 1976, eventually came to the conclusion that capital punishment should be abandoned. Even Justice Sandra Day O'Connor, who joined the Court in 1981 and regularly votes to uphold death sentences and to restrict review of capital cases, noted that "serious questions were being raised about whether the death penalty is being fairly administered in this country." At the time she spoke, over ninety people sentenced to death had been exonerated since the death penalty was reinstated in 1976, leading Justice O'Connor to admit frankly, "If statistics are any indication, the system may well be allowing some innocent defendants to be executed."[6] And several years earlier, in a speech to the American Bar Association, Justice John Paul Stevens pointed out that scientific evidence had conclusively established that a number of innocent people had been sentenced to death; he suggested that one reason was the shabby legal representation appointed for defendants too poor to hire their own lawyers.

George Ryan, the Republican governor of Illinois, had supported the death penalty and other "tough on crime" measures as a member of the Illinois legislature. Early in 2000, however, he expressed dismay at his state's "shameful record of convicting innocent people and putting them on death row" and declared a moratorium on capital punishment.

By the time of these realizations, however, the Rehnquist Court had largely succeeded in giving the states free rein to carry out executions. And other governors not as concerned as Governor Ryan allow the machinery of death to chug on. Texas's busy execution chamber dispatched 152 people during the six-year period George W. Bush was governor. Brad Thomas, Florida Governor Jeb Bush's top policy adviser on capital punishment, expressed his enthusiasm for expediting executions with the comment "Bring in the witnesses, put [the defendants] on a gurney, and let's rock and roll."[7] For those who share such sentiments, the Rehnquist Court has made it easier than ever to dance with death.

Criminal cases, especially capital cases, are often affected by the passions of the moment. This and the enormity of a state's taking the life of a human being should result in more careful scrutiny by the courts of any case in which the death penalty is imposed. The Rehnquist Court, however, has steadily reduced the power of the federal courts to review capital cases and to set aside convictions and death sentences obtained in violation of the Bill of Rights. It has required strict compliance with various technical rules that are not even known by many of the court-appointed lawyers assigned to defend poor people. A lawyer's mistake can, therefore, cost a client his or her life. For example, the Court held that the federal courts could not review issues raised by Roger Keith Coleman, who was condemned to death in Virginia, because his lawyers were late in filing his notice of appeal. In that case, Justice O'Connor opened the majority opinion with the startling sentence "This is a case about federalism," to which Justice Blackmun responded in dissent:

> Federalism; comity; state sovereignty; preservation of state resources; certainty: The majority methodically inventories these

multifarious state interests. . . . One searches the majority's opinion in vain, however, for any mention of petitioner Coleman's right to a criminal proceeding free from constitutional defect or his interest in finding a forum for his constitutional challenge to his conviction and sentence of death.[8]

The Court has also ruled that federal courts may not even address some issues on habeas corpus review, making it easier, even where constitutional violations are found, for federal judges to shrug their shoulders, pronounce the violations "harmless," and affirm the conviction and sentence.[9]

The Rehnquist Court has restricted the power of courts to grant new trials even when it has been discovered after trial that egregious police or prosecutorial misconduct may have contributed to the conviction or that new evidence indicates that the defendant is actually innocent of the crime. In cases where prosecutors have refused to disclose evidence that cast doubt on the defendant's guilt or have misled the jury, the Court requires a showing that the misconduct actually affected the outcome, forcing courts to guess at what would or would not have mattered to a jury at trial and substituting trial by appellate judges for trial by jury. For example, the Court has held that a prosecutor's failure to disclose exculpatory evidence regarding the accuracy of an eyewitness's testimony does not require it to overturn a death sentence.[10]

Even innocence is irrelevant. In a case from Texas, the prosecutor expressly repudiated the version of events he had used to obtain defendant Jesse Dwayne Jacobs's conviction and death sentence. The prosecutor argued at Jacobs's trial that Jacobs had fired the fatal shot. The same prosecutor argued, however, at a subsequent trial involving a second person accused of the same crime that it was the second person who had fired the fatal shot. Indeed, the prosecutor now believed Jacobs's claim that he had not fired the shot or even anticipated that the victim would be shot; the prosecutor also agreed that parts of Jacobs's confession were false. Under the argument advanced at the second trial, Jacobs would not have been eligible for the death penalty under Texas law.[11] Nevertheless, only Justices Stevens, Ginsburg, and Breyer were willing to stay the execution, and Jacobs was executed.

In the few cases where prosecutorial misconduct was so egregious that the Court set aside the conviction, Rehnquist, Scalia, and Thomas dissented.[12] Justice Scalia has written that "in a sensible system of criminal justice" wrongful conviction is avoided at the trial level, not by appellate review. However, the exoneration of many people in noncapital as well as capital cases through the use of DNA evidence—and, in the cases of three persons sentenced to death in Illinois, by the findings of a journalism class at Northwestern University—demonstrates that trials often result in wrongful convictions, and evidence of police or prosecutorial misconduct, incompetent defense lawyering, and innocence sometimes surfaces after trial, during the appellate review and even later.

The Court's restrictions on federal habeas corpus review were not enough for Congress. In the Antiterrorism and Effective Death Penalty Act, which President Bill Clinton signed into law in 1996, Congress added still more procedural barriers, including a one-year time limit for filing federal habeas corpus petitions. These restrictions on federal habeas corpus review rest on the notion that state court judges will enforce the Constitution as well as their federal counterparts. This ignores political realities. An elected judge who suppresses evidence seized in an unlawful search or arrest or who even grants a change of venue to another part of the state where there has been no publicity about the crime, thereby depriving the local community of its chance to exact vengeance, may be ruining any hope of being reelected. More than a few judges have learned this lesson the hard way. In 1994, for example, after the Texas Court of Criminal Appeals reversed a conviction in a particularly notorious capital case, a former chairman of the state Republican Party called for Republicans to take over the court. The voters responded, and by 1998 the court, which had once been made up exclusively of Democrats, was composed entirely of Republicans who were all strong supporters of the death penalty.[13]

In 1996, Justice Penny White was voted off the Tennessee Supreme Court after a decision in a death penalty case led the Republican Party and other groups to oppose her retention. Immediately after the retention election, the governor of Tennessee, Don Sundquist, said, "Should a judge look over his shoulder [in making decisions] about whether they're going to be thrown out of office? I hope so."

Sundquist's effort to intimidate the state judiciary was similar to that of Governor George Deukmejian of California. In 1986, Deukmejian campaigned against three justices of the state supreme court because they had voted to overturn death sentences. All lost their seats, and Deukmejian appointed their replacements. Ever since, the California Supreme Court has had one of the highest affirmance rates in capital cases of any court in the country.

The courts in Texas, Tennessee, California, and other states have sacrificed the rule of law and the independence of their judiciaries to bring about executions. As Supreme Court Justice Stevens once remarked, "It was never contemplated that the individual who has to protect our individual rights would have to consider what decision would produce the most votes." Twenty years ago people sentenced to death in violation of the Constitution in those states could reasonably expect that a federal court, insulated from political pressures, would prevent their execution. As a result of Rehnquist Court decisions, they now have little hope that federal courts will surmount the many barriers and vindicate their constitutional rights.

Restrictions imposed by the Court and Congress on the power of federal courts to review capital cases represent not only a return to states' rights; such restrictions send the message that constitutional violations are inconsequential, show a willingness to tolerate departures from constitutional standards in the quest for convictions and death sentences, and reaffirm the notion voiced so often by politicians that the Bill of Rights is nothing more than a collection of "technicalities" that get in the way of convicting the accused and carrying out their sentences.

The death penalty is frequently imposed not because the defendant committed the worst crime but because he or she had the misfortune of being assigned the worst court-appointed lawyer. Poor people have no control over the legal representation they receive; judges appoint lawyers to defend them. Justice Ruth Bader Ginsburg said in 2001 that she had "yet to see a death case among the dozens coming to the Supreme Court . . . in which the defendant was well represented at trial. People who are well represented at trial do not get the death penalty."[14] At some later, critical stages of appellate review, the poor may not have a lawyer at all, making it impossible for them to gain access to courts that would be open to them if they could afford a lawyer. The Rehnquist Court is responsible for allowing this shameful lack of fairness and equal justice to worsen during a time of unprecedented prosperity in American society and the legal profession.

The right to counsel is the most fundamental constitutional right a person charged with a crime has, because every other right depends upon it. An attorney is also needed to conduct an independent investigation and present the evidence necessary for a fair and reliable determination of guilt or innocence and, in case of conviction, a proper sentence. But many states still do not have public defender systems and pay the lawyers assigned to defend the poor very little. Consequently, the most difficult cases, where the client's life is at stake, attract few lawyers willing to accept wages that are among the lowest in the legal profession. In many states, lawyers defending a capital case are paid less than a paralegal is paid for completing forms for a bankruptcy case. Lawyers appointed to represent the accused often lack the knowledge, skill, and resources and sometimes even the inclination to provide a competent defense. About one-third of the people sentenced to death in Illinois, Kentucky, and Texas were represented at their capital trials by lawyers who were later disbarred, suspended, or convicted of crimes. Courts have even upheld cases when lawyers appointed to represent the defendant were drunk or asleep during trial. One federal judge, in reluctantly upholding a death sentence, observed that, as interpreted by the Supreme Court, the Constitution "does not require that the accused, even in a capital case, be represented by able or effective counsel."[15]

While the Supreme Court has required since 1932 that a poor person facing the death penalty be provided a lawyer at trial, it was not until 1984 that the Supreme Court addressed the quality of legal representation. In the case of David Leroy Washington, who was sentenced to death in Florida, the Court held that, while an accused is entitled to a "reasonably competent" lawyer, a conviction or death sentence should not be overturned even if the lawyer's representation was deficient unless the defendant shows a "reasonable probability" that the lawyer's incompetence affected the outcome.[16] Justice Thurgood Marshall, in dissent, warned that this standard was so malleable that it was meaningless.

He was right. Several years later, Justice Marshall observed that "capital defendants frequently suffer the consequences of having trial counsel who are ill-equipped to handle capital cases" and pointed to numerous cases in which the lawyers "presented no evidence in mitigation of their clients' sentences because they did not know what to offer or how to offer it, or had not read the state's sentencing statute."[17] Justice O'Connor, who in 1984 authored the opinion setting the lax standard, later acknowledged the poor quality of representation, noting that in 2000 a defendant represented by court-appointed lawyers in Texas was 28 percent more likely to be convicted than one who retained private counsel and 44 percent more likely to receive the death penalty when convicted.[18]

Even though it has long been apparent that lower courts have been tolerating levels of representation that make a mockery of the right to counsel, the Rehnquist Court has refused to reexamine the standard. At the same time, the Court has tightened what Justice Marshall described as an "increasingly pernicious visegrip" by adopting strict rules prohibiting consideration of constitutional violations because a court-appointed attorney did not present critical evidence or was ignorant of the law or did not follow a state procedural rule. According to the Court, even when the ignorance or ineptitude of a court-appointed lawyer costs a client vindication of his or her constitutional rights—and thus his or her life—the client's right to counsel has not been violated. The Court has found only once in its history that a lawyer's poor performance violated the right to counsel. In that case, decided in 2000, the Court held that a man sentenced to death in Virginia was denied his right to counsel by the lawyer's failure to investigate the man's background and present evidence that was "indispensable" for the jury's sentencing decision. Even there, Rehnquist, Scalia, and Thomas dissented. They voted to allow Virginia to execute the man.[19]

There are important stages in the review of capital cases following trial at which, as a result of a decision by the Rehnquist Court, a poor person may have no lawyer at all. The Supreme Court held in the early

1960s that a poor person accused of a crime was constitutionally guaranteed a lawyer at trial and for one appeal.[20] After his appointment in 1972 as associate justice, Rehnquist wrote that a poor person is not entitled to a lawyer for the further appeals that many states provide or for petitions to review convictions.

In 1989, in an opinion by Chief Justice Rehnquist, the Court by a 5–4 vote refused to make an exception for people under sentence of death, rejecting the argument that those condemned to death had a special need for counsel in the later stages of review because of the complexity of capital cases, the enormity of the punishment, and the immense time pressures of preparing and filing a petition before an execution date. In *Murray v. Giarratano* Rehnquist wrote: "Virginia may quite sensibly decide to concentrate the resources it devotes to providing attorneys to capital defendants at the trial and appellate stages of a capital proceeding" instead of at later stages of review. At the time of the man's trial, however, Virginia paid lawyers appointed to defend people facing the death penalty less than any other state. It had decided not to apply its resources to providing adequate representation for the poor at *any* stage of the proceedings.[21]

As a result of that decision, Exzavious Gibson, whose I.Q. was found on different tests to be between 76 and 82, stood, totally bewildered and without a lawyer, in front of a judge at his first state postconviction hearing. The case went forward as follows:

The Court: OK, Mr. Gibson, are you ready to proceed?
Mr. Gibson: I don't have an attorney.
The Court: I understand that.
Mr. Gibson: I am not waiving my rights.
The Court: I understand that. Do you have any evidence to put up?
Mr. Gibson: I don't know what to plead.
The Court: Huh?
Mr. Gibson: I don't know what to plead.

Nevertheless, the hearing continued. The state of Georgia was represented by a lawyer who specializes in capital cases and who presented evidence that Gibson was helpless to challenge or cross-examine. Gibson offered no evidence, examined no witnesses, and made no objections. The judge denied Gibson relief by signing an order prepared by the attorney general's office without making a single change. The Georgia Supreme Court held that Gibson had no right to counsel and affirmed the denial of relief. And Gibson is in no way unique. People facing the death penalty in Alabama, Texas, and other states are frequently unable to find lawyers before their deadlines for filing petitions for review.

Thanks to the Rehnquist Court, whether people sentenced to death receive full review of their case before execution is a function of income and luck. A person wealthy enough to hire a lawyer can obtain full review. Virtually all of those on death row, however, are poor. If they are fortunate, a lawyer may volunteer to represent them for free or they may be in a state that provides lawyers during the later stages of review. Very frequently, however, the condemned face death alone without access to the legal system.

The criminal justice system is the part of society least affected by the civil rights movement in large measure because of the hands-off approach to racial discrimination in criminal cases taken by the Rehnquist Court in a capital case in 1987.

A person of color is more likely than a white person to be stopped by the police, to be abused by the police during that stop, to be taken into custody, to be denied bail, to be charged with a serious crime, and to be convicted. He or she is also apt to receive a harsher sentence than a white person. Although people of color are most likely to be victims of crime and to be charged with crime, there are few people of color among judges, prosecutors, and lawyers. Even in communities with substantial African-American or Hispanic populations, the jury may be all white. Often, the only person of color who sits in front of the bar in the courtroom is the person on trial.

Study after study has confirmed that race plays a role in capital sentencing. In 2000, the U.S. Department of Justice examined its own record and found that over three-fourths of the people given the death penalty were members of racial minorities. Over half were African

American. A major reason for these disparities is the vast and unchecked discretion afforded prosecutors. The two most important decisions in a death penalty case are made not by the jury or judge but by the prosecutor. First, the prosecutor decides whether to seek the death penalty, which is always a matter of discretion—the prosecutor is never required to seek death. Second, the prosecutor has complete discretion in deciding whether to offer a sentence less than death in exchange for the defendant's guilty plea. The overwhelming majority of all criminal cases, including capital cases, are resolved not by trials but by plea bargains. In the thirty-eight states that have the death penalty, 97.5 percent of the chief prosecutors are white. In eighteen of the states, all the prosecutors are white.

Although African Americans constitute only 12 percent of the national population, they are victims of half the murders that are committed in this country. Yet 80 percent of those on death row are there for crimes against white people. The discrepancy is even greater in the death-belt states of the South. In Georgia and Alabama, for example, African Americans are the victims of 65 percent of the homicides, yet 80 percent of those sentenced to death are sentenced for crimes against white persons. In Georgia, of the twenty-three people executed between 1976 (when the death penalty was reinstated) and 2000, twenty-one were executed for crimes against white victims.

The racial disparities are stark, undeniable, and disturbing in an increasingly diverse society. Courts seldom, however, address the extent to which those disparities are the result of racial prejudice, whether conscious or unconscious, because the Rehnquist Court held in 1987 that racial disparities in sentencing did not even raise an inference of discrimination. The Court allowed Georgia to continue to carry out executions despite substantial racial disparities in its infliction.[22] In a 5–4 opinion by Justice Powell, the Court found that such disparities were "inevitable" and rejected them as a basis for inferring discrimination. Instead, the Court required defendants to prove that the decision makers in their individual cases discriminated, a virtually impossible task unless the prosecutor or a juror admits as much. The Court justified this impossible burden in part because the claim of racial discrimination in capital cases, "taken to its logical conclusion, throws into

serious question the principles that underlie our entire criminal justice
system." Justice William Brennan, in dissent, characterized this concern as "a fear of too much justice."

The decision frustrated challenges to sentencing disparities in other
areas and even to ugly racial incidents. The Georgia Supreme Court
refused to allow a hearing into why 98 percent of those serving a life
sentence for a second drug offense are African American. Two African-
American men sentenced to death by an all-white jury in Utah were
executed even though jurors received a note that contained the words
"Hang the Nigger's" (*sic*) and a drawing of a figure hanging from a gal-
lows. No court, state or federal, ever conducted a hearing on such
questions as who wrote the note, what influence it had on the jurors,
and how widely they may have discussed it.[23]

Although the Rehnquist Court held in a 5–4 opinion by Scalia in 1989
that mentally retarded persons were subject to capital punishment, the
Court found in 2002 that much has changed and a national consensus
had developed against execution of the mentally retarded.[24] The
Court, by a 6–3 vote, concluded that the execution of mentally retarded people violates the Constitution, because the mentally retarded,
owing to their limitations in the areas of reasoning, judgment, and
control of impulses, lack the same degree of moral culpability as people who are not retarded.

Rehnquist and Scalia both filed dissents that were joined by
Thomas. Scalia's dissent was arrogant, caustic, and sarcastic in its dis-
dain for the majority's reasoning, the universal abandonment of executing the mentally retarded by other countries, and the opinions of
professional and religious organizations. (Scalia dismissed the views of
the leaders of his own religion, saying that Catholic bishops are so far
from being representative, even of the views of Catholics, that they are
currently the object of intense national—and even ecumenical—criti-
cism.) He predicted that capital trials would become a game because
defendants would feign mental retardation. However, a finding of
mental retardation requires that limited intellectual functioning be apparent during childhood. Since mentally retarded persons have a his-

tory of low test scores and special education classes during childhood, it is virtually impossible to feign retardation. This did not prevent Scalia from cynically predicting that capital trials would become a game of those facing condemnation pretending to be retarded.

Scalia's view that world opinion and practices are irrelevant won the votes of four other justices in an earlier case that upheld the death penalty for children who were sixteen or seventeen at the time of their crimes.[25] As a result, since 1990 the United States is one of only six countries that have executed people who were under eighteen at the time of the crime—the other five are Iran, Nigeria, Pakistan, Saudi Arabia, and Yemen. Even in that rather undistinguished company, the United States leads by far in the number executed. The United States is one of only two countries that have not ratified the International Covenant on the Rights of the Child, which among other things would prohibit the execution of people who were children at the time of their crimes; the other country is Somalia.

In declaring a moratorium on executions in Illinois, Governor George Ryan said that the execution of an innocent person would be the "ultimate nightmare." Many supporters of capital punishment argue, however, that society is fighting a "war on crime," and, as in any other war, there will be some innocent casualties. An earlier notion of justice, that it was better for ten guilty people to go free than for an innocent person to be convicted, is being eclipsed. One legacy of the Rehnquist Court will be the replacement of that notion with another, that sacrificing a few innocent lives to wage a war on crime is more important than ensuring the fairness and reliability of a conviction and death sentence. It is a sad commentary on the Court, its members, and the times. Justice Brennan observed in one of his many eloquent dissents, "the way in which we choose those who will die reveals the depth of moral commitment among the living."[26] As Justice Blackmun ultimately concluded, the path the Court has chosen lessens us all.

INDIVIDUAL RIGHTS

The Religion Clauses:
A Study in Confusion

NORMAN REDLICH

When William H. Rehnquist became chief justice of the United States in 1986, the Supreme Court inherited a complicated framework of judicial doctrines developed over four decades of litigation involving the Religion Clauses. Despite the inevitable ebbs and flows in the interpretation of these doctrines, they are justly credited with providing this diverse country with a degree of protection for religious freedom, religious diversity, and religious peace that is unrivaled anywhere else in the world. The critical decisions that guided the Court's interpretations of the Religion Clauses during the first fifteen years of Rehnquist's tenure as chief justice were rooted and decided within the context of these same precedents, although different facts, changes in Court personnel, and the inevitable modifications in positions have left the seminal cases in a state of uncertainty, a result that may be traced in part to the countervailing doctrines these very decisions generated. Litigation has focused primarily on the Establishment Clause (the church-state separation provision), with "free exercise" concerns generally merged with, and subsumed by, issues involving freedom of speech.

When read carefully, the pivotal Establishment Clause decisions, partly because of their vagueness and generality of language, contain various doctrinal seeds that have allowed the Court broad flexibility to move in different directions on a host of issues. In the 1947 *Everson* case, for example, the Court proclaimed that the government could not pass laws "which aid one religion, aid all religions, or prefer one religion over another," but nevertheless upheld state financing of bus transportation to parents of parochial school students, thereby maintaining a degree of flexibility that may not have been predicted or fully understood at the time.[1]

The doctrines in the prayer cases were similarly untidy. In *Engel v. Vitale*, a 1962 case striking down a New York law directing the reading of a so-called nondenominational prayer at the beginning of each school day, the Court carefully limited the opinion to the precise facts before it, opening the way for religious teaching to reenter the public schools through persons distributing religious literature, engaging in prayer on college premises, or allowing student religious publications to be funded by the state and circulated on school grounds.[2]

In essence, then, the Rehnquist Court inherited constitutional doctrines that were sufficiently flexible so that a sharply divided Court could decide cases, even reaching seemingly contradictory results, without explicitly overruling any of the foundational cases that formed the jurisprudence bequeathed to it.

It would be a mistake, however, to view the Rehnquist years as a wholesale undermining of the judicial edifice created in prior years. The strong separationist dicta in *Everson* have not been overruled. Even with the narrowing of the traditional concept of separation of church and state by countervailing doctrines—the necessity of accommodating religious beliefs, concepts of so-called neutrality toward religion, expansion of speech-protecting principles to encompass religious activities that take place in public forums, including public schools—the Court has refused to erase the line prohibiting direct financial aid to religious schools or government promulgation of and support for prayers in schools. Instead we have a multitude of conflicting and contradictory principles that could either topple the delicate constitutional arrangement or reinvigorate the constitutional principles that the Rehnquist Court inherited. The interpretation of the Religion Clauses is still very much up for grabs.

The main building block of the establishment structure bequeathed to the Rehnquist Court was *Lemon v. Kurtzman*.[3] In *Lemon*, with its famous three-part test—secular purpose, religiously neutral effects, and no excessive entanglement with religion—the Court refused to allow the government to subsidize the salaries of teachers employed by parochial schools. Without addressing the question whether the principal or primary effect of the programs was the advancement of religion, the Court held that the "cumulative impact of the entire relationship arising under the statutes . . . involves excessive entanglement between government and religion." Because the teachers subsidized by the government could use the aid to engage in religious teaching rather than to cover textbook or transportation costs, as allowed in prior cases, the state was constitutionally obligated to take precautions to guard against that happening.

But by instituting needed safeguards to prevent government resources from being "diverted" for religious use, the state would inevitably run afoul of the "excessive entanglement" prong of the test. "These prophylactic contacts," the *Lemon* ruling held, "involve excessive and enduring entanglement between state and church." Some justices, prominent among whom was then-Justice Rehnquist, decried the Catch-22 thus created. In their view, government support provided to religious schools was deemed by the majority to create an impermissible risk of advancing religion through behind-the-door diversions of state resources to religious uses, thus running afoul of the "effects" test. Any attempt to prevent such a diversion, however, would be barred by concerns about "excessive entanglement."

Thus, courts were required to decide whether a particular form of aid fell on the textbook and transportation side of the line or whether it was sufficiently "divertible" to place it within the range of objections that applied to government subsidization of teacher salaries. The complexity of this line-drawing enterprise was well illustrated in *Wolman v. Walter*, a 1977 case in which the Court upheld government provision of secular textbooks, standardized testing and scoring, and therapeutic services but barred state aid in the form of loans of audiovisual equipment and transportation for field trips. The Court concluded that TVs and VCRs could be used for religious teaching and that field trips presented opportunities to inculcate religious lessons.[4]

The Rehnquist Court (or a majority therein) was clearly impatient with the approach it inherited, with its fine distinctions on the issue of divertibility and its stringency. Yet the Court did not squarely overrule *Lemon*. It did, however, substantially modify its application in various contexts. Whereas the precedents in the pre-Rehnquist era had demonstrated a deep and abiding concern about the diversion of government resources for religious use, fearful that a message of symbolic church-state union and government endorsement of religion might be communicated, the Rehnquist majority was less troubled than its predecessors when the aid was first given to private individuals who then decided to channel the aid to religious purposes. Hence, the Rehnquist Court, with echoes of *Everson*, found no constitutional defects in a student's decision to use government vocational assistance to study at a Christian college to become a pastor (*Witters*) or in a state's provision of sign language interpreters for students who attended a Roman Catholic high school (*Zobrest*).[5] The Court gave great weight to the fact that the aid that ultimately flowed to religious institutions did so only as a result of the genuinely independent and private choices of aid recipients, even though there was no dispute that the government-financed interpreter would be "diverted" to translate the religious message taught in class or that the vocational assistance might be "diverted" to allow the aspiring pastor to attend a class on the New Testament taught by a Baptist minister.

Perhaps the most important modification the Rehnquist Court effected in applying *Lemon* was a repudiation of the assumption that certain types of government aid are more "divertible"—and therefore more objectionable—than others. In the process, the Court undid the Catch-22 created by prior cases. Absent compelling evidence to the contrary, the Rehnquist Court operated on the assumption that public school and sectarian school teachers alike would heed constitutional limits and not funnel government resources, of whatever form, toward religious teaching. Pervasive monitoring was thus unnecessary, and the possibility of excessive entanglement between church and state was therefore eliminated. Using this modified framework, in 1997 the Court, in *Agostini v. Felton*, overturned an injunction issued twelve years earlier in *Aguilar v. Felton* that had barred the use of federal funds to pay the salaries of public employees who taught in parochial schools.[6] There would no longer be any per se legal bar to these forms of state aid.

Then, in *Mitchell v. Helms*, decided in 2000, a majority of the Court concluded that the Constitution does not prohibit the government from lending instructional materials and equipment to religiously affiliated schools—even in classes taught by teachers hired by, and under the supervision of, sectarian schools.[7] *Wolman*, with its classification of various types of aid depending on their "divertibility," was expressly overruled.

What the Rehnquist Court did not do, however, is as important as what it did do. While a plurality of the Court would elevate "neutrality" or "evenhandedness" as the sole inquiry—allowing government aid to be diverted to religious use as long as aid recipients are not defined by reference to their religion and the substance of the state aid itself does not contain religious content—this position failed to garner the requisite five votes. As a result, the doctrines in this area remain muddy and contentious. Both concurring and dissenting justices make clear that diversion of government resources to religious instruction, if the violation can be proved, is still barred under current law, with the possible exception being cases where the aid passes through a private party who independently decides to direct the government aid to religious use. Finally, the level of permissible constitutional violations remains uncertain. Notwithstanding verifiable instances of impermissible diversion in *Helms*, for example, the majority refused to invalidate the assistance program, finding these violations "de minimis."

Yet the basic *Lemon* approach survives. Neutrality has not triumphed as the ultimate touchstone, probably because it is unworkable. The wall of separation has, however, become conspicuously more porous. While the Rehnquist majority did not overrule the foundational cases in this area, other decisions—notably *Wolman* and *Aguilar*—that gave shape and content to that doctrinal foundation were unabashedly renounced.

Given this Court's willingness to overturn disfavored precedents, the future direction of religion-funding cases remains in doubt. Still, at least for now, the Establishment Clause has bite or at least a threatening bark. Direct cash grants to religious schools remain unconstitutional, even though similar secular organizations qualify. Widespread diversion of government aid to religious use, if the violations can be proven, continues to be constitutionally barred, even though the type of aid in question is distributed without regard to religious affiliation by the government under a broad-based secular program. As important as are the justices' disagreements in the funding cases, these disputes should not obscure the crucial role the Establishment Clause has played in separating politics and religion, despite the efforts of the Christian right and certain religious leaders and opportunistic politicians to breach the barrier the clause has erected.

In the 1962 case of *Engel v. Vitale*, the Supreme Court held that "it is no part of the business of government to compose official prayers for any group of the American people to recite as a part of a religious program carried on by government." New York, therefore, could not require a school prayer—even a nondenominational one (a religious impossibility)—to be recited in class at the beginning of each school day. Since then, the Court has been vigilant in guarding this clear prohibition from erosion. In *School District of Abington v. Schempp* (1963), the Court expanded the reach of *Engel* by invalidating a Pennsylvania law requiring "at least ten verses from the Holy Bible . . . be read, without comment, at the opening of each public school on each school day," even though the law provided that "any child shall be excused from such Bible reading, or attending such Bible reading, upon the written request of his parent or guardian" and even though the particular verses were to be chosen by the students reading the verses, without the participation of teachers.[8] The Court recognized this as an exercise with "a devotional and religious character." It was not designed to present the Bible objectively as a work of history or literature but was a state-sponsored religious observance.

These cases led to more subtle and sophisticated attempts by states to introduce religion back into the public schools. Alabama, for example, enacted a statute in 1981 providing for a moment of silence "for meditation or voluntary prayer." No religious exercise was involved, only a brief opportunity for students to pray if they so wished. Or so the state argued. In *Wallace v. Jaffree*, however, the Court carefully examined the background and legislative history behind the enactment and found that the goal was "an effort to return voluntary prayer to the public schools," with the explicit reference to "voluntary prayer" indicating the state's "endorsement"—a result at odds "with the established principle that the government must pursue a course of complete neutrality toward religion."[9]

These skeptical attitudes and probing examinations into the statutory purpose continued even after Rehnquist became chief justice. In *Edwards v. Aguillard* (1987), for example, the Court struck down Louisiana's Creationism Act, which required teachers who taught evolution to teach "creation science" as well.[10] The Court rejected the state's contention that the act, under the banner of academic freedom, merely sought to guarantee the evenhanded presentation of scientific evidence to schoolchildren. Cutting through the thicket of verbiage, the Court recognized that the act was intended "to narrow the science curriculum . . . by counterbalancing its teaching at every turn with the teaching of creationism."

Five years later, in *Lee v. Weisman*, the Court banned graduation prayers in a public school—even though the prayers were allegedly nondenominational and were delivered by invited members of the clergy otherwise unconnected to the school.[11] The Court expressed concern about the potential for coercion of high school students and about the symbolic message of state endorsement that might be communicated. In rejecting the school's free-speech claims, the Court recognized a special role for the Establishment Clause. "Speech is protected by ensuring its full expression even when the government participates," the Court wrote. "In religious debate or expression the government is not a prime participant. . . . The Establishment Clause is a specific prohibition on forms of state intervention in religious affairs with no precise counterpart in the speech provisions."

Given such strong language and the constraint imposed by a relatively unbroken line of precedents barring prayers and religious teaching in the public schools, the Court's recent decision in *Santa Fe Independent School District v. Doe* (2000) is unsurprising.[12] The Court refused to allow student-led, student-initiated prayers at football games, finding that these invocations were implicitly authorized by government policy and took place "on government property at government-sponsored school-related events." Echoing *Lee*'s concerns about coercion of students who might object to participating in the religious exercise and "the actual or perceived" endorsement of religion that would be conveyed by the intimate association of church and state, the Rehnquist Court refused to allow the prayers even though the students voted to have them. The government could not, in the Court's words, establish "a governmental electoral mechanism that turns the school into a forum for religious debate."

Despite these cases, it would be a mistake to conclude that prayers and religious instructions are now completely expelled from public schools. One cannot predict, for example, whether a pure moment of silence, without the incriminating bits of legislative history that infected the laws in *Wallace* and *Aguillard*, would withstand constitutional challenge. Moreover, recent developments have cast doubt on the scope of the Court's prayers cases, as schools throughout the country try various ways to evade the constitutional prohibition. In *Adler v. Duval County School Board*, high school seniors were permitted to vote on whether to include opening and closing "messages" at graduation and to elect the student speaker to deliver an uncensored speech.[13] The Eleventh Circuit approved this practice because it concerned only generic graduation "messages" not "invocations," religion was not at the core of the arrangement, and, unlike in *Santa Fe*, school officials could not censor the student's speech. Despite *Lee*, *Santa Fe*, and similar cases that appear to have established clear principles, another line of precedents seems to permit religion to reenter the public schools through another route.

Establishment concerns seem to retreat into the background when pitted against free-speech values. In *Widmar v. Vincent*, decided in 1981, the Court struck down a university regulation prohibiting the use of university buildings or grounds "for purposes of religious worship or religious teaching."[14] The university defended its policy on establishment grounds—maintaining church-state separation—but the Court found that there were no establishment dangers under the *Lemon* test and that the university's policy discriminated against religious groups on the basis of their religious message, thereby violating the Free Exercise and Free Speech Clauses. To accomplish this result, the Court in *Widmar* characterized prayers as ordinary speech and ignored the special role reserved for the Establishment Clause as evidenced in the school prayer cases. But religious speech, as we have seen, is different from secular speech when the government is involved. By conceptualizing prayers that take place in government-supported public forums as ordinary speech, the Court chipped away at the independent force of the Establishment Clause.

In addition to equating prayers with everyday speech, the Court, in requiring equal access to facilities by religious groups, concluded that "an open forum in a public university does not confer any imprimatur of state approval on religious sects or practices." This concept elevated neutrality as a crucial, if not decisive, factor in the inquiry. But neutrality in the prayers and funding cases is an elusive standard. Clearly, the government cannot pay the salaries of ministers and rabbis simply because there is a broad-based program distributing money to leaders of similarly situated secular groups. A principal cannot invite a cleric to lead a graduation prayer even if the school invites other prominent members of the community holding contrasting viewpoints to give graduation speeches. In emphasizing neutrality here, the Court has substituted confusion and uncertainty for reasoned analysis. Moreover, the presence of a "public forum"—the condition that triggers the requirement of neutrality in these cases—has defied clear definition despite decades of case law.

The confusion is evident in *Rosenberger v. Rector and Visitors of the University of Virginia*, a 1995 case invalidating the university's guidelines withholding support payments from any group that "primarily promotes or manifests a particular belief in or about a deity or an ultimate reality."[15] Invoking the regulation, the university denied financial assistance to a student newspaper, *Wide Awake*, that espoused a Christian perspective. In striking down the regulation on free-speech grounds, a 5–4 majority of the Court, arguing that the university had violated neutrality principles governing speech in "limited public forums," expanded the definition of "public forum" from a purely physical concept with tangible geographical boundaries (*Widmar*) to a more amorphous concept of support and assistance. By creating a common fund to support student activities, the university had created a "public forum," the Court found, rejecting the distinction advanced by the university between access to facilities and provision of funds. If, as *Rosenberger* strongly suggests, neutrality is the touchstone and the government must be neutral as between religious and secular groups in the provision of funds, nothing stands in the way of unrestricted state funding of religious activities, as long as religious groups are not favored.

The Rehnquist Court has done little to sort out the resulting confused state of affairs. In *Good News Club v. Milford Central School* (2001), the Court affirmed the reasoning of *Widmar* and *Rosenberger* without clarifying the relationship these public forum cases have with other doctrinal areas and without reconciling any of the tensions between establishment and free-speech concerns.[16] The policy in *Good News Club* authorized district residents to use the school building after school for, among other things, "instruction in education, learning, or the arts," as well as "social, civic, recreational, and entertainment uses pertaining to the community welfare." The school denied use of the facility to the Good News Club on the grounds that the club's purpose was to conduct religious instruction and that granting it access would violate the Establishment Clause. Following *Rosenberger*, the Court struck down the policy on free-speech grounds, finding that the school had created a limited public forum and that excluding the religious group would constitute impermissible viewpoint discrimination.

The Court in *Good News Club* ignored the factual similarity to the funding and prayers cases. Children were the primary members of the audience in *Good News Club*, as in *Lee* and *Santa Fe*, raising the distinct possibility that children might misperceive state endorsement of religion from the simple fact that religious activities were taking place on school premises. Moreover, there existed a potential for students to feel subtle coercion to participate, even though the afterschool lessons, like a graduation ceremony or a football game, were not technically part of the required curriculum.

Good News Club purported simply to follow *Rosenberger*'s neutrality requirement concerning "public forums," but it ignored the significance of the expansion of the public forum's concept to classroom space. Speech in a public school setting, however, troubled the Court in the funding and prayers cases because of the possible divisiveness and coercion when the *government* sponsors a public forum in which religious issues are debated—whether in the form of an electoral mechanism, as in *Santa Fe*, or in the form of an afterschool religion class outside the core curriculum, as in *Good News Club*.

Hence, despite the apparent neatness and consistency in the doctrines concerning school prayers (*Lee* and *Santa Fe*, which rather uniformly held that prayers are impermissible) and the doctrines concerning public forums (*Widmar, Rosenberger, Good News Club*, which rather uniformly held that public forums must be made available to religious groups), the doctrines, when viewed together, become very blurred. These two lines of cases cannot be hermetically sealed off. The Rehnquist Court's failure to address their relationship has maintained and increased chaos at the margin. While *Good News Club*, because of its similarity to *Rosenberger*, was treated as a public forum case, it could easily be viewed as a funding case, in which the religious group impermissibly "diverted" a government resource (classroom space) toward religious use, or a school prayers case, with all the attendant dangers of subtle coercion and symbolic union of church and state.

These public forum and free-speech cases, decided with broad church-state implications, demonstrate the confusion and uncertainty that results when cases are decided separately within the boundaries of artificial categories that lack defensible content or structure.

As in the free-speech and public forum cases, the Rehnquist Court has compartmentalized free-exercise claims without considering whether the recognition by a government of a "freedom of religion" exception to a statute constitutes an establishment of religion. Thus, the theoretical tension that may exist between free-exercise and establishment concerns does not appear to have caused the Court to deviate from its practice of evaluating free-exercise claims in terms that appear quite unrelated to the Establishment Clause. For example, when the Rehnquist Court, in perhaps its most important free-exercise case, the 1990 decision in *Employment Division, Department of Human Resources v. Smith*, upheld Oregon's denial of employment benefits to a Native American fired for ingesting peyote, it made no reference to the argument that granting the exception might constitute an establishment of religion.[17] Instead, the Court treated the free-exercise claim in isolation and considered only the question of whether, in evaluating free-exercise claims, it should apply a "compelling state interest" standard or the more lenient "rational relationship" standard. Departing from earlier cases that had invalidated state laws for failing to meet a "compelling state interest" test, the Rehnquist Court allowed states far more leeway in restricting religious practices as long as governments could provide a meaningful "rational relationship" for upholding the statute. Indeed, in its most prominent case upholding a free-exercise claim, *Church of the Lukumi Babalu Aye, Inc., v. City of Hialeah*, the Court struck down an ordinance enacted to prevent members of the Santeria faith from performing animal sacrifices, a principal tenet of their religion.[18] Since the ordinance was not a statute of general applicability and therefore differed from zoning or unemployment insurance laws, the Court had little difficulty concluding that the statute demonstrated hostility against the Santeria religion and therefore violated the Free Exercise Clause.

It is commonly asserted that the Free Exercise and Establishment Clauses are in conflict because a ruling that a government program violates the Establishment Clause arguably violates someone's free-exercise rights, and the recognition of a free-exercise claim usually creates a preference for a religious practice in violation of the Establishment Clause. As a result, the Court has not invoked the Establishment Clause as a basis for rejecting a free-exercise claim, and it has not invoked the Free Exercise Clause in rejecting an Establishment Clause claim. Instead, the Court seems determined to decide Free Exercise and Establishment Clause issues without consideration of the consequences that a decision under one clause might have on the other. For example, although *Smith* has been widely criticized for its cavalier treatment of the free-exercise claims of peyote users (applying a standard of mere rationality to laws that allegedly infringe on free exercise), the Court narrowed the scope of free-exercise protection and did not bolster its conclusion by arguing that the state's exemption might have created Establishment Clause problems. Similarly, in *City of Boerne v. Flores*, the Court rejected a federal statute, the Religious Freedom Restoration Act (RFRA), by significantly narrowing Congress's powers to enforce the Fourteenth Amendment and did not contend, as it was urged to, that RFRA was an unconstitutional establishment.[19] And, in the *Hialeah* case, the Court found a free-exercise violation without contending, as it might have done, that upholding the practice of ritual sacrifice would have violated the Establishment Clause. Although these three free-exercise cases—*Smith, Hialeah,* and *City of Boerne*—can be criticized for their failure to address the tension between establishment and free-exercise issues, they send a clear message that the Court intends to treat Free Exercise and Establishment Clause issues separately, without addressing the tension that the clauses create. Indeed, this compartmentalization may reflect the reality that the two clauses, which appear to be in conflict, are in their separate ways protective of religious freedom.

This theme of uncertainty continues as one examines cases dealing with the display of religious symbols in public places. In *Stone v. Graham* (1980), the Court invalidated a Kentucky statute requiring the display of the Ten Commandments in every public classroom, because the Court did not believe the posting had a legitimate secular purpose.[20] The significance of this ruling was quickly limited four years later, however, in *Lynch v. Donnelly*, in which the Court upheld the display of a crèche, or Nativity scene, as part of the city of Pawtucket's Christmas celebration.[21] The Court found that the display served a secular purpose: "celebrat[ing] the Holiday and . . . depict[ing] the origins of that Holiday." Even though the government-sponsored display might provide an "incidental benefit" to religion, this was not enough to invalidate the practice, and the display did not produce an excessive entanglement between church and state.

Once again, these pre–Rehnquist Court cases failed to lay down any bright-line rules, merely declaring that the issue is necessarily one of line drawing because "total separation [of church and state] is not possible in an absolute sense. Some relationship between government and religious organizations is inevitable."

The fact-intensive nature, as well as the hopelessly amorphous quality, of the inquiry became quite evident in the 1989 case *Allegheny County v. ACLU*.[22] The Rehnquist Court was faced with the constitutionality of two religious displays: a crèche on the grand staircase of the county courthouse, and an eighteen-foot menorah next to a forty-five-foot Christmas tree and a sign saluting liberty—all placed in front of the city-county building. After a detailed description of the decoration, the Court first found that the display of the crèche communicated impermissible government endorsement of "a patently Christian message." Among the factors analyzed were the floral arrangement surrounding the crèche and the location of the crèche in "the main and most beautiful part of the building."

With respect to the menorah, the Court reached the opposite conclusion. It found that "in the shadow of the tree, the menorah is readily understood as simply a recognition that Christmas is not the only traditional way of observing the winter-holiday season" and was unlikely to convey an impermissible message of endorsement.

Once again, while the structure of the *Lemon* test was preserved in this line of cases, its application, as evidenced by the Court's struggle to draw a principled line in *Allegheny*, is anything but straightforward. What seemed to be a clear-cut prohibition in *Stone* became a far more nebulous and unpredictable inquiry, with the ultimate outcome depending heavily on the particularities of each case—including details that one would think only interior decorators would notice and analyze—and the views of five justices at the particular moment.

At the end of the 2001–02 term, two issues in the area of religion remained heavily contested. The first was vouchers. The second was charitable choice. How would they fare constitutionally? Would the rush toward the elusive goal of "neutrality" sweep away the barriers created by the Court's interpretation of the Establishment Clause?

It is not difficult to understand the appeal of school vouchers to certain parents and politicians. Designed to maximize choice and competition, they would allow more parents the financial ability to make schooling decisions for their children, including placing them in religiously affiliated private schools. Also, the Rehnquist Court had made it much easier for vouchers to pass constitutional muster. *Mitchell v. Helms*, which allowed the government to lend equipment and instructional materials to private schools, widened the door. In addition, vouchers, unlike equipment loans, are given directly to parents, who then exercise the independent choice to direct the aid to religious educational institutions.

Not surprisingly, a narrowly divided Supreme Court, on the last day of the 2001–02 term, upheld the Cleveland school voucher program while at the same time distinguishing the voucher case from earlier cases that had invalidated direct financial assistance to religious schools. In his opinion in *Zelman v. Simmons-Harris*, Chief Justice Rehnquist, writing for a 5–4 majority, emphasized the concept of "neutrality," and the fact that the voucher program involved decisions by individual parents rather than direct grants, such as had been held invalid in *Lemon*. Relying on *Mueller v. Allen*, *Zobrest*, *Witters*, and *Agostini*, the chief justice's opinion upheld the voucher program without overruling or even mentioning *Lemon*. Both the opinion of the Court and Justice O'Connor's concurrence distinguished the voucher program from financial grants and argued that it was similar to other programs of direct financial assistance, disregarding the fact that the voucher program enabled substantial sums of money to flow directly to the religious schools. Thus, the most eagerly anticipated Establishment Clause case since *Lemon* was treated by the chief justice and by Justice O'Connor as a case that added nothing to Establishment Clause jurisprudence and, indeed, was compelled by precedents.[23]

As was to be expected, the four dissenting justices (Stevens, Souter, Ginsburg, and Breyer) emphasized in their opinions that the voucher program was a thinly disguised attempt to funnel public money directly to religious schools.

Having passed constitutional muster, voucher programs can be expected to flourish and, when combined with the types of financial assistance that were upheld in *Mitchell v. Helms*, direct extensive infusions of public money to religious schools. Only the financial and political limitations on state spending, as well as the continued objections to vouchers by advocates of public education and church-state separation, stand in the way of a drastic shift in the financing of primary education from public to religious schools.

These impediments may not apply to charitable choice, although that, too, has begun to encounter political resistance. Still, it is difficult for political leaders to object to programs that, for example, provide drug treatment assistance to heroin addicts or counsel teenage mothers in crisis.

Nevertheless, charitable choice programs are highly vulnerable on constitutional grounds—perhaps more so than school vouchers—for they place religion at the center of government-funded programs, thereby raising major establishment concerns. According to preliminary details, the government, at least in some cases, would be directly funneling money to religious organizations to help them provide useful social services. Therefore, unlike the sign language assistance program in *Zobrest*, the vocational assistance program in *Witters*, or even school vouchers, there is no buffer between church and state.

Coercion, moreover, may be involved in some situations, as when a homeless person, for example, is placed in a situation where he or she feels a compulsion to join in a prayer before receiving a meal in a soup kitchen. With the government's role in the welfare area rapidly shrinking, the homeless person might not be able to find a nearby government-run kitchen. And even if homeless persons are not required to pray—just as no one is required to bow one's head in the pre–football game prayer—the element of coercion is undoubtedly present, especially given the vulnerable position that the homeless frequently endure.

Another danger is the possibility of communicating a message of state endorsement. The close partnership between church and state conveys a symbol of church-state union that is not unlike the display of a cross or a Nativity scene in front of city hall.

Mitchell v. Helms, *Agostini*, and *Zelman* indicate clearly that "neutrality" can destroy rather than preserve the constitutional separation of church and state. The Establishment Clause, apart and beyond the free-speech and free-exercise provisions, must be kept as an independent barrier against the diversion of government funds to religious use. The confused state of the law that the Rehnquist Court has left us gives cause for concern, particularly since the constitutionality of charitable choice remains very much an open question and the separationist position seems to command only a narrow and fluctuating Court majority. Also open are the efforts of certain religious groups to seek government money and to insert religion into various aspects of public life. To those for whom the separation of church and state is a unique and important aspect of religious diversity, freedom, and peace, a future that depends on the decisions of one or two Supreme Court justices is a terrifying prospect.

The First Amendment:
The High Ground and the Low Road

JAMIN B. RASKIN

Compared with its astonishing decision in *Bush v. Gore*—which established that truth can do irreparable harm, burdens on pregnant chads are more suspect than burdens on pregnant women, poor dimpled chads have a right to equal treatment across county lines that poor dimpled children do not, the remedy for hypothetical potential variations in counting a few ballots is the disenfranchisement of tens of thousands of people, and Supreme Court decisions can be good for the evening of publication only—the Rehnquist Court's performance thus far in First Amendment cases would seem to merit something like a standing ovation.

Rather than turning back the clock on freedom of expression, in several landmark cases—especially *Hustler v. Falwell, Texas v. Johnson*, and *Rosenberger v. Rector and Visitors of the University of Virginia*—the Court has continued to spell out the commanding theme of modern free-speech jurisprudence: the state shall not deliberately repress expression, however extreme, based on its content or viewpoint.[1] It even propelled this principle into cyberspace with libertarian Internet decisions like *Reno v. ACLU*, which established that, when it comes to sex talk, grown-ups can take care of their own children and need not be treated like children themselves, and *Ashcroft v. Free Speech Coalition*, which struck as overbroad Congress's attempt to criminalize "computer-generated" images that create the appearance of minors having sex.[2]

At the level of principle and rhetoric, shifting majorities on the Court have thus far taken the high ground on speech, even when the hard-right justices, such as Chief Justice William H. Rehnquist, have filed curmudgeonly dissents. This rhetorical speech friendliness has both historical and contemporary causes. The Court's libertarian course was set in earlier cases like *New York Times v. Sullivan, Cohen v. California*, and *Brandenburg v. Ohio*.[3] In the Rehnquist Court, Justice David Souter is a powerful intellectual force for free expression, and Justice Anthony Kennedy, often joining with the moderate-liberal bloc, has emerged as a lucid champion of free speech and viewpoint neutrality—well, sometimes at least.

But for fascinating political reasons, even the authority-worshiping hard right of the Court occasionally finds itself defending free speech. The ferocious right-wing backlash against "political correctness" and campus hate-speech codes in the late 1980s and the 1990s gave free-speech grievances an unprecedented halo in conservative circles during the Rehnquist era. In *R.A.V. v. St. Paul*, where the Court unanimously struck down a municipal anti-cross-burning ordinance, Justice Antonin Scalia wrote a haughty opinion, clearly animated by anti-PC sentiment, insisting that, while fighting words generally can be criminalized, *racist* fighting words cannot be selectively targeted.[4] The conservative justices' plutocratic identification of unrestrained campaign spending with political expression, which dates back to *Buckley v. Valeo*, has further convinced them that they are now the true champions of free expression, holding the line against political censorship by liberal reformers.[5] For the antichoice justices—Rehnquist, Scalia, and Clarence Thomas—a number of edgy cases where obstructionist "prolife" street protestors have invoked the First Amendment against prosecution have clinched their sense of free-speech martyrdom on the cross of political correctness.[6]

These "culture war" crosscurrents came to a head in 2000 in *Boy Scouts of America v. Dale*, where the solid conservative bloc of five, over the dissent of Justices John Paul Stevens, David Souter, Ruth Bader Ginsburg, and Stephen Breyer, found that the Boy Scouts, as a private group exercising associational rights, could exclude gay scoutmasters.[7] The liberals argued, a bit oddly, that the Boy Scouts had never really taken an expressive position against homosexuality. But the real issue was not whether the exclusion of gays was an expressive associational statement but whether a state could treat the Boy Scouts as a public accommodation like a hotel or restaurant. There are interesting arguments both ways that never really appeared in the case, but the die had probably been cast already in *Hurley v. Irish-American Gay, Lesbian, and Bisexual Group of Boston*, where Justice Souter found that since the private organizers of the St. Patrick's Day parade in Boston had a right to define their own message, they could exclude an unwanted formal contingent from the Boston Gay, Lesbian, and Bisexual Group.[8] A good answer to these anachronistic homophobic expressions by private groups in civil society is political counterpressure and boycott, effective strategies that are currently costing the Boy Scouts dearly.

But the conservatives' preening free-speech rhetoric in high-profile pet cases where they *like* the speech they are protecting masks a complex and demoralizing system of speech repression they have shaped for the rest of society. When citizens have challenged censorship and viewpoint discrimination in major social institutions such as schools, public television networks, electoral systems, and federally funded programs, the Rehnquist majority has habitually deferred to government and rolled over the rights of the people. Thus, while certain kinds of extreme speech and exclusionary policies have won larger-than-life symbolic victories in the Rehnquist Court, ordinary speech has suffered terrible defeats and reversals at the level of institutional practices (including the practice of electoral democracy), where Americans need the First Amendment most. The Court has grabbed the rhetorical high ground but has usually taken the low road when it really counts.

To give the devil its due, however, the Rehnquist Court has quite faithfully rejected frontal attacks on offensive speech in public places by way of the criminal and civil law. The classic decision in this vein is *Texas v. Johnson* (1989), where a five-justice majority made up of Justices William Brennan, Thurgood Marshall, Harry Blackmun, Scalia, and Kennedy struck down the criminal conviction of Gregory Johnson, a member of the Revolutionary Communist Party, for "desecrating" an

American flag at the 1984 Republican National Convention.[9] In *Texas v. Johnson*, Justice Brennan revived the spirit of Justice Robert Jackson in his famous 1943 opinion in *West Virginia v. Barnette*, which invalidated West Virginia's compulsory Pledge of Allegiance and flag salute.[10] Echoing Jackson's syntax and enunciating a kind of political free-exercise principle, Justice Brennan wrote: "If there is a bedrock principle underlying the First Amendment, it is that the Government may not prohibit the expression of an idea simply because society finds the idea itself offensive or disagreeable."

Making essentially literary and sentimental arguments, the dissenters wanted the Court to elevate its loyalty to the flag over its loyalty to free speech. Rehnquist, joined by Byron White and Sandra Day O'Connor, excerpted flowery passages of flag-related poetry and fiction to show that "the American flag has occupied a unique position as the symbol of our Nation, a uniqueness that justifies a governmental prohibition against flag burning in the way Johnson did here." It evidently did not matter to them that the First Amendment contains no exception for censorship of speech about "unique" patriotic symbols, because, as Rehnquist put it, "millions and millions of Americans regard [the flag] with an almost mystical reverence."

Also dissenting, Justice John Paul Stevens, ordinarily well grounded in the First Amendment, echoed the call to suspend conventional rules of constitutional analysis: "Even if flag burning could be considered just another species of symbolic speech under the *logical* application of the rules that the Court has developed in its interpretation of the First Amendment in other contexts, this case has an *intangible* dimension that makes those rules inapplicable." He likened the claimed right to burn flags in protest to "a federal right to post bulletin boards and graffiti on the Washington Monument." The problem with the analogy is that we have but one Washington Monument, all of it public property; if it is defaced, it is ruined for all. But we have tens of millions of flags, the private property of citizens who can do with them what they will without harming their fellow citizens' enjoyment of their own flags or the government's control of its own supply.

In 1988, the year before *Texas v. Johnson*, the conservatives joined the liberals in deciding *Hustler v. Falwell*, which will be another enduring statement of free-speech values. In *Hustler*, there was no American flag to hypnotize the conservatives, and Chief Justice Rehnquist actually wrote the opinion for a unanimous Court. *Hustler* had lampooned Jerry Falwell, leader of the Moral Majority, insinuating in an advertisement that parodied celebrity "first times" that a drunken Falwell had lost his virginity to his mother in an outhouse. The piece had a disclaimer reading "ad parody, not to be taken seriously," so it was clearly not meant to be taken as a statement of biographical fact. But Falwell sued *Hustler* in Virginia and recovered on the nouveau tort of intentional infliction of emotional distress.[11]

Rehnquist found that the right of political cartoonists and satirists to poke fun at public figures was at stake even if the caricature of Falwell in *Hustler* was "at best a distant cousin" to most journalistic cartoons. There was, he said, no coherent way to "separate" the political highbrow from the pornographic lowbrow and "the pejorative description 'outrageous' does not supply one."[12] Because the right of aggressive political satire is protected, the Court found that public figures could not recover for the intentional infliction of emotional distress— this is what comedians, cartoonists, and satirists do for a living—without first proving that a false statement of fact had been made with "actual malice," as *New York Times v. Sullivan* puts it. Here, the Court edged toward the epiphany that the First Amendment protects *all* speech against purposeful government efforts to silence it.

In *Rosenberger v. Rector and Visitors of the University of Virginia*, the Court in 1995 struck down the University of Virginia's practice of reimbursing the publishing costs of all student-produced newspapers and magazines except those having a religious purpose or identification. In a 5–4 split, with the conservatives now on the free-speech side, Justice Kennedy held that the university's publishing program established a limited public forum for student speech and its policy disfavoring religiously inflected speech was viewpoint discrimination.

In a speech market dominated by secular viewpoints, Justice Kennedy wrote, religion furnishes an alternative premise and perspective, a different "standpoint from which a variety of subjects may be discussed and considered." Despite the fact that the university thought it was avoiding Establishment Clause problems by refusing to subsidize publications like the plaintiff's *Wide Awake* Christian newspaper, it was actually effecting "a sweeping restriction on student thought and student inquiry." This understanding followed from the Court's 1981 holding in *Widmar v. Vincent,* which invalidated a public university's exclusion of religious groups from use of school facilities held open to all other student groups.[13] Although the liberals in dissent—Justices Souter, Stevens, Ginsburg, and Breyer—thought the university's selective ban was indeed required by the Establishment Clause to prevent state funding of religious proselytization, the majority found there was no compelling interest in excluding religious publications because a program that funded all journals equally would actually be "neutral toward religion." It is a First Amendment requirement, not offense, to allow religious speakers to have their say in public forums.

While the Court in *Rosenberger* determined that stripping certain subjects and speakers from a public forum is, almost by definition, the suppression of speech, the conservatives' understanding of this point has vanished in major institutional settings where they want to defer to administrative power over unwelcome expression. This acquiescence to bureaucratic censorship has dramatic antidemocratic consequences throughout society.

For example, in *Arkansas Educational Television Commission v. Forbes* (1998), the Court's conservatives and Justice Breyer (unfortunately) upheld by a 6–3 vote the commission's exclusion of Ralph Forbes, an Independent running for Congress, from a televised debate on its public TV channel that included his Democratic and Republican rivals.[14] This was a disappointing decision, not just because the censorship of political viewpoint was so blatant but because the government's interference in the campaign almost certainly changed the outcome of the election.

Forbes had been an irritant to the Republican Party establishment before leaving the party, but he was not a joke, as Justice Kennedy portrayed him. In 1990, Forbes had run for lieutenant governor on a hard-right platform and captured a winning 46.8 percent of the vote in a three-way Republican primary race, taking a clean majority in fifteen of sixteen counties in his congressional district. Thus, when he sued the public cable TV network *pro se* in his First Amendment case—to which he gave the irresistible caption *Forbes v. The Arrogant Orwellian Bureaucrats of the AETN, the Crooked Lying Politicians, and the Special Interests*—he won in the Eighth Circuit Court of Appeals, where Chief Judge Richard Arnold found that the televised debate was a "limited public forum."[15] In such a forum, a speaker may not be excluded without compelling reason. As a balloted candidate, Forbes properly belonged to the class of speakers invited, and AETN's rationale for excluding him—its standardless and tautological judgment about his political "viability"—violated the First Amendment because his viability was a "judgment to be made by the people of the Third Congressional District, not by officials of the government in charge of channels of communication."

Justice Kennedy did not see things this way. Squinting hard, he wrote that AETN "did not make its debate generally available to candidates for Arkansas' Third Congressional District seat" but rather "reserved eligibility for participation in the debate to candidates for the Third Congressional District seat [as opposed to some other seat]. At that point . . . [AETN] made candidate-by-candidate determinations as to which of the eligible candidates would participate in the debate." Thus, the debate was really a "nonpublic forum."[16]

In the "nonpublic forum," government can make "reasonable" and viewpoint-neutral exclusions. But why was the exclusion of Forbes reasonable and viewpoint-neutral? No policy or criteria for invitation were ever announced. AETN simply invited the major party candidates and rejected the Independent. The freewheeling "candidate-by-candidate determination" method that Justice Kennedy invoked as proof that the debate was a nonpublic forum was itself the essential violation of Forbes's First Amendment rights. For there were no objective viewpoint-neutral standards used in making these selections, only unregulated and standardless decisions.

Justice Kennedy dangerously eroded the doctrine of viewpoint neutrality by sanctioning the practice of government officials making ad hoc judgments about a balloted candidate's "viability." Of course, even assuming that the officials were clairvoyant and could foretell the election results, what made Forbes not "viable" was his perceived unpopularity. But *Texas v. Johnson* taught us that unpopular viewpoints must receive equal free-speech protection. So what is the relevance of viability anyway? Even in a two-person race, one candidate is certain to lose, but we do not consider the debate a waste of time for that reason. After facing Stephen Douglas in eight celebrated debates all over the state of Illinois in the 1858 Senate race, Abraham Lincoln lost the election. But his debate performance laid the groundwork for his successful presidential run two years later.

Justice Kennedy thought there was no viewpoint discrimination because the trial jury determined that Forbes's exclusion was not based on "objections or opposition to his views."[17] But this reliance badly confused the doctrine of viewpoint discrimination. The factual question of whether the network objected to Forbes's views does not control the legal question of whether his exclusion was viewpoint-based. The test of First Amendment viewpoint neutrality is an objective test that focuses on the nature of a governmental classification treating two classes of speakers differently, not a subjective test that focuses on the motivations of specific government actors in suppressing someone's speech. Subjective animus may be evidence of objective viewpoint discrimination, but it is not an element of it.

In *Rosenberger*, for example, there was no allegation of animosity toward religious students, but Justice Kennedy himself found that religiously motivated expression provided a distinctive viewpoint that could not be blocked from public debate. The University of Virginia bore no malice toward religion, but its rule effectively silenced a distinctive body of opinion. In the same way, the whole purpose and effect of excluding Forbes was to block out presentation of a political viewpoint and candidate deemed unpopular. This is the essence of viewpoint discrimination, which is the cardinal First Amendment sin.

The Court's transparent embrace of the Democratic-Republican "two-party system" in *Forbes* permeates its treatment of election cases. In *Timmons v. Twin Cities Area New Party* (1997), the New Party challenged Minnesota's 1901 "anti-fusion" law as a violation of the First Amendment associational rights of party members who wanted to cross-nominate a Democratic-Farmer-Labor candidate, State Representative Andy Dawkins, on the New Party line. Dawkins agreed but faced a law that prevented "fusion" candidacies, the kind that gave life in the nineteenth century to numerous progressive and populist parties in the Midwest and West.[18] The Eighth Circuit upheld the challenge, finding that the fusion ban was a "severe" burden on the New Party's "freedom to select" its own "standard-bearer" and its right to "broaden the base of public participation in and support for [its] activities."[19]

But by a vote of 6–3, the Supreme Court reversed and rejected the plaintiffs' claims. Slicing the bologna very fine, Rehnquist distinguished the conceded right of the New Party to nominate its own standard-bearer from its right to place its nominee's name on the ballot, a right that he said is not absolute. The New Party could endorse Dawkins and campaign for him, but Minnesota could keep his name off the New Party's ballot line. In other words, the ballot belongs to the government, not the people. In this sense, the decision echoes the equally troubling *Burdick v. Takushi*, where the conservatives upheld Hawaii's ban on write-in votes, finding that the government could shape the ballot to provide for selection among preapproved candidates.[20]

Although the Constitution says nothing of a two-party system, Chief Justice Rehnquist in *Timmons* came close to constitutionalizing it: "The Constitution permits the Minnesota legislature to decide that political stability is best served through a healthy two-party system." Of course, a "healthy two-party system" is a fluid arrangement open to challenge, the kind that gave rise to Lincoln's Republican Party prior to the Civil War. But the kind that Minnesota sought to entrench is a fortified political establishment built on violation of other citizens' rights. Many people were shocked by the Rehnquist Court's partisan intervention into the 2000 election in *Bush v. Gore*, but why should a Court that had already gone beyond the text of the Constitution effectively to establish a two-party system have any qualms about maintaining that system and simply dropping one of the parties?

No case better exemplifies the shift from the Warren Court's defense of speech in America's institutions to the Rehnquist Court's acquiescence to administrative censorship than the 1988 decision in *Hazelwood School District v. Kuhlmeier*, which sharply undercut the Court's watershed 1969 holding in *Tinker v. Des Moines School District*.[21] In *Tinker*, the Court reversed the suspension of thirteen-year-old Mary Beth Tinker, a Quaker who wore a black armband to school to protest the Vietnam War. The Court found that "state-operated schools may not be enclaves of totalitarianism" and that students enjoy "freedom of expression" unless it "materially" disrupts the educational process or violates other students' rights. Justice Abe Fortas, writing for the majority, was emphatic that students must be able to bring their own thoughts and feelings to school and "may not be confined to the expression of those sentiments that are officially approved."

This understanding began to unravel in 1986 with Chief Justice Burger's decision in *Bethel School District No. 403 v. Fraser*, which upheld discipline against a student for making lewd remarks in a student council nominating address.[22] But in *Hazelwood*, the Court set up a far more sweeping counterprinciple to the famous *Tinker* rule. There, the conservative majority upheld a principal's censorship of two student-written articles that were scheduled for publication in the school newspaper, one about the impact of parental divorce on high school students and the other about the problems faced by teenage mothers. The articles were deemed "inappropriate." The students felt their worthy journalistic efforts gave them an open-and-shut case on *Tinker* grounds, but the Court held that school officials can "exercise editorial control" over the "content of student speech" in all "school-sponsored activities," including newspapers, yearbooks, and theater, for any "legitimate pedagogical" purpose at all. The message sent to students is that their schools are training them not for participatory citizenship but for submission to bureaucratic power. The result in many parts of the country has been a crackdown on student speech and the development of private Web sites by students to castigate their censors, a trend that has predictably produced a lot of district court litigation.

The principles of viewpoint and content neutrality, embraced by majorities of five justices each in *Texas v. Johnson* and *Rosenberger*, lose their hold when government discriminates against speech in programs it funds, especially where conservatives favor the discrimination. This is the lesson of *Rust v. Sullivan*, where the Court upheld antiabortion regulations promulgated by the first President Bush's Department of Health and Human Services regarding family-planning groups that receive Title X funding.[23] The so-called gag rules banned all abortion counseling and referrals of pregnant patients by doctors, required physicians to refer pregnant clients "for appropriate prenatal and/or social services by furnishing a list of available providers that promote the welfare of the mother and the unborn child," and prohibited any projects receiving Title X funds from engaging in activities that "encourage, promote or advocate abortion as a method of family planning." The Court viewed these restrictions not as unconstitutional conditions compelling speech or forbidding it but rather as a funding and policy choice to prefer childbirth over abortion. As Chief Justice Rehnquist put it, "The Government has not discriminated on the basis of viewpoint; it has merely chosen to fund one activity to the exclusion of another."

In a powerful dissent joined by Justices Marshall and Brennan and in part by O'Connor, Justice Blackmun argued that the ban on abortion counseling was a direct assault on the free-speech and privacy rights of both women and their physicians. He also stated, "By refusing to fund those family-planning projects that advocate abortion *because* they advocate abortion, the Government plainly has targeted a particular viewpoint."[24] Reliance on the fact that these are funding decisions "simply begs the question," he wrote, since it is clear that the government could not, for example, distribute funds to clinics "upon considerations of race." According to Justice Blackmun, "ideological viewpoint is a similarly repugnant ground upon which to base funding decisions."

In fairness, it should be said that abortion politics have also at times distorted the free-speech principles of liberals on the Court. In one significant case, the liberals let their fears of admittedly spooky anti-abortion protestors dilute their commitment to free speech in the "traditional public forum" of the public sidewalk. In the rather shocking 5–4 decision of *Hill v. Colorado* (2000), where they were joined by Justice O'Connor, the liberals upheld a remarkable state law ban in Colorado against "knowingly approach[ing] another person within eight feet of such person . . . for the purpose of passing a leaflet or handbill to, displaying a sign to, or engaging in oral protest, education, or counseling with such person in the public way or sidewalk area within a radius of one hundred feet from any entrance door to a health care facility."[25] Everything about this law, from its legislative history to its text to its enforcement, tells us that it was a content- and viewpoint-based effort to suppress antiabortion activities outside of clinics. But the majority, validating for the first time in the First Amendment context a social interest in being left alone (outside the home), upheld the law as a reasonable place-and-manner regulation. *Hill* now stands as a template for local governments to develop regulations to stifle the expression of unpopular views in public places. One assumes the liberals will quickly return to their senses, but in the meantime the labor movement should beware.

The case that might have forced the justices to choose loyalties between the viewpoint-discrimination principle upheld in *Rosenberger* and the principle that government may selectively subsidize speech activities was *National Endowment for the Arts v. Finley*. The case brought to a head a decade-long public controversy over provocative NEA-funded art, such as Robert Mapplethorpe's homoerotic photography and Andres Serrano's much-maligned *Piss Christ*. Congress passed a statutory provision requiring the chairperson of the National Endowment for the Arts to ensure that, in the grants application process, "artistic excellence and artistic merit are the criteria by which applications are judged, taking into consideration general standards of decency and respect for the diverse beliefs and values of the American public."[26] An overly eager challenge to the law brought before it took effect by performance artist Karen Finley and other NEA-grant hopefuls elicited an ambiguous result. By an 8–1 vote, the majority upheld the new standard on the theory that the NEA, reading the provision as "merely hortatory," viewed it as stopping "well short of an absolute restriction." The majority thus interpreted the language only to make the NEA take "decency and respect" (whatever the terms might mean) into consideration in a general way in forming selection panels and not on a dispositive case-by-case basis with respect to applications.[27] If the NEA converted the general admonition into a specific "penalty on disfavored viewpoints, then we would confront a different case."

Justice Scalia, joined by Justice Thomas, concurred in the result but slammed the majority for changing the plain meaning of the act. He wrote: " 'The operation was a success, but the patient died.' What such

a procedure is to medicine, the Court's opinion in this case is to law.
. . . The most avid congressional opponents of the provision could not
have asked for more." He viewed it as "100% clear that decency and
respect are to be taken into account in evaluating applications" and
found there to be absolutely nothing wrong with this kind of viewpoint
discrimination.[28] Indeed, his opinion is a panegyric to the virtues of
viewpoint discrimination in government-funded programs, where the
government can spend its money however it wants.

Justice Souter's lone dissent provided the most intellectually honest
perspective in the case. He agreed strongly with Justice Scalia that the
statute embodied a requirement of viewpoint discrimination in consideration of specific grant applications, but he saw this as blatantly unlawful. Even if interpreted to be a command of only general and
diffuse consideration by the NEA, Justice Souter argued, the "decency
and respect" provision was no more legitimate than a requirement of
"taking into consideration the centrality of Christianity to the American cultural experience," or "taking into consideration whether the
artist is a communist," or "taking into consideration the political message conveyed by the art," or "taking into consideration the superiority
of the white race." Justice Souter rejected Justice Scalia's claim that
this was just a case of government itself being the speaker, the conservative paradigm in *Rust*, since it was clearly acting as an arts patron
subsidizing private speech by artists. The NEA was in the same position as the University of Virginia when it paid for student speech. Justice Souter's unflinching defense of free speech and his unwillingness
to paper things over mark him as the great champion of the First
Amendment on the Rehnquist Court and the proper heir to Justice
Brennan.

The most recent government funding case, *Legal Services Corporation
v. Velazquez*, was a 5–4 win for free speech when Justice Kennedy joined
the liberals to invalidate outrageous restrictions Congress imposed on
the Legal Services Corporation, which distributes federal funds to
groups providing free legal assistance to the poor.[29] Congress blocked
any funding of groups that represent clients challenging the validity or
constitutionality of a welfare law, and if a problem with the law sur-
faced after representation began, Congress required the lawyer to with-
draw from representation. Finding that this restriction caused a "severe

impairment of the judicial function," the majority saw it as "designed to insulate the Government's interpretation of the Constitution from judicial challenge." Amazingly but not uncharacteristically, the four other conservatives who defended the fundamentalist Christian student newspaper in *Rosenberger* against government manipulation of speech found the legal services restriction to be an unobjectionable *Rust*-style decision by government on how to spend its own funds.

There are enough historical and ideological forces at work to keep Chief Justice Rehnquist and his allies from gutting the First Amendment in the way they have worked over equal protection. Indeed, because of the politics of antiabortion protest, campaign finance reform, hate-speech regulation, and the always simmering controversy over "political correctness," conservatives both on and off the Court have of late affected a kind of wounded First Amendment pride about standing up for unpopular speech. This microchip on the shoulder is all to the good, and we can only hope (against hope) that their newfound interest in free expression lasts during the speech-hostile environment accompanying the war on terrorism.

The problem is that the healthy doctrines of viewpoint and content neutrality sketched out in cases like *Rosenberger* never go to work for ordinary people who dare to challenge the authority of those who run our social institutions. You are far better off appearing before this Court as a student editing a fundamentalist Christian newspaper or even a hopeless teenage Maoist burning flags in the street than as an organizer of a new political party that might threaten the two-party system, an intellectually engaged student speaking uncomfortable truths to the community in the high school campus newspaper, or a poor woman in a federally funded family-planning clinic who wants to talk to her doctor about a life choice the conservatives wish would just go away. The problem with the Rehnquist Court lies not so much in its high principles and rhetoric but rather in its malleable, unsystematic doctrines and its concrete sympathies, which tilt hard to the right and remain depressingly constant over time.

Gay Rights

CHAI FELDBLUM

Shortly before William Rehnquist became chief justice, the Supreme Court issued an opinion in the case of *Bowers v. Hardwick* that upheld the constitutionality of Georgia's sodomy law.[1] In the years of the Rehnquist Court, it has decided only three other cases dealing with gay rights. The pace and substance of change in this country's attitudes toward equality for gay people are well reflected in these cases, however. The tone of the Court's opinions, whether the result has been a "win" for the gay rights party or not, has been relatively respectful of those who are gay, lesbian, or bisexual. Moreover, the increasing number of cases that have come to the Supreme Court raising issues of gay equality reflect the rise in gay rights activism and visibility. But the narrow loss for James Dale, the openly gay scoutmaster who lost his bid to remain in the Boy Scouts by a one-vote margin in the Supreme Court, reflects as well how the next few appointments to the Supreme Court will shape the future of gay legal rights.[2]

The underlying theme in these Supreme Court cases has been the justices' views regarding the morality of gay sexual conduct. As long as most of them believed homosexual conduct was *inherently* immoral, gay rights claims were necessarily doomed to failure. But as the country's attitudes began to shift regarding the inexorable connection between immorality and gay sexual conduct and, with them, the attitudes of some of the justices, the outcomes of gay rights cases became less easy to predict. No justice has yet been willing to write a decision based on a stated belief that homosexual conduct is morally equivalent to heterosexual conduct. But a majority of the justices are no longer willing to accept that homosexual conduct is inherently and necessarily *immoral*.

Of course, liberals like to believe that moral judgments should ordinarily have little relevance anyway for purposes of governmental actions and judicial decisions. Under a liberal view of "equality" and "individual rights," individuals should have a right to intimate association and privacy that should not be restricted by the government, as long as the individual's behavior harms no one else. A majority of people in a society may dislike, or even hate, a particular behavior in question, but a liberal, neutral government is designed to protect the right of an individual to engage in such behavior, regardless of how morally perverse it may seem to others in society.

In reality, however, legislative and judicial decision making is often shaped by the moral assessments of legislators and judges. Thus, if gay sexual conduct is viewed by a majority in the society as morally reprehensible, and consequently to be condemned if not eradicated, it will be next to impossible for individuals engaged in such conduct to gain nondiscrimination protection based on sexual orientation in either the legislative or the judicial arena. The only way they can achieve acceptance, tolerance, and ultimately true equality is for the public moral assessment of homosexuality to change. Nothing makes this clearer than the progression of Supreme Court cases dealing with gay rights.

In 1986, in *Bowers v. Hardwick*, the Supreme Court considered the constitutionality of a Georgia sodomy statute that criminalized oral or anal sex engaged in by any two individuals, regardless of the individuals' gender or sexual orientation. Thus, under Georgia law, a married couple who engaged in oral or anal sex were engaging in as equally criminal activity as a gay man who had oral or anal sex with another man.

The question whether the Georgia statute was constitutional would not necessarily have been an easy question to answer under the Court's constitutional jurisprudence to date. The Court had previously found a general "right to privacy" in the Constitution, which has been held to prohibit a state from criminalizing the use of contraception, abortion, or other family-planning decisions—for married couples or unmarried couples. The question in *Bowers v. Hardwick*, therefore, should have been whether this "right to privacy" also prohibited a state from criminalizing certain types of sexual conduct—that is, oral or anal sex—whether practiced by married or unmarried couples or by gay or heterosexual couples.

But Justice Byron White, who wrote the Court's majority opinion, framed the question in a manner that made the answer obvious to him (and presumably, any reader) as soon as he posed the question. To Justice White, the question in the case was whether "the Federal Constitution confers a fundamental right for *homosexuals* to engage in *sodomy*." As Justice White explained, the right of privacy had previously been extended by the Court to protect such areas as child rearing, family relationships, marriage, and procreation. The moral distinction between such areas of life and the relationships engaged in by gay people was patently clear to him. As he noted, "no connection between family, marriage, or procreation on the one hand and homosexual activity on the other has been demonstrated." Therefore the answer to the question had to be no.

Justice White was also not willing to extend a more limited "right to be let alone" to protect any consensual gay sexual conduct practiced in the privacy of a home. The Court had previously recognized such a right in prohibiting a state from criminalizing the reading of obscene materials inside the privacy of one's home. But Justice White could not envision how homosexual conduct would then be distinguished, "except by fiat," from private sexual conduct such as "adultery, incest, and other sexual crimes committed in the home."

Justice Blackmun's dissenting opinion in *Hardwick* was a remarkably progressive one in many ways. It is worth observing, however, that he did not argue that gay sexual conduct should be protected under the right of privacy because gay couples embody the same moral values as heterosexual couples. In a previous case, in which the government had been constitutionally prohibited from interfering with family and marriage relationships, the Court had waxed eloquent on the virtues of heterosexual coupling within the marriage context: "Marriage is a coming together for better or for worse, hopefully enduring, and intimate to the degree of being sacred. It is an association that promotes a way of life, not causes; a harmony in living, not political faiths; a bilateral loyalty, not commercial or social projects."[3] But Justice Blackmun did not invoke this opinion to argue that committed gay couplings should be protected against government intrusion because such relationships partake equally of the importance and good of heterosexual couplings within marriage. Instead, he focused on the "right to be let alone" aspect of the right of privacy. As noted, under this aspect of privacy, the government is constitutionally prohibited from interfering with those activities that occur in the privacy of one's home and do not harm others (such as reading pornography at home). As Justice Blackmun put it, quoting an earlier case, " 'a way of life that is odd or even erratic but interferes with no rights or interests of others is not to be condemned because it is different.' "[4]

Almost ten years passed before the Supreme Court again considered a gay rights case fully on its merits. During that time (1986–95), the country witnessed an increase in activism and visibility on the part of the gay community, as deaths from AIDS ravaged it, encouraging increased fear and prejudice. But the disease also politicized hundreds of individuals and involuntarily "outed" many others as gay. Thousands of people were suddenly confronted with the fact that they *did* know someone who was gay, often a close family member or personal friend. Gay people who had been hiding their sexual orientation for years began to "come out," trading invisibility for integrity and pride.

One symbolic aspect of this push for visibility was efforts by gay, lesbian, and bisexual descendants of Irish immigrants to march in the St. Patrick's Day parades in New York City and Boston. The message these marchers intended to send was clear: "Irish is good. Gay is good. Irish gay is good." Each year, however, parade organizers excluded the gay Irish groups. Clearly, they wanted nothing to do with the message conveyed by such groups. In 1995, the Supreme Court concluded in *Hurley v. Irish-American Gay, Lesbian, and Bisexual Group of Boston* that the Boston parade organizers had a constitutional right not to be forced by a state antidiscrimination law to include a gay Irish group among its march contingents.[5] Although the decision was greeted with dismay by some gay rights advocates, its tone reflected a sea change in the Court's attitude toward homosexuality.

Justice David Souter, writing for a unanimous Court, explained that most parades are intended to express something. And although the Boston St. Patrick's Day parade hosted various and often cacophonous contingents and messages, each contingent's expression, at least in the eyes of the parade's organizers, comported with what merited celebration on that day. The gay Irish group had a message as well. The presence of organized marchers under the gay Irish banner, Justice Souter explained, would "suggest their view that people of their sexual orientations have as much claim to unqualified social acceptance as heterosexuals and indeed as members of parade units organized around other identifying characteristics."[6]

It is hard to imagine the majority in *Hardwick* understanding that gay people might want to march in a parade to convey the message that gay people are morally and socially equivalent to heterosexuals. That would have seemed preposterous. It would have seemed to the *Hardwick* majority like a group of adulterers or a group of people who engage in incest marching to send a message of pride and integrity about adultery or incest! But to Justice Souter, it seemed reasonable that a contingent of gay people would want to march to express a message of pride and integrity about being gay and Irish. Moreover, he described that desire respectfully and thoughtfully. The problem, from his perspective, was that the parade organizers did not wish to send such a message, and the First Amendment precludes the government from forcing people to utter speech they do not wish to utter.

Justice Souter emphasized that the objective of the state's antidiscrimination law based on sexual orientation was legitimate: to ensure that individuals are not denied access to private businesses and groups simply because they are gay. But in this case, the parade organizers had not barred individual gay people from marching in the parade. Rather, they had a rule barring an organized gay Irish *group* from marching in order to send a message through the parade about the goodness of being Irish and gay. Under the First Amendment, a state antidiscrimination law could not force a private entity to send such a message.

While gay Irish groups never managed to obtain permission from

parade organizers to march in either the Boston or the New York parade, the acceptance of gay people living their lives openly and with
integrity increased over time. Together with visibility and a sense of
"belonging" came the passage of local and state antidiscrimination
laws that prohibited government, private employers, and private businesses from using sexual orientation as a basis for adverse actions. Between 1990 and 1995, approximately 80 cities, counties, or localities
passed such laws and ordinances; by 2001, the number had reached
134 (prohibiting discrimination in private employment) and 239 (prohibiting discrimination in public employment).

Proponents of these antidiscrimination laws do not argue for their
passage on the grounds that homosexual conduct is morally equivalent
to heterosexual conduct. Rather, they take pains to assert that such
laws are neutral regarding the morality of being gay and that they simply ensure equality for all people—gay or straight. Nevertheless, there
has often been a backlash to these laws, spurred in part because the liberal rhetoric of neutrality used in advocating them ignores the moral
disagreements that still exist over gay sexual conduct. That is, people
who believe homosexuality is morally wrong also believe employers
and businesses should be able to refuse to associate with people whose
conduct they find morally reprehensible.

Interestingly enough, the opponents of these laws have rarely attempted to get them repealed by asserting a virulent view regarding the
immorality of homosexuality. (This is a mirror image of the reticence
of gay rights supporters who do not advocate the passage of such laws
because of a putative moral equivalence of homosexuality and heterosexuality.) The fact is, as more gay people have begun to live ordinary,
honest, and open lives, the previously assumed societal belief that
homosexuality is inherently immoral has itself come under question.
Most people in America today do not believe that homosexuality is an
inherent evil that must be eradicated. Most people also do not
believe that responsible gay sexual conduct is morally equivalent to responsible heterosexual conduct (and thus, for example, should be supported by the government in the way that heterosexual coupling is
supported through marriage and other benefits). But a clear majority
are now uncomfortable with the idea that private parties should be al-

lowed to deny individuals housing or employment based solely on their sexual orientation.[7]

Thus, the approach taken by those who oppose antidiscrimination laws is to describe them as bestowing "special rights" for gay people. For example, in Colorado, where the cities of Aspen and Boulder and the city and county of Denver banned discrimination based on sexual orientation in a range of areas, opponents sponsored a ballot initiative to amend the Colorado constitution to repeal all such existing protections and to preclude the adoption of any further protections. Known as Amendment 2 and passed by a vote of 54 percent, the provision precluded Colorado, all its localities, and any of its agencies from adopting any rule that provided "homosexual, lesbian, or bisexual orientation, conduct, practice, or relationships" any claim of "minority status, quota preferences, protected status, or claim of discrimination." The campaign to pass Amendment 2 was peppered with claims that gay people were seeking to obtain special rights through the passage of such laws.

In 1996, in the case of *Romer v. Evans*, six justices of the Supreme Court concluded that the people of Colorado had violated the Constitution's guarantee of "equal protection under the law" when they passed Amendment 2. The opinion, written by Justice Anthony Kennedy, stressed the breadth of the protection removed by the amendment and the narrowness of its focus on gay people. Unlike any other group that might need protection from discrimination and could approach their cities, localities, and state for such protection, gay people were precluded from seeking it. Justice Kennedy concluded that the sheer breadth of the amendment seemed "inexplicable by anything but animus toward the class it affects; it lacks a rational relationship to legitimate state interests."[8]

Justice Antonin Scalia, joined by Justices Rehnquist and Clarence Thomas, was vigorous in his dissent and incredulous at the majority's reasoning. From the dissent's perspective, the Court's opinion in *Hardwick* had pronounced it constitutionally permissible for a state to make homosexual conduct criminal. Given that, surely it was permissible for a state to pass laws that simply disfavored homosexual conduct; even further, surely it was permissible for a state not to confer special protection on homosexual conduct by prohibiting discrimination specifically on that characteristic.

It also seemed eminently reasonable to Justice Scalia that the people of a state might want to ensure that special protections based on sexual orientation were never passed anywhere in their state. He noted that the majority opinion had contained grim, disapproving hints that the people of Colorado were guilty of "animus" toward homosexuality, "as though that has been established as un-American." But, as he observed, "I had thought that one could consider certain conduct reprehensible—murder, for example, or polygamy, or cruelty to animals—and could exhibit even 'animus' toward such conduct. Surely that is the only sort of 'animus' at issue here: moral disapproval of homosexual conduct, the same sort of moral disapproval that produced the centuries-old criminal laws that we held constitutional in [*Hardwick*]."[9]

Justice Scalia was absolutely correct, of course, that certain animus is permissible in our society. That is why the liberal rhetoric of neutrality that asserts that antidiscrimination laws simply establish basic equality and nothing more is somewhat disingenuous. While such laws may not condone any particular behavior, they certainly establish that particular types of animus are no longer considered permissible. Indeed, as Justice Scalia correctly noted, they effectively stand for the proposition that discrimination based on homosexuality is as reprehensible as discrimination based on race or gender.

But the majority justices in *Romer*, presumably reflecting public opinion in the country by 1996, presumed that a locality might indeed wish to make animus based on sexual orientation illegal in its jurisdiction. Moreover, they presumed that a state constitutional amendment that broadly denied gay people in that locality, and all other localities, the right to seek and benefit from such laws reflected inappropriate animus for purposes of the Equal Protection Clause.

These justices never said they believed homosexuality and heterosexuality were morally equivalent, nor did they probably even view their opinion as morally condoning homosexual conduct. Nevertheless, the logic of their opinion required them to view gay sexual conduct as morally distinct from the immorality of murder, polygamy, or cruelty to animals.

The breadth of Colorado's Amendment 2 and the fact that gay people were denied the right to seek protection from their own local, friendly localities were clearly factors for Justices Kennedy and Sandra Day O'Connor in joining the *Romer* majority. Indeed, while it was deciding *Romer*, the Supreme Court had pending before it a case that raised essentially identical issues to those presented in *Romer*. In *Equality Foundation of Greater Cincinnati, Inc. v. City of Cincinnati*, the appellate court upheld the validity of an amendment to Cincinnati's city charter that repealed a city council ordinance prohibiting discrimination based on sexual orientation and denying the council the right to pass such ordinances in the future.[10] Ordinarily, one would have expected the Supreme Court to summarily reverse the *Equality Foundation* case, based on its recently released *Romer* decision. Instead, the Court sent it back to the appellate court for "further review" in light of *Romer*.

The appellate court's subsequent review and decision were a shock to gay rights advocates. The court concluded that the *narrowness* of the city charter amendment (all it did was affect the city council ordinances) distinguished it from Amendment 2 in Colorado and that it was reasonable for the people of Cincinnati to want to eliminate the public and private costs that might accrue from lawsuits arising under the council's ordinance. Indeed, a significant portion of Justice Scalia's legal reasoning in his *Romer* dissent made its way into the appellate court's majority decision, which largely parroted Justice Scalia's opinion, also in dissent (joined in by the other *Romer* dissenters), from the Supreme Court's remand decision.[11]

Gay rights advocates sought review of the second *Equality Foundation* ruling in the Supreme Court, but the Court refused to hear the case, thus letting the appellate court ruling stand. In the ordinary course of events, not too much should be read into the Supreme Court's refusal to hear a case. Indeed, in this instance three justices (John Paul Stevens, Souter, and Ruth Bader Ginsburg) wrote an accompanying statement pointing out that the Court may refuse to hear a case simply because specific facts make it inappropriate for Supreme Court review. But the fact that the Supreme Court allowed the ruling in *Equality Foundation* to stand felt like a splash of cold water to gay rights advocates after the euphoria of the *Romer* decision. To some observers, it seemed to indicate that Justices Kennedy and O'Connor, the two moderate justices who had respectively written and joined *Romer*, were not willing to extend gay rights too far.

This interpretation seemed to be validated in the case the Supreme Court decided in June 2000, *Boy Scouts of America v. Dale*. New Jersey had passed a public accommodations law that prohibited a range of businesses and associations from discriminating on the basis of sexual orientation. The New Jersey Supreme Court concluded that the Boy Scouts of America were covered under that law as a public accommodation, a ruling the Supreme Court had no authority to review because it was based on an interpretation of state law. But the Boy Scouts argued to the Supreme Court that the Constitution precluded the state from forcing the organization to comply with a state antidiscrimination law that required it to retain an openly gay scoutmaster, James Dale. The Boy Scouts viewed themselves as like the St. Patrick's Day parade organizers in *Hurley*. If the Boy Scouts were forced to retain James Dale, they would be forced to send a moral message about homosexuality that was contrary to their own chosen and expressed viewpoint about homosexuality.

Chief Justice Rehnquist, joined by Justices Kennedy, O'Connor, Scalia, and Thomas, agreed. He concluded that the Boy Scouts needed to exclude James Dale as a scoutmaster to preserve their expressive views regarding homosexuality and that the government's interest in prohibiting discrimination was not sufficient to override the Boy Scouts' First Amendment expressive rights.

The Boy Scouts' actual view on homosexuality, however, was a seriously contested issue in the case. According to the Boy Scout Oath and Law, scouts must be "morally straight" and "clean." "Morally straight" is defined in the *Boy Scout Handbook* as being a "person of strong character," and "guid[ing] your life with honesty, purity, and justice." There was nothing in the Scout Oath or *Handbook* that stated that being gay was incompatible with being "morally straight." Writing for the majority in *Dale*, Chief Justice Rehnquist was forced to observe that the Scout Oath never expressly mentioned either sexuality or sexual orientation and indeed that the terms "morally straight" and "clean" were not self-defining. As he explained, "Some people may believe that engaging in homosexual conduct is not at odds with being 'morally straight' and 'clean.' And others may believe that engaging in homosexual conduct is contrary to being 'morally straight' and 'clean.' "

Having acknowledged that there was not a universal societal view regarding the immorality of gay sexual conduct, Rehnquist then simply asserted that the Boy Scouts fell into the latter category of those who believe homosexual conduct is inconsistent with being morally straight and clean. To Rehnquist and his colleagues, this conclusion was simple: the organization had stated such a position about homosexuality in a memo to the Boy Scouts executive committee and had told the Supreme Court in its brief that this was its view.

In previous cases, in which groups such as the Rotary Club or the United States Jaycees had been forced to defend their policies of excluding women as members, the Court had been able to identify specific practices on the part of the organization (such as inviting women as junior members or as guests) that undermined their asserted expressive interests in excluding women as full members. By contrast, in *Dale*, all the Supreme Court had before it was the Boy Scouts' bald assertion that admitting homosexuals as scoutmasters would be incompatible with the organization's mission. Nevertheless, given the current public state of moral views on homosexuality, these five justices presumably considered it reasonable that a respected American organization would consider gay sexual conduct to be incompatible with being "morally straight," and hence it was easier for these justices to accept the Boy Scouts' simple assertion to that effect.

In response, the four dissenting justices, led by Justice Stevens, took the majority to task for accepting, with little critical analysis, the Boy Scouts' assertion that they had a clear, coherent viewpoint that being gay was morally wrong. The dissenting justices did not doubt that many people held such a view, including people who were senior Boy Scouts officials. Nor did they believe that whether such a view was correct or reasonable was relevant to the Court's legal analysis, a point Justice Souter emphasized in a separate opinion. The problem for them was that it was difficult to discern this viewpoint about homosexuality from the way values were actually taught in Boy Scouts settings. There was no mention of homosexuality in the Scout Oath or *Hand-*

book; scoutmasters were told to refer questions about sexuality generally to those better able to handle them (religious counselors or parents), and a number of the entities that sponsored Boy Scouts chapters had expressed policies of nondiscrimination based on sexual orientation and, hence, presumably did not share the same moral views on homosexuality as did the Boy Scouts executive committee.

As the dissenting justices emphasized, it was irrelevant to their legal analysis whether they agreed with the Boy Scouts' moral message. The First Amendment protects the rights of groups to organize in order to convey their viewpoints—even viewpoints that might be heartily disliked by others. But society's changing moral assessment of homosexuality meant that the Boy Scouts could not simply require that scouts live lives of "honesty, purity, and justice" and then presume that this was understood to include a requirement not to engage in gay conduct. As Justice Stevens observed, although unfavorable opinions about gay people are ancient and "like equally atavistic opinions about certain racial groups . . . have been nourished by sectarian doctrine," over the years "interaction with real people, rather than mere adherence to traditional ways of thinking about members of unfamiliar classes, have modified those opinions." For example, he noted, some religious communities had clearly altered their views on the morality of homosexuality, including some of the religious groups that sponsor Boy Scouts chapters.

Despite the loss for James Dale and other gay scoutmasters, the fact that the issue of whether gay conduct was contrary to being "morally straight" and "clean" was seriously contested is itself an important reflection of society's changing moral assessments of homosexuality. These changing assessments are a direct reaction to the real lives of gay people—lives that are lived openly, honestly, and right next door in suburbia, urban areas, and the countryside. Moreover, the continued visibility of such lives—both in the media and in real life—shows no sign of decreasing.

The narrow victory for the Boy Scouts in *Dale* has not ended the public conversation regarding gay conduct and morality. To the contrary, the Boy Scouts' position that engaging in gay conduct is necessarily contrary to being moral has come under attack—or, at least, strict scrutiny—by parents, boys, and families across the country. Once one accepts that individuals do not choose to be gay (a fact validated by all reputable scientific and psychological work), it is hard to justify the morality of denying gay people the opportunity to love other human beings. The public conversations about Boy Scouts, morality, and love will ultimately only enhance the possibility of equality for all gay people.

The courts have always been a locus of public debate, both as a reflection of the current state of beliefs on a particular issue and as a catalyst for further examination of such beliefs. In the area of gay rights, everything from membership in the Boy Scouts to recognition of same-sex marriage has been debated in the courts. In each case, legal decisions have helped move the conversation forward, even if the particular outcome has not been favorable to the gay plaintiff's position. For example, in 1999, the Vermont Supreme Court ruled that gay couples in Vermont have a right under the state constitution to have their relationships recognized by the state in some form equal to that of heterosexual relationships.[12] This decision was possible only because the conversation on the morality of gay coupling shifted.

Future rulings from the Supreme Court will in large part depend on future appointments of justices. Socially conservative justices will presumably be more willing to assume that homosexuality is immoral and hence that discrimination based on sexual orientation is legitimate; liberal or moderate justices may be more skeptical of the assumption that gay conduct is necessarily immoral. But regardless of the composition of the Supreme Court, as an increasing number of gay people live open and honest lives, the public view of the morality of gay conduct will continue to undergo change. And that change, ultimately, will be the most revolutionary one of all.

The Politics of Abortion

SUSAN ESTRICH

For the last two decades of the twentieth century, feminists sought to draw a link between the presidential election, the Supreme Court, and reproductive freedom. "You vote for the Court when you vote for president. You're voting on *Roe v. Wade*."[1] That's what they say, every four years. And we said it again in 2000.

In one sense, of course, it was immediately true this time around: the Supreme Court did decide the election and, depending on your perspective, it did so on a partisan or at least a political basis. Would the same majority have stepped in to block a recount ordered by the state court if doing so would have made Al Gore president? It was remarkable enough that they did it for George Bush, ideologically speaking.

But as a strategy, tying an election to the Supreme Court and thence to *Roe v. Wade* rarely works, and as a prediction, it oversteps the mark. In the 2000 election, while there was certainly a significant gender gap and certainly a correlation between views on abortion and voting, Al Gore got fewer votes than the prochoice position does on most polls. Ralph Nader's support was almost entirely composed of prochoice voters who were reconciled to Bush's election, and Bush received substantial backing among prochoice white women, particularly those who were married.

As a political matter, the last thing President George Bush wants is to turn either future mid-term elections, and particularly the 2004 re-election, into an actual referendum on abortion, which is why the prediction is part doomsday, part wishful thinking.

The good news is that middle-class women are unlikely to lose their rights to a safe early abortion. The bad news is that they are unlikely to rise up politically to demand their rights, much less the rights of less fortunate women.

Legally speaking, the story of abortion can be seen as a tale of two cases. The first was *Roe v. Wade*, decided in 1973. Prior to *Roe*, each state decided for itself whether to allow abortion; Massachusetts didn't (unless you had two doctors attesting to mental instability) and New York did, and women used to chip in to buy bus tickets when girls got pregnant.

Then everything changed. In one of the most criticized opinions in modern jurisprudence, the United States Supreme Court held that a Texas law prohibiting all abortions except when necessary to save the life of the mother violated the Constitution. Justice Harry Blackmun's painstaking opinion divided a pregnancy into trimesters, holding that during the first trimester state prohibitions could not limit a woman's right to choose, in consultation with her doctor, to terminate a pregnancy; that during the second trimester this right could be limited only to protect her health; and that only after the fetus reached the stage of viability in the third trimester, the stage where the baby could survive outside the womb, did the state have a compelling interest in protecting potential human life.

The smart boys had a field day with *Roe*. A generation of young constitutional scholars ate Justice Blackmun for lunch, finding nothing in the Constitution or its penumbra to justify the Court's articulation of a constitutional right to choose. The trimester approach was criticized as having neither a medical nor a legal basis; it is a construct, an invention, testament to the legislative judgments that inform abortion regulation. What kind of constitutional right comes with a trimester analysis? None, of course.

Yet there was always a logic to *Roe* that was more substantial than its doctrinal basis. Years of discussing, debating, and teaching abortion have taught me that this is not a subject where anyone changes anyone else's mind, where intelligent argument is anything more than that, where politics works. It is a matter of belief, tempered with experience, almost immune from outside influence. The decision to terminate a pregnancy is one that in our society can only be left to the individual: there is no collective judgment that could be tolerably enforced. The argument against *Roe* in the academy was never that the Court had reached the wrong result but rather that someone else should have reached it. The inelegant answer to that complaint and the ultimate raison d'être for the decision was that unfortunately no one else was stepping up to the plate. Justice Blackmun did what needed to be done, inelegantly, perhaps, but effectively. This is why *Roe* has survived, despite itself.

In 1989, in *Webster v. Reproductive Health Services*, four justices of the Supreme Court seemed to give notice that they were ready to overrule *Roe*.[2] The Missouri law at issue in *Webster* declared that life begins at conception, prohibited using government funds or facilities for the purpose of "encouraging or counseling" a woman to have an abortion, and required a test of "viability" before abortions would be allowed after twenty weeks of pregnancy. The Court upheld the statute, without a majority opinion. Chief Justice William Rehnquist, writing for himself and Justices Byron White and Anthony Kennedy, criticized the twin pillars of *Roe*: trimesters and viability. The rigid *Roe* framework, he wrote, is hardly consistent with the notion of a Constitution cast in general terms. As for viability, Rehnquist opined, "we do not see why the State's interest in protecting potential human life should come into existence only at the point of viability, and that there should therefore be a rigid line allowing state regulation after viability, but prohibiting it before viability." Justice Antonin Scalia wrote separately, emphasizing that the plurality opinion "effectively would overrule *Roe v. Wade*. . . . I think that should be done," he added, "but would do it more explicitly." In Scalia's judgment, the failure to overrule *Roe* "needlessly prolongs this Court's self-awarded sovereignty over a field where it has little proper business since the answers to most of the cruel questions posed are political and not juridical."

And so prochoice activists raised the alarm, louder than ever. Four votes to overrule *Roe*. And that didn't include Sandra Day O'Connor, who concurred in the result with the Rehnquist group but refused to enter the discussion as to whether or not *Roe* should be overruled, saying there would be "time enough to reexamine *Roe*" when a state passed a law, presumably one prohibiting abortion, whose constitutionality actually turned on *Roe*. And it didn't take account of the newly appointed justices: between the time of the Court's *Webster* decision and its ruling three years later in *Planned Parenthood of Southern Pennsylvania v. Casey*, Justices William Brennan and Thurgood Marshall had been replaced by Justices David Souter and Clarence Thomas.[3] The solicitor general of the United States used the Pennsylvania law at issue in *Casey* as an opportunity to argue that the Court should overrule *Roe*.

"Liberty finds no refuge in a jurisprudence of doubt." In a joint opinion by Justices O'Connor, Kennedy, and Souter, the Court upheld not the logic of *Roe*, not its doctrine, not its approach, but its result. Throwing away trimesters, but bowing to precedent and affirming the value of a woman in the room, the Court held that a woman retained a right to decide whether to terminate a pregnancy prior to viability and that the state, while free to pursue its preference for birth over abortion, could not impose an "undue burden" on the woman's right to decide for herself.

In states whose legislatures are antichoice, abortion statutes are regularly loaded with all kinds of time, place, and manner restrictions, consent forms and waiting periods, and even bans on procedures, like the legal creation of the concept of a "partial-birth abortion."[4] Then the Supreme Court sorts them out, upholding most, throwing out only the very worst. In *Casey* itself, the Court upheld a waiting period for adult abortions; earlier, it had upheld informed-consent provisions that, in the eyes of some, constitute nothing less than a sermon against abortion. Parental-consent laws, provided there is some form of judicial override, have been upheld now for most of the last two decades. Since *Casey*, it is only the prohibition of "partial-birth abortion" that has risen to the level of an undue burden.

"Life's not fair," Jimmy Carter declared when the Supreme Court upheld the right of state and local governments to deny public funding to poor women seeking abortions. In the years since, it's gotten more unfair, but the truth is that law is only part of the problem. The continued vitality of *Roe v. Wade* means that if you're lucky enough to live in a place where doctors aren't afraid to do abortions and you have the money to pay for one, you don't have to bring cash in a plain envelope. If it's provided and you can pay for it, an abortion is safe and legal, until viability. In Los Angeles, you can open the phone book, make an appointment, and bring a credit card.

On the other hand, if the Catholic hospital is the only one in town, or you're under eighteen or poor, or live in North Dakota rather than Santa Monica, or don't notice your period is late because you're just a kid, you may have real troubles. You may have to bring suit if you're a teenager, even if it's a relative who raped you; you may be too late for an early abortion and then have to sort through the obstacles and regulations that start kicking in with force. In most states, if you're poor and depend on Medicaid for health care, it'll provide everything but an abortion. In much of the country, outside urban areas, access matters more than law: finding a local doctor, hospital, or clinic is simply impossible; in 86 percent of all counties, most of them rural, and in some states, there are none. If you have money, you can go to another state.

It is said that the country is less prochoice than it used to be, and that's probably so. It's easy to be troubled by the idea of abortion when it's a theoretical issue for you or when you have in your mind's eye the image of a much-wanted baby on a sonogram. I have lost babies at seven and twelve weeks, and they were in my soul. Then again, I'm not fourteen, or a college freshman on the verge of her life, or an at-the-end-of-her-rope struggling mother of four or five. I'm not the girl in the dorm room next door who hemorrhaged on the way home in the bus.

Today's young people may be less ardently prochoice, but they have also grown up in a world in which the choices are theirs to make. Take that away and see if they still feel the same.

Now imagine that the Court had come down the other way in *Casey*. Imagine that the Court were to revisit its decision. The impact on the political sphere would be enormous. Overruling *Roe* would make politics matter more. If *Roe* were actually to be overruled, every state would be required to go through a full-blown debate about whether and when to permit or prohibit abortions. Congress would have to go through the same sort of debate.

Such a debate would have to empower women. Could a room full of men get away with deciding whether to make abortion a crime without even pretending to listen to a woman now and again? Imagine what would happen if they tried. Every time a man stood up to give a speech about what he thinks, there'd be women laughing in beauty shops across America. I can't think of an easier way to motivate women to take over American politics, to recognize that they have the power to do it.

And then imagine what a real movement of women using their power could accomplish—not only on the issue of reproductive freedom but on issues of health care, education, the environment, human rights . . . That's my pipedream of course, what's behind those election-year speeches every four years.

Which is reason enough that it won't happen. Consider the abortion issue from George W. Bush's perspective. I believe that he really is against abortion. I saw former President Bill Clinton shortly after his first Oval Office meeting with his successor, and his assessment of then-Governor Bush rings true: he thought Bush was much more conservative than people assumed, and also much cannier.

Antiabortion activists value the fight for its own sake, even if, indeed sometimes especially if, they lose. Is there any explanation, after all, for the fact that they so often refuse to add the mediating "life and health of the mother" language that would render their restrictions less vulnerable to constitutional attack? Unlike politicians, who prefer to ask for less and win, activists often opt to demand more, even if it means grabbing defeat from the jaws of victory, in the hopes of pushing the larger debate forward.

Would antiabortion activists like to make presidential campaigns referendums on abortion? Certainly, even if they lose them. It puts their issue at the center of the fight, holds everyone's feet to the fire, allows them to demonstrate their clout and make their case.

At the 1992 Republican convention, only the pragmatists, the hacks, the nonbelievers viewed the takeover by the religious right as a signal of doom. Everyone else there had a great time. Best convention

ever, people kept telling me, at least the ones who didn't call me a
"babykiller." George W. Bush was also there, first learning the lesson
that Karl Rove, now his senior political adviser, would repeat after-
ward, that his father had been undermined by his loss of support on
the right, a mistake Rove was determined not to repeat. The younger
President Bush has been very good to the religious right on abortion,
giving them John Ashcroft as attorney general and the executive orders
they wanted, not to mention a decision on stem-cell research that posi-
tioned the administration substantially to the right of that well-known
liberal Orrin Hatch. But none of that has served to turn abortion into
a highly salient issue for the broader public, a fact that is also a measure of Rove's political skill. The first round of the Bush administration's antiabortion executive orders, limiting the ability of international
family-planning organizations that accept federal funds to use their
own money for abortion, came on the same day that Ashcroft was
pledging allegiance to *Roe v. Wade* as the law of the land in his confirmation hearings on Capitol Hill. The stem-cell decision, welcomed by
antiabortion activists who saw it as the victory it was, was packaged
with enough care to make it appear far more generous to researchers
than it was.

As for the rank inconsistency between Bush's support for government aid to churches, where the answer to the entanglement argument
is that the church uses government funds for its public activities and
private funds for its religious ones, and his refusal to apply the same approach to family-planning organizations—his administration simply
chooses to ignore it. And to a large extent, the issue does go away. Thus
far, those most harmfully affected by the administration's actions on
abortion are poor women abroad and United States servicewomen,
who can no longer get a safe abortion at a military hospital. Previously,
at least the option existed even though they were required to pay for it
themselves. Exactly where does a servicewoman in Saudi Arabia go if
not to a military facility? Or how about Pakistan? Still, foreign women
and women serving abroad hardly provide the needed fodder, or army,
for a domestic political revolution. Something akin to the fight over
Robert Bork's nomination might stoke the flames, which is why we are
unlikely to see a Robert Bork. Conservatives, absolutely. But a closely

divided Senate only makes it easier for Bush to resist the calls for the most conservative nominees in favor of a relative liberal like Orrin Hatch. Code language like "respect for precedent" will signal a nominee who will ultimately toe the Anthony Kennedy line on abortion, uphold virtually all restrictions, but maintain the basic constitutional right recognized in *Roe v. Wade.*

I worked on my first abortion case twenty-three years ago when I was a law clerk for Justice John Paul Stevens; the issue was Massachusetts's parental-consent law. My students are now litigating parental-consent laws across the country; what is striking to me is how little has changed in two decades, legally speaking—same sorts of issue, same sorts of argument, with more and more of the effort reserved for the swing votes in the middle who are engaged in that precarious task of burden measuring. The promise of a solution in the form of RU-486 has yet to materialize; administration of the oral abortion pill still requires medical supervision and in any event is not appropriate except in the early weeks.

Meanwhile, the political climate has changed dramatically. During the Carter administration, feminists fought to include in the Democratic platform, over the opposition of President Carter himself, the same language that Attorney General Ashcroft has used. Today, Democratic candidates trumpet their support for abortion rights, while Republicans at the national level are struggling to figure out how to hold on to the right without losing the middle, particularly the moderate, female middle. Democrats win not because abortion is an issue but because for most voters it isn't one; since their rights are protected, such voters are free to think what they want and vote how they choose, and they feel no need to give high priority to an issue that could affect them but doesn't. Can you blame them for ignoring activists who make the prochoice argument every four years? When I say, on the eve of an election, that *Roe* is on the ballot, it is not because I really think I or my students will lose their rights. It is because for me it is enough that poor women and foreign women and teenage girls continue to lose their rights. The political majorities don't exist for taking our rights away, and the courts—the "rule of law"—provide ample cover for Republican politicians like Bush and Ashcroft to avoid the attempt.

This campaign dilemma inevitably raises the question of whether we on the prochoice side have actually succeeded in the courts too well. We have taken advantage of the right wing's unwillingness to add the clauses that could save their statutes and thus have won more than we have lost in the lower courts and even in the Supreme Court. The surprise here is not that we are still fighting the same war but that after so much time with the Rehnquist Court, with six of its members appointed by Republicans, we haven't lost it yet.

Overruling *Roe v. Wade* would mean turning abortion exclusively into a political issue, a result that might, both in the short term and in the long run, aid in the election of prochoice candidates. But it would come at the expense of the life and health of those women who still depend on the law and on the courts, even if the protection is tattered. And for most of us, who are in fact very much both prochoice and prolife, that would be an unacceptable trade-off.

THE ASSAULT ON

FEDERAL POWER

The States' Rights Assault on Federal Authority

HERMAN SCHWARTZ

The five conservative justices on the Rehnquist Supreme Court have intensified Ronald Reagan's assault on the New Deal, on the Great Society, and on other congressional efforts to improve the lives of ordinary Americans. Their weapon of choice has been a professed passion for states' rights in the name of liberty, democracy, and efficiency. But just as the states' rights doctrine was used during the New Deal to block federal efforts to combat with the Depression, the Rehnquist Court's embrace of this constitutional theory, which seems nonideological, is merely a fig leaf to cover up more tangible interests like race, wealth, and power. As *Bush v. Gore* so clearly shows, the devotion to states' rights is quickly abandoned when vital interests are at stake like winning a presidential election and determining one's own successors on the Court.

This is not new. Though states' rights is a very pliable doctrine and liberals are not averse to invoking it, federalism has been used most often for regressive causes. It was the slaveholders' favorite strategy before the Civil War and the segregationists' after it and a weapon in the judicial assault on the New Deal. But concern for states' rights was noticeably absent when the states themselves passed social legislation intended to deal with the ravages of America's post–Civil War industrialization and conservative judges, again led by the Supreme Court, struck down almost two hundred of these laws.

By the beginning of the twentieth century it was obvious that the problems of a huge, modern industrial society could be dealt with only on a national scale, and the federal government began to enact legislation to correct some of the worst abuses. One was child labor, which the states had been unable to cope with on their own. In 1916, Congress passed the Child Labor Act, but it was quickly struck down as unconstitutional in 1918 by a 5–4 majority, over a Holmes-Brandeis dissent. Child labor was a "purely local matter . . . entrusted to local authority," declared the Court, and the federal government had no business dealing with it. A second effort to restrict child labor through the taxing power met the same fate four years later.[1]

Then the Depression came. To pull the nation out of it, President Franklin D. Roosevelt's administration created the New Deal with its many federal programs and agencies. One result was a massive transfer of power to the federal government.

The New Deal was intended to do more than bring recovery to the economy and restore the status quo. FDR wanted also to provide basic economic security for the average American and to prevent a repeat of the Depression's ravages. This obviously required a bigger government, higher taxes, and a redistribution of wealth. It inevitably outraged conservatives and produced a deep political cleavage that persists to this day.

During FDR's first term (1933–36) a five-member conservative majority of the Supreme Court consistently struck down his programs and policies for purportedly exceeding federal authority and encroaching on states rights.[2] In 1937, things changed, as Justice Owen Roberts switched sides, voting to uphold New Deal initiatives like minimum-wage laws, Social Security, and other economic programs. Then, as the conservative justices left the Court and New Deal appointees took their places, the Commerce Clause of the Constitution was interpreted to allow federal regulation to extend to anything even marginally affecting the economy.[3] Over the next six decades, the Supreme Court used both the Commerce Clause and the post–Civil War Fourteenth Amendment to confirm the New Deal's shift of power to the national government. The matter seemed to be settled.

But not really. Though the states' rights resurgence attained its full vigor only with the Rehnquist Court, conservative sniping at federal authority began with the Burger Court in the early 1970s, especially after William H. Rehnquist and Lewis Powell became justices in 1972. Raised in a Roosevelt-hating family, Rehnquist has been an archconservative since childhood. While a law clerk to Justice Robert H. Jackson in 1952, he argued that the separate-but-equal doctrine "was right and should be reaffirmed." At his confirmation hearing as chief justice in 1986, he denied that this represented his own view, but lied about this, as Jackson's secretary and others have confirmed and as his whole career shows. Additional evidence comes from a memo he wrote in a case that year, which did not come to light during the 1986 hearings:

> It is about time the court faced the fact that the white people in the South don't like the colored people; the Constitution restrains them from effecting this dislike through state action, but it most assuredly did not appoint the court as a sociological watchdog to rear up every time private discrimination raised its admittedly ugly head.[4]

And while a lawyer in Phoenix, Arizona, he opposed modest public accommodation and school desegregation proposals.

Rehnquist's first opportunity to strike at federal power came in 1976, in *National League of Cities v. Usery*, a case involving the 1974 amendments to the Fair Labor Standards Act, which extended minimum-wage and maximum-hours requirements to state and local governments.[5] Cobbling together a 5–4 majority, Rehnquist got the Court to strike down the 1974 amendments. For authority, he looked to the Tenth Amendment, which provides that "the powers not delegated to the United States by the Constitution . . . are reserved to the states." Since the amendment does not specify what is in fact "reserved," Rehnquist created a new doctrine based on the "policy" of the Tenth Amendment, which he said authorized judges to prohibit Congress and the federal government from regulating the states' "traditional functions," if doing so "impaired their sovereignty" and "their ability to function effectively in a federal system." The result was judicial confusion, as courts struggled with these vacuous criteria. After nine years, the Court overruled the decision in *Garcia v. San Antonio Metropolitan Transit Authority* (1985).[6]

National League of Cities was not Rehnquist's first use of states' rights against social welfare legislation. Two years earlier, in anticipation of cases using the Eleventh Amendment to expand state sovereign immunity, he had written for a 5–4 majority in *Edelman v. Jordan* an opinion that denied aged, blind, and disabled Social Security recipients the right to sue Illinois officials for wrongfully withholding their payments.[7] And in 1985, the same year that the Court decided *Garcia* and overturned *National League of Cities*, the four dissenters in *Garcia*, now joined by the increasingly conservative Byron White (virtually the same majority as in *Edelman*), dismissed a Rehabilitation Act suit against a state hospital for discriminating against a partially blind diabetic, because Congress had not *explicitly* authorized such a suit even though Congress's intent to allow such suits was clear.[8] Congress could not, of course, have anticipated that the Court would require it to go further and make an explicit statement to that effect when its intent was obvious, but the diabetic still lost his lawsuit.

In 1991, Clarence Thomas joined Rehnquist, Anthony Kennedy, Sandra Day O'Connor, and Antonin Scalia, making a virtually solid conservative majority. The constitutional assault on federal power now went into high gear with two targets: federal power and use of the courts by private individuals and public interest organizations—often called "private attorneys general"—to enforce federally created rights, especially those related to social welfare. This attack on private suits, a vital component in the enforcement of such laws, has long been championed by Justice Scalia, who seems to believe that only the executive branch should have that authority—even though (or perhaps because) it is clear that the executive branch has neither the resources nor sometimes even the will to enforce these laws effectively.

The first target came in 1992, the year after Thomas joined the Court: a statute regulating disposal of radioactive waste. No state wants to have radioactive waste stored on its territory. To forestall direct federal regulation, the states bargained among themselves and with the federal government, working out a plan proposed by the National Governors Association that called for various interstate agreements and obligations. An appropriate law was passed, but after it went into effect, New York changed its mind and challenged the statute. It won in *New York v. United States*.[9]

As in *National League of Cities*, the conservatives were unable to rely on any provision in the Constitution, so this time they used their own new conception of the constitutional "framework" and "structure" to bar the federal government from "commandeering" state officials to implement federal laws, in the process ignoring numerous historical examples of state implementation of federal laws. "Accountability is . . . diminished" by such state enforcement, wrote Justice O'Connor, because state officers who have to implement burdensome federal directives would be blamed for them. The Court used the same "accountability" reasoning five years later in *Printz v. United States* to slap down the Brady gun control bill's requirement that local law enforcement officers check the backgrounds of prospective gun purchasers, even though the argument is patently ludicrous—people in the radioactive-waste business knew the rules were set by the federal government, and are there gun owners or buyers anywhere who don't know the Brady bill is a federal law?[10] If there are, surely a sign to that effect would give enough notice, and local officials would certainly not be bashful about telling them.

Four years after *New York v. United States*, the trickle of antifederal decisions became a flood.

The Commerce Clause is the source of federal power over the national economy. Recognizing the interrelatedness of almost all parts of the economy, the Supreme Court had upheld every assertion of federal power under the Commerce Clause since 1937. In 1995, that changed. In *United States v. Lopez*, the now-usual 5–4 majority, again in a Rehnquist opinion, struck down a federal law criminalizing the possession of guns in a school zone because the justices saw no "economic" transaction in the situation and there was no specific congressional finding of an effect on interstate trade.[11] The obvious impact of school violence on the national economy was dismissed, and the fact that most guns moved in interstate trade was ignored.[12] In 2000, the same 5–4 majority used the same argument to strike down the Violence against Women Act (VAWA). Domestic violence is not an "economic" matter, wrote Rehnquist, even though there was, in Justice Souter's words, "a mountain of data" that violence against women costs the economy billions each year. The Court also ignored overwhelming state support for the act.[13]

The Constitution does presuppose a line between interstate and local commerce, but in today's world it is impossible to draw the line with any precision. There is also no way to distinguish clearly between "economic" and "noneconomic" matters, as the VAWA case makes clear, for any large-scale phenomenon will have economic effects and there are no manageable judicial standards for drawing the line between inter- and intrastate commerce in any but the easiest cases. Whenever the Court has tried to draw a line limiting federal authority over the economy on behalf of states' rights, reality has soon washed it away.

The implication is that virtually everything is subject to federal power and that in practice the federal government is not really a government of limited powers. That is probably true for the national economy, which can be dealt with only on a national scale. We act on that understanding all the time. As the Court recognized in *Garcia*, meaningful protections for the states can only be political and they are usually quite sufficient.

But there is one instance in which the courts can impose meaningful limits on the national government and that is when federal power encroaches on individual rights. Then the Court can indeed impose limits that are both needed and usually workable.

In 1996, the Rehnquist Court turned its fire on a private person's ability to enforce his or her rights against state violations, the private attorney general suit, resurrecting the Eleventh Amendment and a state sovereign immunity doctrine that had been repudiated just seven years earlier. The amendment denies *federal* courts jurisdiction over suits by citizens of *one state* against *another* state. Nevertheless, over the next five years the conservative bloc developed a state sovereign immunity doctrine that is based on the discredited "The king can do no wrong" philosophy, allowing a state to prevent money damage suits against itself, even by its *own* citizens, even in *state* courts, and even if the state engages in ordinary private business activities that wrongly damage a private competitor and violate federal law.[14] Although nothing in the language of the Constitution touches on any of these three situations, and certainly not for rights created by Congress, that did not faze these justices, each of whom has regularly excoriated liberal judges as "activists" when they sought to promote individual rights or did not stick closely to the text of the Constitution.[15]

Despite this ban on private suits against states, since 1908 people injured by state officials who violate either the Constitution or federal law have been able to get a federal court order against those officials to prevent continuing violations.[16] This doctrine, the so-called *Ex parte Young* remedy, has never been challenged. Yet even that is being chipped away by a new rule that if the federal law in question establishes a particular structure for enforcing that law, the remedy is not available unless Congress makes clear that it is.[17] Those special statutory enforcement structures are, however, often unavailable to private parties, being reserved to the federal government. The practical effect is to deny any private remedy for violations of rights by state administrators even though victims of such violations have long relied on such remedies; several lower courts have used this new doctrine this way, though at this writing, one has been reversed.[18] And since the federal government is usually too busy or has other reasons for not strictly enforcing the statutory remedy, the effect is to deny any relief at all, no matter how blatant or egregious the violation.

Suits by the federal government against a state are not supposed to be affected by sovereign immunity, but even when there is federal enforcement, the conservative justices have managed to strike at national authority. In *Federal Maritime Commission v. South Carolina State Ports Authority* (2002),[19] the commission tried to enforce the antidiscrimination provisions of the federal Shipping Act of 1984. The commission used a trial-type hearing between the complainant and the Ports Authority as a way for the commission to decide whether to get a court order against the authority. This, Justice Thomas wrote for the usual 5–4 majority, was like a private suit against a state defendant and therefore barred by state sovereign immunity. But as Justice Breyer's dissent pointed out, it was still the federal executive agency that decided whether and how to enforce the act. It could have used other methods but these would have required use of the commission staff, and like most enforcement agencies, the commission is understaffed. The Court's approach, Breyer warned, could undermine enforcement of many worker safety and health laws as well as the effective handling of complaints against state hospitals for improper medical care.

In their assault on private enforcement suits, the conservatives have also turned on the Reconstruction Amendments. Section 5 of the Fourteenth Amendment empowers Congress to enforce the provisions of that amendment "by appropriate legislation." In 1976, the Court declared that because these amendments effected a major transfer of power to the federal government from the states, suits against states brought under them and under laws passed pursuant to Section 5 (and Amendment XV, Section 2) would be exempt from Eleventh Amendment immunity. This seemed like a likely vehicle for the survival of many private suits, since the Fourteenth Amendment and the Civil Rights Act of 1983 cover a great many areas, particularly unlawful discrimination. That door to the federal courts was soon shut.

In 1990, in *Employment Division v. Smith*, the Court narrowly adopted a Scalia opinion overturning a twenty-seven-year-old rule that allowed religious groups not to comply with generally applicable statutes if those laws imposed unnecessary burdens on important religious practices. The case involved the Native American Church's sacramental use of peyote, a drug banned by the Oregon drug law (though not in other states or by the federal government). Congress responded by promptly and almost unanimously passing the Religious Freedom Restoration Act (RFRA) to reinstate the pre-*Smith* rule.

But RFRA didn't last long. In *City of Boerne v. Flores* (1997), the Court first cut back on congressional power by ruling that Section 5 gave Congress no right to "interpret" the Constitution by protecting religious freedom beyond the limits the Court had set in *Smith*—a view contested by many constitutional experts.[20] Moreover, the Court said, even if RFRA involved no new interpretation but only a remedy under Section 5 for judicially established interpretations, it failed in that regard as well because it went too far, burdening too many state activities too heavily. A Section 5 remedy had to be "proportionate and congruent," wrote Justice Kennedy for the usual five-member majority. And here the obligations that RFRA imposed on the states were considered too burdensome, even though the states had lived comfortably for more than a quarter century with the pre-*Smith* rule that RFRA tried to reinstate.

During the next four years, the conservative majority turned back efforts to use Section 5 in suits under the Age Discrimination in Employment Act, the Violence against Women Act, the Americans with Disabilities Act, and the patent and trademark laws.[21] In the VAWA case, the 5–4 majority ruled that Section 5 did not apply to the states' unconstitutional *failures* to enforce their own laws on violence against women, even though the attorneys general of thirty-eight states supported the federal act because, as they told Congress, those failures resulted from sex discrimination. According to Chief Justice Rehnquist, relying in his argument on now-discredited 1875 cases that had not involved the state in any way, Section 5 was limited to affirmative state abuses.

In *Garrett*, a Disabilities Act case, Rehnquist, again writing for the majority, recognized that Section 5 gives Congress leeway in how to enforce the Fourteenth Amendment, particularly when it comes to finding the facts and shaping a remedy. But then he cavalierly dismissed thirteen congressional hearings, a report by a national task force that heard more than thirty thousand people in all fifty states, census results, and other studies, as well as three hundred specific examples of state discrimination against the disabled (all laid out in Justice Stephen Breyer's dissent). Even if all this did show a pattern of discrimination, Rehnquist wrote, Congress hadn't proved either that the discrimination was "irrational," which the Court has defined as "patently arbitrary," or that there were a great many such instances. But to provide such proof, Congress would have to hold the equivalent of a full-blown trial for a very large number of cases of discrimination, an obvious impossibility never before demanded of any legislative body. As a result, states can now violate with impunity many congressionally created rights for the elderly, pregnant women, the mentally retarded, the mentally ill, and others.

There have been a few isolated losses for the states' rights bloc: Kennedy jumped ship to make a 5–4 majority to strike down a state term limits law, and in 2000 the Court upheld a law banning the sale by states of private data collected from driver's license applications.[22] But such decisions have been few and far between.[23]

Is there any justification for this exaltation of states' rights at the expense of the federal government? In her opinion for the Court in *Gregory v. Ashcroft*, Justice O'Connor set forth the advantages she saw in strong state sovereignty:

> This federalist structure of joint sovereigns preserves to the people numerous advantages. It assures a decentralized government that will be more sensitive to the diverse needs of a heterogeneous society; it increases opportunity for citizen involvement in democratic processes; it allows for more innovation and experimentation in government; and it makes government more responsive by putting the States in competition for a mobile citizenry. . . . Perhaps the principal benefit of the federalist system is a check on abuses of government power.[24]

Unfortunately, these "advantages" are frequently unrealized and offset by very real disadvantages. Unless they are directly involved, few citizens pay much attention to state issues or even to local ones. Media coverage of state activities is spotty at best and often nonexistent. Voter turnout in state and local elections is even lower than in national elections. Indeed, few voters even know the names of their local representatives other than their mayor, and they know even less about their state representatives. Most voters, however, know who their congressional representatives and senators are and what they are doing. Whatever the opportunities for citizen involvement at the state and local levels, few seem interested in taking advantage of them.

Moreover, state sovereignty is hardly necessary either for citizen involvement or for most of what states do. Decentralization without sovereignty offers many opportunities for meaningful local participation and governmental responsiveness.[25] Indeed, we have two ubiquitous examples in this country—city and county government, including school and zoning boards. Yet both cities and counties are but creatures of the state, without sovereignty or indeed any constitutional status at all.

As for the "principal benefit" of checking "abuses of power," historically that kind of check has come not from the states on the federal government but the reverse, as James Madison predicted in *Federalist Paper* No. 10; discrimination against blacks, women, and gays and encroachments on free speech are obvious examples. In fact, much and perhaps most of the time, states' rights have been a weapon of reaction. Moreover, when the national government suffered from McCarthyism and similar "abuses of government power," the states did not check the abuses but exacerbated them.[26]

There is, however, one area where state sovereignty is necessary: social and other experimentation, especially where the federal government is unable to act. State and local action on tobacco, gun control, prescription drug pricing, consumer safety, campaign finance, and other issues requires truly independent state authority, for decentralization alone would subject these initiatives to the same forces that block national action. These instances do not justify the Supreme Court's states' rights decisions, however, for they have been made in cases where the federal government has indeed acted. Moreover, on more than a few occasions the states have sued the federal government for relaxing environmental standards and other matters.[27]

Nor is experimentation always a good thing. At least some state experimentation has involved a "race to the bottom," not only in corporate affairs, as in Delaware, but in lowered wages, worse safety conditions, child labor, discrimination, and other matters.

There are also issues of efficiency and of corruption. Although many state legislators now work full-time their sessions are still relatively short—the Texas legislature, for example, meets only once every two years for just four months. Much important legislation is rushed through in the waning minutes of a session, unread by most legislators. Conflicts of interest are rife: a recent study found that 20 percent of state legislators "help regulate their own business or professional interests, [or] have financial ties to organizations that lobby state governments, and many receive income from agencies they oversee."[28]

State and local governments are often hostile to those down on their luck, particularly if they are racial minorities. That is one reason the Republican Party's Contract with America pushed so strongly for more state and local control at the expense of the federal government.[29] For example, in 1999 New York City conceded in court that workers at "job centers," formerly welfare offices, illegally prevented or discouraged people from applying for food stamps and Medicaid. Despite a court order, the city was still doing so a year later.[30] Many states have made it so onerous to apply for food stamps, which the states administer, that many needy people do not even apply.[31]

The hollowness of the conservatives' concern for states' rights was revealed in *New York v. United States*. The radioactive waste law was not a federal initiative but was conceived and promoted by the states. When the dissenters on the Supreme Court pointed this out, Justice O'Connor responded that the anticommandeering principle was not for the benefit of the states but to preserve "the liberties" of the people; the states' consent to the law was irrelevant. But how are the people's liberties protected when the wishes of their elected representatives are ignored? And is not accountability diminished if those representatives cannot act as they believe their constituents want?

This indifference to state interests is not a rare phenomenon. The Court's conservatives struck down hundreds of state and local affirmative action plans, voluntary desegregation plans, and electoral districting plans that created majority-black districts. Nor have Rehnquist, Scalia, and the others hesitated either to strike down zoning and environmental laws in order to protect property rights or to rule that federal law has preempted state tort law when business interests are at stake. Their allies in Congress, who also proclaim their undying loyalty to states' rights, likewise have no problem with proposing legislation barring assisted suicide, gay marriage, limits on tort recovery, and other matters that are usually considered quintessentially local.[32]

Academic commentators disagree on how harmful the conservatives' federalism rulings have been. They have unquestionably spawned confusion and litigation, thereby overburdening a federal judiciary that is already creaking. Moreover, conservative judges on the lower courts have used the Supreme Court decisions that blurred established law on *Ex parte Young* and the Spending Clause to dismiss class action suits by Medicaid and Social Security Act beneficiaries.[33] If the decisions taken by these lower courts are approved by the Supreme Court, the effects could be devastating for the poor, the disabled, and all the other intended beneficiaries of the New Deal and Great Society programs.

Some years ago, a University of Chicago law professor, one of the leaders of the current states' rights movement, announced the goal of the movement in unequivocal terms: to overturn the New Deal and to shrink the federal government to just a few functions. Given the accumulated history and law of the last sixty years, as well as the events of September 11, 2001, that goal is not likely to be achieved. But except in certain areas directly related to national defense, the Supreme Court's conservative majority is also not likely to abandon its campaign against federal power and citizen suits. Enemies of federal authority on and off the Court rarely abandon their crusade, as history shows again and again. In 1918, while German armies were rolling toward Paris, the Supreme Court's five-member conservative majority struck down the Child Labor Act. During the worst of the Depression, conservative justices struck down almost every major federal effort to pull us out of it. Moreover, Rehnquist, Scalia, and their colleagues are not likely to see much of a link between suits by welfare, Social Security, and Medicaid beneficiaries, or victims of discrimination, and war-induced needs.[34]

Because of *Bush v. Gore*, the next appointments to the Supreme Court may not differ much from the current Court majority. It may take a constitutional crisis similar to that of the 1930s and a change in the White House before the current assault on those shortchanged by birth and by fortune is thwarted.

The Roles, Rights, and Responsibilities of the Executive Branch

DAVID C. VLADECK AND ALAN B. MORRISON

In a democratic system governed by the rule of law, government—and particularly the executive branch—must be accountable to the citizenry for its policies and actions. Under our constitutional system of checks and balances, Congress can impose a direct check on specific executive branch actions by oversight and legislation, but citizens can do so only indirectly, either by voting the president out of office or by invoking the power of the judiciary to review executive action. For the latter approach to be successful, however, citizens must know what the executive branch is doing, must have the right to use the courts to challenge actions they believe violate the law, and must have judges willing to compel the executive branch to obey the law.

The 1966 Freedom of Information Act (FOIA) is arguably the most important tool ordinary Americans have to oversee the workings of their government. The Rehnquist Court has made it increasingly difficult for citizens to use the act. At the same time, by narrowing the rules of standing and in some cases overturning congressional efforts to broaden access, the Court has made it harder for private citizens to challenge illegal government actions in federal court. Also, it has increasingly insulated agency action from judicial review when the challenges are made by public interest plaintiffs, while it has expanded judicial review when the challenges come from business interests. Its sympathy for business has also led it to ignore the federalist inclinations that it professes in other contexts and frequently to strike down state regulations when they are more rigorous than federal ones. All in all, the Rehnquist Court has been a boon to business and not a friend to the ordinary citizen.

Under the FOIA, any person has the right to request any record in the hands of a federal agency other than the president, Congress, or the judiciary, subject to nine exemptions that permit the government to withhold sensitive records. The hostile attitude of the Burger Court toward the public's efforts to obtain government documents has been adopted by the Rehnquist Court. In no more than a handful of the thirty-two FOIA cases decided by the Court since 1966 has it sided, even in part, with the requester.

Under the FOIA, courts are supposed to balance privacy rights against the public's right to know, tipping the scale toward disclosure in close cases. Nevertheless, the Court has often accepted claims that disclosure might jeopardize an individual's privacy rights that, to put it charitably, are far-fetched. A low point came with *Department of Justice v. Reporters Committee for Freedom of the Press* (1989).[1] The Reporters Committee asked for the arrest records of certain persons alleged to have been involved in organized crime and illegal dealings with a corrupt congressman. Holding that the records were exempt from disclosure under the FOIA's privacy exemption, the Court dismissed the fact that the information had already been made public. Most significantly, however, it narrowed the scope of the public interest to be considered in the FOIA balancing process by limiting it to "the core purpose of the FOIA," namely, to "shed light on an agency's performance of its statutory duties." Thus, even if government documents are important for other reasons, such as exposing corruption or even criminal misconduct, they may be withheld so long as the government can point to virtually any privacy interest, no matter how remote or implausible.

The Court more fully developed the rule of *Reporters Committee* in its follow-up decision in *Department of State v. Ray* (1991).[2] At issue in *Ray* were notes made by State Department personnel on the treatment of Haitian refugees who had been involuntarily returned to Haiti. The request was made by an immigration lawyer who wanted the notes, including the names of the returnees, both to bolster the claim that returnees were being subjected to political reprisal and to facilitate their reinterview by human rights advocates. Applying *Reporters Committee*, the Court allowed the State Department to withhold the names to protect the privacy of the interviewees because the release of personal identifiers "would not shed any additional light on the Government's conduct of its obligation." In a classic Catch-22, the refugees' own privacy interests were cited as justification to thwart access to their records by lawyers trying to assist them in developing their cases for asylum.

There is one significant Rehnquist Court FOIA ruling that benefits requesters, but it has a limited reach. In *Department of the Interior v. Klamath Water Users Protective Association* (2001), the Court rejected the government's argument that the FOIA's exemption for intraagency records shielded from public disclosure documents exchanged between the Department of the Interior and the Klamath and other Indian tribes regarding disputed water rights because the department's special role as trustee to Indian tribes made the tribes more like government consultants than like outsiders.[3] The Court rejected this and other prosecrecy arguments. Though this suggests that the Court will not automatically rubber-stamp government claims, it does not signal any measurable shift in the Court's FOIA cases.

Following the Supreme Court's lead, lower courts have clamped down on access under the FOIA, weakening significantly the ability of the citizenry to hold their government accountable. The tragic events of September 11 have only accelerated this trend.

The Rehnquist Court has left a mark on the judicial review of federal agency decisions in two distinct ways. First, it has further insulated the executive branch from attack by cutting back on the Court's "standing" jurisprudence, which makes it harder for parties complaining of noneconomic harm (such as environmental groups) to get into court; second, it has redefined the law relating to deference to agency action in a way that frees the courts, in cases brought mainly by business interests, to superintend the regulatory process more closely.

Under Article 3 of the Constitution, federal courts may adjudicate only actual "cases" and "controversies." Injuries that neither have occurred nor are imminent are not sufficient to trigger the exercise of federal judicial power. A party who cannot show actual or imminent "injury," as defined by the Court, lacks "standing" and may not sue in federal court. Until 1990, the Court had held that someone contesting an agency's decision in environmental cases could generally establish personal injury and overcome the standing hurdle by showing that the challenged conduct was likely to harm the environment. But then the Rehnquist Court repudiated this liberal standing doctrine, and it is now much more difficult for a party claiming noneconomic harm to be heard in court, primarily as a result of *Lujan v. National Wildlife Federation* (*Lujan I*) and *Lujan v. Defenders of Wildlife* (*Lujan II*).[4]

Justice Antonin Scalia, writing for the Court in both cases, brushed aside the plaintiffs' arguments on injury. In *Lujan I*, he faulted the plaintiffs, who alleged that they used a park for hiking and other recreational purposes, for not specifying that they actually used the very portions of the park that the Department of the Interior had opened up to mining. In *Lujan II*, the plaintiffs were wildlife experts who had regularly traveled abroad to view species threatened with extinction in their natural habitats. Rejecting the plaintiffs' claim that they were harmed because they would not be able to see the species endangered by a proposed Egyptian dam rehabilitation project, Scalia observed that it is "pure speculation and fantasy" to "say that anyone who observes or works with an endangered species, anywhere in the world, is appreciably harmed by a single project affecting some portion of that species."

When Congress passed the Endangered Species Act it recognized that the law was not self-enforcing and that court compulsion might be necessary. To enable individual citizens to serve as private attorneys general to force compliance with important laws, Congress often enacts "citizen suit" provisions, and the Endangered Species Act contains such a provision. Prior to *Lujan II*, the Supreme Court had accepted the proposition that Congress could confer such a right, the deprivation of which gave rise to injury sufficient to provide standing. But in *Lujan II* the Court ruled that Congress could not "convert the undifferentiated public interest in executive officers' compliance with the law into an 'individual right' vindicable in the courts." In so ruling, the Court made it far more difficult for ordinary citizens to compel the executive branch to obey the law.

Six years later, the Court reaffirmed its get-tough policy in *Steel Company v. Citizens for a Better Environment.*[5] The Steel Company had repeatedly failed to comply with the reporting requirements of the Emergency Planning and Community Right-to-Know Act, and the citizens group alerted the company of its intention to bring suit to force it to obey the law. The company then submitted its reports to the Environmental Protection Agency—six years after they were due but before the suit was filed. When citizens sued to ensure future compliance with the act, the Court, again in an opinion by Justice Scalia, ruled that past harms were not sufficient to constitute present injury, even though there was no assurance that the company would not again disregard the law as soon as the lawsuit was dismissed.

The Court somewhat tempered this ruling in *Friends of the Earth, Inc. v. Laidlaw Environmental Services (TOC), Inc.*[6] There the Court held, over a Scalia-Thomas dissent, that the plaintiffs had standing to maintain a suit under the Clean Water Act where the defendant ceased its violations *after* the lawsuit was brought. But nothing in *Laidlaw* prevents companies from ignoring their legal obligations until they learn of a potential lawsuit and then, before the suit is filed, bringing themselves into compliance and thereby avoiding litigation, with little risk of sanction.

Another opinion curtailing the right of citizens to have a court check agency action is just as important. In *Ohio Forestry Association, Inc. v. Sierra Club* (1998), the Court rejected, on "ripeness" grounds, a challenge to the EPA's overall land-use plan for a major forest area in Ohio because only the *implementation* of certain aspects of the plan could trigger harm, according to the Court, not just the adoption of the plan.[7] Litigation would have to wait until the logging and road-building activities that the plaintiffs wanted to prevent were imminent.

Taken together, these cases deal a serious blow to the ability of citizens who suffer noneconomic injuries at the hands of executive branch agencies to bring suit, particularly environmentalists, preservationists, and animal rights activists.

The Court's decisions on judicial deference to administrative agencies, however, suggest that the Court is not willing to protect these executive branch agencies when businesses challenge their actions. The terrain in this area of law was marked, some thought for good, by the Supreme Court's 1984 ruling in *Chevron, U.S.A., Inc. v. Natural Resources Defense Council, Inc.*, which held that courts owe considerable deference to any authoritative agency interpretation of the statutes the agency administers.[8] Statutory ambiguities were to be left to resolution by the executive branch, so long as the agency's interpretation was consistent with a reasonable reading of the statute.[9]

The first crack in the *Chevron* wall was the Court's 2000 ruling in *Christensen v. Harris County*, where the Court suggested that an informal agency position, as set forth in a letter, for example, may not warrant *Chevron*-style deference.[10] The wall did not crumble, however, until 2001 and *United States v. Mead Corporation*.[11] That case involved the mundane question of what deference, if any, should be given to rulings made by the United States Customs Service. Mead imports diaries and day planners, merchandise that for years entered the country duty-free. Then the Customs Service's headquarters office shifted ground and classified Mead's three-ring binder products as "bound diaries" subject to tariff. Mead challenged the ruling and succeeded. Formally adopted agency positions, either through a notice-and-comment rule making or through an adjudicatory proceeding, the Court ruled, are entitled to *Chevron* deference, but informal agency statements, such as in an opinion letter, policy statement, or amicus brief, are not; at most they deserve respect based on the persuasive power of their reasoning. In other words, unless an agency position is formally adopted, reviewing courts will no longer be obligated to uphold it even though that position is reasonable and not at odds with the text of the statute.

The consequences of *Mead* are far-reaching, as Justice Scalia pointed out in his lone dissent. The decision tells courts to give far greater scrutiny to agency action, at least in those cases where the agency's position has not been formally adopted. Indeed, *Mead* can be seen as uprooting part of *Chevron*'s foundation because it suggests that, at least where the agency has not officially adopted an interpretation, it is the courts and not the executive branch that should take the lead in resolving statutory ambiguities. Since many if not most agency pronouncements fall into the informal category, the court's powers are vastly enlarged under *Mead*.

Mead is a big victory for any party challenging agency action, especially big business. Because the Rehnquist Court's standing restrictions have driven down the number of nonbusiness challenges to agency action, most lawsuits against federal agencies are now filed by businesses complaining of overregulation. *Mead* gives those challengers a boost because it tells reviewing courts that they have an important role to play in ensuring the fairness and rationality of the regulatory process and that they need not tilt the scale in favor of government. It remains to be seen whether challenges from environmental and consumer advocates will benefit from *Mead* as well.

Two pre-*Mead* cases also warrant mention. First is the Court's controversial 5–4 decision in 2000 in *FDA v. Brown & Williamson Tobacco Corporation*.[12] The FDA claimed authority to regulate tobacco products as "drugs" under the Food, Drug and Cosmetic Act because of the industry's manipulation of the nicotine content in cigarettes and chewing tobacco. This is a question on which the agency would ordinarily receive substantial deference under *Chevron*. Nevertheless, the Court ruled that the FDA lacked authority over tobacco products because Congress had never explicitly given the agency the power to regulate them.

The ruling is result-oriented adjudication at its worst. Congress does not usually specify the products an agency may regulate; it describes them categorically and lists any exclusions, and the Food, Drug and Cosmetic Act is no exception. The majority could not plausibly find that nicotine failed to meet the statutory definition of a drug because, in fact, it is a drug, and even the industry did not seriously contest that fact. Instead, the Court pieced together a congressional "intent" to *deny* the FDA authority over tobacco even though, despite many opportunities to do so, Congress had never said in a statute or other pronouncement that tobacco was off-limits to the FDA. A more charitable explanation is that tobacco regulation is so politically volatile that the Court thought that Congress, not an administrative agency, ought to tackle the job. If so, *Brown & Williamson* is an unalloyed act of judicial activism, the sort of activism that conservatives normally decry.

Despite its probusiness tilt, this Court has its limits. In *Whitman v.*

American Trucking Associations (2001), the question was whether Congress intended that when the EPA sets air quality standards under the Clean Air Act, it may look at health concerns alone, or must also consider the costs of regulation.[13] The Court unanimously upheld the EPA on this key question, ruling that the text of the act did not permit a reviewing court to read in a cost-consideration requirement. Had industry prevailed, cost/benefit concerns would have inevitably dwarfed other factors in rule making, and unless an agency could justify its regulatory decisions in hard economic terms, those decisions would have been at high risk of judicial invalidation.

The Constitution divides government into three parts and envisions that each branch will operate in a way that checks the inevitable tendency of institutions—here, the other branches of government—to aggrandize their own power. The Burger Court had been accused of reinvigorating the separations of powers doctrine by being overly rigid and formalistic in keeping each branch within its respective spheres. In a pair of celebrated cases the Court had overturned efforts by Congress to give power to the executive branch but to retain control over the exercise of that power.[14]

The Rehnquist Court has shown a more pragmatic and flexible approach in evaluating the constitutionality of claimed interbranch encroachments. In *Morrison v. Olson* (1988), it upheld the independent counsel law against claims that denying the president and attorney general control over the appointment, the supervision, and, to a significant degree, the firing of a high-level prosecutor to investigate and, if necessary, prosecute charges of criminal wrongdoing by senior government officials fundamentally interfered with the powers of the executive branch.[15] Written by Chief Justice Rehnquist, *Morrison* rejected the Burger Court's notion of iron-clad separation and sustained a scheme that, everyone acknowledged, permitted the judiciary to carry out powers—like appointing and supervising a prosecutor—that historically had been the responsibility of the executive branch. The Court was obviously influenced by Congress's determination that an independent prosecutor was essential to a public perception that the laws were being equally and fairly enforced in the course of investigations of high-ranking administration officials, including the president.

The Rehnquist Court's pragmatist bent has its limits, however. In 1996, Congress gave President Clinton what presidents have wanted for many decades—a line-item veto. The constitutions of more than forty states give their governor some form of line-item veto, but there is no comparable provision in the U.S. Constitution. Congress understood that the bill had serious constitutional problems, and so it included a special provision allowing an immediate and expedited challenge by members of Congress, who would be injured in their capacity as legislators by the grant of power to the president. A suit was filed, but the Supreme Court ruled in *Raines v. Byrd* (1997) that members of Congress lacked standing.[16] According to the opinion written by Chief Justice Rehnquist, they suffered no personal injury, and any harm to them in their legislative capacities was not the kind of injury that could be redressed in the federal courts. This was an important victory for the executive branch because it sharply limited, if not eliminated, cases in which members of Congress might sue the executive branch for violations of the Constitution.

The president's victory, however, was short-lived. A year later, in *Clinton v. City of New York*, the Court agreed that the line-item veto statute was an unauthorized end run around the Constitution.[17] Although counter to the Rehnquist Court's emerging pragmatism, the decision was clearly influenced by the majority's concern that the law shifted to the president unprecedented and excessive power that Congress could not effectively check.

Finally, in 2001, in *Whitman v. American Trucking Associations*, the Court unanimously rejected the claim that Congress had failed to give the EPA sufficient guidance on how to write pollution standards under the Clean Air Act and that the EPA regulations should therefore be struck down. Industry's main argument was that Congress, in directing the EPA to reduce air pollution without reference to the costs involved, failed to give the agency sufficiently concrete principles within which to act, thereby conferring on it the power to regulate the economy "back to the stone age."

Justice Scalia's opinion seems to put to rest, perhaps permanently, the notion that the courts should tell Congress how it should delegate its rule-making power to executive agencies. As he put it, the Court has "almost never felt qualified to second-guess Congress regarding the permissible degree of policy judgment that can be left to those executing or applying the law." So long as the delegation falls somewhere between these distant poles, the Court will uphold it.

This ruling's implications go well beyond the confines of the case and solidify the view that the Rehnquist Court will not usually tread on power-sharing arrangements between the branches. Congress routinely identifies a difficult problem and gives the agency some degree of direction, but leaves many of the hard choices to the agency to decide. To have agreed with industry in this case would have forced Congress to fine-tune each delegation of authority to an agency—a process that would tie Congress in knots and render it unable to tackle the difficult issues that face our nation, like fighting air pollution.

Preemption is a lawyer's word—no ordinary person would use it in conversation. But the concept is simple: the Supremacy Clause of the Constitution says that if there is a conflict between state and federal law (the Constitution, a statute passed by Congress, or a rule of a federal agency), federal law controls or "preempts" state law. Cases arise because Congress or a federal agency has been unclear about whether the federal and state schemes can coexist. These disputes generally fall into two categories: first, where a state wants to regulate activities or conduct (such as the sale of cigarettes to minors) that is also subject to federal regulation; second, where a person is suing for damages under state law for injuries caused by conduct of the defendant and the defendant claims that, because the conduct is regulated by federal law, state law cannot be the basis for liability.

The executive branch plays a pivotal role in this dynamic between the application of federal or local law. Most statutes enacted by Congress are not self-executing; they are implemented and enforced only when a federal agency takes some form of regulatory action. Congress, for example, may decree that no car may be sold in the United States unless it meets safety standards issued by the National Highway Traffic

Safety Administration (NHTSA), the federal agency that regulates auto safety. But until NHTSA takes action, the statute has little practical meaning. Moreover, because the federal agencies are presumed to understand the relationship between their rules and local law, the Supreme Court looks to the agencies to provide guidance on whether they intend that their regulation preempt state law.

The main battle in regulatory preemption cases is between businesses that are regulated by both the federal and the state governments and state governments that want to enforce their laws. States often seek to do this in instances where their laws are more stringent than the federal ones and they are concerned that the lax federal rules may not provide sufficient protection. Almost invariably, the defendant will claim that federal law trumps state law and that the state is foreclosed from enforcing its law. Time and again, the Rehnquist Court has sided with business (often supported by the federal government) to find state laws preempted.

A cigarette advertising case best illustrates this point. On the final day of the 2000–01 term, the Court concluded in *Lorillard Tobacco Company v. Reilly* that the Federal Cigarette Labeling Act preempted efforts by Massachusetts to limit cigarette advertising near parks and playgrounds.[18] The federal law was designed to ensure that the warnings set forth on cigarette packaging and labeling were uniform and not subject to diverse content requirements by states. The Court concluded that the federal law applied as well to the location of advertising and that it barred states from imposing limitations on where cigarette advertising could be placed. Under the Court's ruling, states would be disabled from preventing tobacco companies from erecting billboards across the street from elementary schools and playgrounds.

Lorillard typifies the problems with the Court's regulatory preemption cases. The Court's mechanical and wooden reading of the labeling law is wholly divorced from any appreciation of the purpose of the law or the adverse consequences of its own ruling. It bodes ill for future cases of this kind and suggests that the Rehnquist Court, despite its professed allegiance to states' rights, will be quite willing to find for regulatory preemption, especially when that frees business from regulation it finds burdensome.

In claims for damages, when injured consumers are pitted against the manufacturers of federally regulated products, the manufacturers almost invariably argue that federal law preempts state tort law. The function for the Supreme Court in these cases is to determine whether Congress, when it enacted the federal regulatory program, intended to displace state law remedies. Historically, the Court has been wary of finding preemption under these circumstances because tort law has long been seen as a necessary state law supplement, providing compensation to injured parties and imposing another discipline on the marketplace.

The Rehnquist Court's approach in this area can be seen in two recent cases. In *Buckman Company v. Plaintiffs' Legal Committee*, it rejected a state tort claim by an individual injured by defective orthopedic bone screws who argued that a company acting on behalf of the manufacturers of the defective device had committed fraud on the FDA in gaining approval for the device and should be held liable.[19] The Court, backed by the FDA, concluded that policing fraud against the FDA was up to the agency alone and not a matter of local concern, even where, as here, the fraud allegedly allowed a defective device on the market that resulted in serious injuries to thousands of people.

In *Geier v. American Honda Motor Corporation*, the Court upheld a preemption claim, wiping out the state tort law claim of a young woman injured in a car accident where the car had only a manual seat belt and no air bag.[20] The issue was whether a federal standard, which required some but not all cars to have either a passive seat belt or an air bag during the early 1990s, preempted a state law claim that the manufacturer should have installed an air bag in the woman's car. The federal agency involved, the NHTSA, did not purport to preempt state tort laws when it issued the standard gradually requiring air bags. Nonetheless, the Court held that state tort law was inconsistent with the NHTSA phase-in approach, leaving the victim without any legal claim.

These cases suggest that where Congress's instructions about preemption are less than crystal-clear, the Court may be shifting away from safeguarding the rights of injured parties to seek compensation under state law and toward the idea that federal regulation frees corporations of tort liability under state law. This is disturbing. Federal agencies cannot provide the protection the public needs, and state tort law is necessary not just to provide remedies to injured parties but to impose discipline on the market and impose safety across the board.

Many of the cases discussed here were decided by a razor-thin 5–4 margin, and the replacement of a single sitting justice could have profound effects. Even with that cautionary note in mind, two overarching conclusions may be drawn about the Rehnquist Court and its relation to the executive branch.

First, it is sympathetic to big business. It has moved decisively to insulate commercial interests from tort litigation in damages preemption cases, it has shielded business from simultaneous federal and state regulation in its regulatory preemption cases, and it has enabled business to challenge federal regulation more effectively by stripping away the judicial deference that historically has been accorded to agency action. Second, the Rehnquist Court has hobbled the ability of ordinary citizens seeking stricter regulation of commercial activity to sue federal agencies, showing little sympathy for the role citizens play in shaping our democracy.

Individually, the Court's rulings are troubling. But taken as a whole, they signal a real hostility to allowing courts to hold the government accountable under the laws and the Constitution on behalf of ordinary citizens.

Environmental Law

JAMES SALZMAN

Modern environmental law is now more than thirty years old, no longer a new legal field but a mature area with its own practicing bar, shelves of regulations and statutes, and thousands of reported opinions. Environmental law's radical innovation of the "citizen suit" has created a key role for ordinary citizens, not just for the government, to use the courts as private attorneys general to enforce our laws. Its integration of ecological principles into legal doctrine has helped reshape our conceptions of legitimate restrictions on the use of private property. These developments, just to mention a few, have contributed greatly to our legal system, forcing a reassessment of basic assumptions. This may well explain why the most influential decisions in the field of administrative law have been environmental cases.

Unlike many of the other topics covered in this volume, the Rehnquist Court's treatment of environmental law defies meaningful labeling. Indeed, the best description that comes to mind is neither "proenvironment" nor "prodevelopment" but, rather, "indifferent." Despite the indisputable rise of environmental concerns on the public agenda, environmental law has played the role of Zelig in the Supreme Court's chambers, observing great events but playing little part in their unfolding.

Consider the research findings of Professor Richard Lazarus, who has analyzed the Supreme Court's decisions over the past three decades, covering all of the Rehnquist Court and almost all of the Burger Court. In reviewing more than 240 cases where environmental issues were raised, Lazarus concluded that "environmental protection concerns implicated by a case appear, at best, to play no favored role in shaping the outcome, which is a sharp departure from what many judges in the 1970s conceived of as the proper judicial function in environmental law. . . . [For] most of the Court most of the time environmental law raises no special issues or concerns worthy of distinct treatment as a substantive area of the law."[1] Deputy Solicitor General Edwin Kneedler shared this view, observing that "in almost every case, the environmental issue is overtaken by some other aspect of the Court's jurisprudence which disposes of the case."[2]

As evidence of the Rehnquist Court's lack of environmental focus, can you guess who has written the most environmental opinions, by far, over the past thirty years? Not Justice William O. Douglas, whose proud rhetoric championing environmental protection on behalf of the public interest is still reprinted in many environmental law casebooks. No, the prize for the leading opinion writer goes to Justice Byron White, hardly one identified with an environmental agenda of *any* kind. And his environmental opinions seem no different from his Commerce Clause, First Amendment, or equal protection opinions—unemotional, analytic, and workmanlike.

In the Rehnquist Court (and Burger Court, for that matter), environmental law has largely served as nondescript wrapping paper, delivering issues for the Court to consider but torn off and discarded while the Court assesses the administrative law, standing, criminal law, and other doctrinal fields contained within them. To be fair, advocates before the Court on environmental issues have not been ideologically consistent, either. In the Reagan era, for example, out of concern that the federal government lacked the will to enforce environmental laws aggressively, states led the way in strengthening environmental protections and environmental groups championed federalism arguments for greater state authority. Under the Clinton administration nearly the opposite was true, with these same groups arguing for stronger federal powers.

This is not to say, however, that particular justices' decisions in environmental cases have been random; it is just that their traditional labels as "liberal" or "conservative" provide little predictive power of how they will vote. Lazarus found only two justices with consistent voting records in environmental cases—Justices Antonin Scalia and Clarence Thomas. Their consistent antienvironment votes, and the voting patterns of other justices, can better be explained by focusing on more basic views rather than on overarching political alignments. As a general guide, justices who believe in a preeminent role for the executive branch in enforcing the law, in a sharp limit on the power of Congress to regulate at the state level, and in the primacy of private property rights over state uses will more likely decide cases against environmental protection. This can be seen in debates over three major issues reshaping environmental law—citizens' access to courts, the scope of private property rights, and Commerce Clause jurisprudence.

Environmental law's greatest contribution to our legal system has likely been its development of the citizen suit, allowing people to sue polluters when they cause harm and the government when it fails to fulfill its mandate of environmental protection. Virtually all our major environmental laws contain citizen suit provisions, creating a legion of private attorneys general to supplement the government's role in enforcing our laws. The once radical idea that private citizens, not just the government, can use the courts to enforce the range of environmental laws has been a powerful force for protection over the last thirty years, ensuring the compliance, both directly and indirectly, of literally thousands of companies and our most powerful government agencies.

For citizen suits to vindicate the protections promised by our laws, however, private parties must be able to get into court in the first place. And to do that they must satisfy the requirements of a doctrine known as "standing." Plaintiffs must demonstrate (1) that they have suffered a recognized harm, (2) that they have suffered it by an act forbidden under the law, and (3) that the court can provide redress. While seemingly easy to satisfy as a result of decisions over the last decade these three requirements have in fact become increasingly difficult for environmental plaintiffs to meet.

Environmental harms fit awkwardly within our common-law notions of injury. Unlike traditional tort harms, like whacking someone on the head, environmental harms are often attenuated, resulting from cumulative, multiple causes over some time. It is unusual for a harm resulting from pollution to be traced back to a single emission source. More generally, the degradation of air and water quality occurs over a long period of extended pollution from multiple sources. Given such remote causation, and wanting to achieve an overall "acceptable" level of pollution, environmental law generally regulates specific emissions at classes of sources, therefore not having to prove the harm caused by each specific emission. In simple terms, it has transformed the common law of nuisance into a comprehensively regulated field that avoids the harm *ex ante* by limiting pollution at its source.

Environmental harms do not just include harm from pollution, of course. What about injuries people sense from the commercial development of a forest or mountainside? Since the landmark 1972 case *Sierra Club v. Morton*, such nonphysical harms have satisfied standing's injury requirements.[3] In that case, the Sierra Club sued to prevent Disney from constructing a ski resort in the Sequoia National Forest. Broadening the scope of harm to include noneconomic injury, the Court held that the requirements of standing may be satisfied by injury to aesthetic and environmental values, even if suffered by many. Over time, however, this standard has been cut back.

In two of the Court's most significant decisions of the nineties, the *Lujan* cases, Justice Scalia, writing for the majority, stated that plaintiffs must demonstrate specific links of causation between the challenged act and the claimed harm to them.[4] In the case of actions alleged to threaten endangered species, he required them to show they had a particular economic or physical connection to the species, and he expressly ruled out aesthetic or recreational injuries. The net effect was to restrict citizens' access to the courts. Some lower courts have since denied standing to plaintiffs unable to show particular harm from a polluter's specific discharge. But we know that this is well-nigh impossible because the harm resulting from pollution can rarely be traced to a single source.

The doors to the courthouse became even tougher to open in the 1998 case *Steel Company v. Citizens for a Better Environment*.[5] In 1995, Citizens for a Better Environment (CBE) filed a citizen suit against the Steel Company for its failure over the previous six years to submit a series of compliance forms required by law. In a citizen suit of this kind, plaintiffs must first inform a defendant of its alleged violations and then wait sixty days before filing suit. During the sixty days before CBE filed its suit, Steel Company submitted its long-overdue forms. CBE went ahead with the case, but on appeal to the Supreme Court it was told that it had failed to meet the redressability requirement for standing. In a Scalia opinion, the Court held that the remedy available in this case, payment of civil penalties to the U.S. Treasury, could not redress injury to CBE or its members. As he put it, "Although a suitor may derive great comfort and joy from the fact that the United States Treasury is not cheated, that a wrongdoer gets his just desserts, or that the nation's laws are faithfully enforced, that psychic satisfaction is not an acceptable Article III remedy because it does not redress a cognizable Article III injury." In other words, because the statute required penalties to be paid to the Treasury rather than to the plaintiffs, the redressability requirement of standing could not be met for the simple reason that the harms suffered by the plaintiffs would not be compensated.

This decision was a body blow to the whole concept of citizen suits, where the primary goal is environmental protection rather than personal enrichment. If the EPA and state agencies presented little credible threat of enforcement to certain industries (and this has certainly happened), companies could simply violate environmental laws and come into compliance, perhaps just temporarily, when forewarned of a citizen suit.

Consistent in its lack of consistency, the Court then reversed its holdings on environmental standing in midstride. In *Friends of the Earth, Inc. v. Laidlaw Environmental Services (TOC), Inc.* (2000), the Court breathed new life into citizen suits.[6] Friends of the Earth had brought a citizen suit under the Clean Water Act against Laidlaw, the operator of a hazardous-waste incinerator that discharged wastewater into the Tyger River in South Carolina. The organization alleged that the facility had violated its permit requirements hundreds of times. It submitted affidavits of several of its members stating that they had stopped using the Tyger River because of health concerns. The district court had found that Laidlaw had violated the mercury effluent permit limits 489 times, the monitoring requirements 420 times, and the reporting requirements 503 times and had been assessed $405,800 in civil penalties. The Fourth Circuit Court of Appeals, though, following the holding of *Steel Company v. Citizens for a Better Environment*, vacated this opinion, in part because the civil penalties awarded in citizen suits did not meet the redressability requirement of standing.

Laidlaw provided a stark example of how, if the government did not act, the Supreme Court's decisions could eviscerate the protection of citizen suits and effectively allow polluters to violate requirements with impunity. Perhaps shocked by the consequence of their earlier decision, the Court now reaffirmed the status of aesthetic and recreational injuries that it had recognized in earlier cases such as *Sierra Club v. Morton*. Eliminating the need for precise tracing of cause and physical effect, the Court stated that the plaintiff's reasonable concern about the effects of toxic pollutants released by Laidlaw on recreational, aesthetic, or economic interests was sufficient for standing. This would make it easier for a plaintiff to demonstrate injury. As to redressability, the Court argued that all civil penalties have a deterrent effect. *Steel Company* was distinguished rather than overturned, with the Court noting that *Steel Company* had denied standing for citizen suits seeking civil penalties for *wholly past* violations, whereas the violations in this case were ongoing and could continue undeterred. Thus plaintiffs must be able to show the likelihood that violations will continue in the future. Justices Scalia and Thomas, it should be noted, strongly dissented, arguing that the Court had sanctioned a "generalized remedy" and ignored the *Steel Company* decision.

While *Laidlaw* reversed the trend of weakening citizen suits, the issue is far from resolved, for it is driven by a fundamental disagreement. The underlying logic for closing the courtroom doors to many environmental concerns lies in differing conceptions of the separation of powers. In his opinions on standing, Justice Scalia has argued that the burden to ensure that laws are faithfully executed lies solely with the executive branch, not the public or the courts. If citizens are concerned over agencies' poor compliance with statutory mandates, the opinions have suggested, they should go to Congress for a legislative fix or the executive branch for a political resolution. As Scalia wrote in *Laidlaw*, "in seeking to overturn that tradition by giving an individual plaintiff the power to invoke a public remedy, Congress has done precisely what we have said it cannot do: convert an 'undifferentiated public interest' into an 'individual right' vindicable in the courts. . . . By permitting citizens to pursue civil penalties payable to the Federal Treasury, the Act . . . turns over to private citizens the function of enforcing the law."[7]

The problem with this pat answer is that Congress provided for citizen suits expressly to ensure that the executive branch *did* enforce the laws. Had the Reagan administration's neutering of the EPA under Anne Gorsuch been forgotten in the mists of time? Citizen suits certainly can force agency agendas, and this does raise concerns over whether the executive branch's discretion to enforce the laws has been unduly limited. But citizen suits normally arise when the government is *not* enforcing the laws. Indeed, usually the federal government can overfile and take over the case. Scalia's advice that, in the face of nonenforcement, citizens should go to Congress or the executive branch for a political resolution rings hollow. Why go to Congress when it has already provided for citizen suits to address this very situation? Why go to the executive branch when it already is not enforcing the law? All that's left of Scalia's strategy is to vote the bums out of office.

The second major fault line—protection of private property rights—runs through what are called takings cases. The Fifth Amendment of the Constitution provides that private property cannot be taken for public use without just compensation. Environmental law raises takings concerns precisely because it alters our vision of property and the legitimacy of government's constraints on its use. As the public's appreciation of and demands for environmental quality increase, our notions of what constitutes reasonable use evolve as well. Use of a private resource, such as housing construction along a coastline, can adversely affect the environment by increasing coastline erosion. To protect the public's interests, the government may restrict such property development for the public benefit of coastal conservation. Yet if the government had to compensate every landowner whose property value diminished *at all* as a result of such zoning, the cost of enforcing such restrictions would be prohibitive and could never take place because of the costs. The difficulty of line drawing, of course, lies in determining when restrictions are so complete and unfair that they constitute a "taking" for which the property owner must be compensated.

The Rehnquist Court has applied the Takings Clause aggressively and shifted the balance toward greater compensation for property owners. For example, in the important decision *Lucas v. South Carolina Coastal Council*, written by Justice Scalia in 1992, the Court required compensation for regulations that deprive the property owner of all economically valuable use of the land unless the government can prove the restriction is necessary to prevent what has traditionally been recognized as a common-law nuisance.[8] This not only switched the burden of proof onto the government to justify its restrictions but, in another part of the opinion, left the lower courts the option of requiring compensation for less than total diminution (and some are already doing so). The net result has been expanded protections for private property owners and cost constraints on legislatures seeking to protect public resources. The case had a slim majority, so new appointments to the Supreme Court will surely affect the trajectory of future takings jurisprudence.

The third major debate shaping environmental law is the reach of congressional authority. This plays out through the Commerce Clause of the Constitution. The Constitution grants Congress several sources of authority to regulate activities in the states, including the power to tax and spend and the power to provide for the common defense. The single most important source of authority for environmental law has been the power to regulate interstate commerce, provided by the Commerce Clause. Congressional reliance on the Commerce Clause seems obvious in a statute like the Clean Air Act, for instance, since air pollution routinely travels across state lines. The same is true for water pollution as well. The Commerce Clause has also been used to justify protection of isolated wetlands. The Clean Water Act forbids the dredging and filling of navigable waters without a permit. How, though, could this be justified under the Commerce Clause if the wetlands are not linked to other waters—such as prairie potholes or other seasonal wetlands? The answer, traditionally, has been migratory waterfowl. Duck hunting is a multibillion-dollar business. Because ducks and geese stop off in such wetlands to feed during their migration, under the Migratory Bird Rule the EPA and the Army Corps of Engineers have justified protection of wetlands as a significant concern of interstate commerce.

In 1995, the expansive breadth of the Commerce Clause was directly challenged for the first time in more than fifty years in *United States v. Lopez*.[9] The Court held that a federal statute regulating private activity exceeded the authority of the Commerce Clause. The challenged statute, the Gun-Free School Zones Act, prohibited the possession of firearms within a thousand feet of a school. In a 5–4 majority, Rehnquist wrote that the activity of possessing a gun in or near a school is not inherently economic or commercial in nature; that the act in question had no express element that explicitly affected interstate commerce; that Congress made no specific findings that possessing a gun in or near a school would affect interstate commerce; and that the suggested connections to interstate commerce were extremely attenuated and could "destroy the Framers' system of enumerated and reserved state powers." The Court went on to hold that the Commerce Clause covers only activities that "substantially affect" interstate commerce. This decision sent shock waves through the environmental community for the same reasons that the *Lujan* decisions had. Direct causation is exceedingly difficult to prove in the environmental context.

The holding of *Lopez* was driven home in the 2000 case *United States v. Morrison*, which struck down part of the Violence against Women Act.[10] Writing for the same five-member majority as in *Lopez*, Rehnquist held that neither law was directed at regulating economic or commercial activities. Despite several years of data gathering by Congress to document the interstate economic effects of violence against women, the Court argued that, in order to maintain the "distinction between what is truly national and what is truly local," the threshold of substantially affecting interstate commerce must be high.[11] If after *Lopez* the Court's scrutiny of Congressional enactments under the

Commerce Clause was unclear, after *Morrison* it was plainly evident. It was also historic. As Professor Michael Gerhardt has observed, "In the past 5 years, the Rehnquist Court has struck down 23 federal laws, including 11 for exceeding Congress' authority under the U.S. Commerce Clause, section 5 of the Fourteenth Amendment, or both. Not since the titanic conflict between Congress and the Court in the 1930s over the fate of the New Deal has the Court been as active as it has in recent years in enforcing federalism-based limitations on Congressional power."[12] Shortly after *Lopez* was decided, Justice Thomas commented that he believed the Migratory Bird Rule fails to satisfy the Commerce Clause.[13] Five years later, it appeared that the entire Court would face this issue when certiorari was granted in *Solid Waste Agency of Northern Cook County (SWANCC) v. U.S. Army Corps of Engineers*.[14] SWANCC, a consortium of twenty-three suburban Chicago cities and villages, had petitioned to develop a disposal site for solid waste in a 553-acre former sand and gravel pit that had been abandoned for almost thirty years. The site had gradually developed into a successional stage forest, with the old trenches turning into permanent and seasonal ponds that ranged in size from one-tenth of an acre to several acres. The Army Corps of Engineers refused to issue a permit to fill the ponds, stating that as many as 121 bird species, including both endangered and migratory birds, had been observed at the site.

In a 1985 decision, *United States v. Riverside Bayview Homes*, the Court had held that the Clean Water Act covered wetlands adjacent to navigable waters.[15] In *SWANCC*, Rehnquist, writing again for the same 5–4 majority as in the *Lopez* and *Morrison* cases, sidestepped the Commerce Clause issue and decided the case on statutory grounds, distinguishing the *Riverside* decision by holding that the Migratory Bird Rule applied only to navigable waters and that waters with no hydrologic connection to open waters (that is, isolated wetlands) were not "navigable waters." The decision has been decried by environmental groups, concerned that it may have put one-fifth of America's bodies of water in jeopardy. The decision also raises the question of whether any of the Clean Water Act (including its pollution provisions) applies to isolated waters. In a district court case in New Jersey, for example, lawyers argued that the Army Corps of Engineers lacked jurisdiction over wetlands owned by a company because they were geographically distant from navigable waters.

While not a Commerce Clause decision, *SWANCC* raises similar concerns over federalism. The Court held that the agency was not entitled to the deference courts normally give to administrative agencies that promulgate federal regulations under *Chevron*.[16] In dicta, the Court noted that a broad reading of the Clean Water Act could impinge upon states' rights to control land and water issues. As Rehnquist wrote,

> Where an administrative interpretation of a statute invokes the outer limits of Congress' power, we expect a clear indication that Congress intended that result. This requirement stems from our prudential desire not to needlessly reach constitutional issues and our assumption that Congress does not casually authorize administrative agencies to interpret a statute to push the limit of congressional authority. This concern is heightened where the administrative interpretation alters the federal-state framework by permitting federal encroachment upon traditional state power. . . . Twice in the past six years we have reaffirmed the proposition that the grant of authority to Congress under the Commerce Clause, though broad, is not unlimited. See *United States v. Morrison*, 529 U.S. 598 (2000) and *United States v. Lopez*, 514 U.S. 549 (1995).[17]

Echoes of the *Lopez* decision continue to sound. Whether undercutting laws by statutory interpretation or Commerce Clause jurisprudence (or Article 5 of the Fourteenth Amendment, for that matter), the Court's majority views the issue as the same—the allocation of authority between the states and federal government. Notwithstanding its contrary decision in *Bush v. Gore*, the Rehnquist Court has established a clear preference to favor state over federal exercise of authority. What are the implications for environmental protection?

From a historical perspective, one would conclude that environmental protection will suffer. One of the main reasons for the development of federal environmental law in the 1970s was the historic failure of states to implement and enforce tough environmental standards. State agencies have traditionally been threatened by the possibility of co-optation by the industries they are supposed to regulate. Perhaps things have changed, though, in the last thirty years. After all, today political candidates reflexively define themselves as environmentalists. The most recent test for the greening of local politics has been the response of states to the *SWANCC* decision. According to the Environmental Law Institute, at least nineteen states reacted to the newly created gap in Clean Water Act protection of isolated wetlands by either enacting or recommending the enactment of laws to protect these areas. While that is a promising development, it is worth remembering that not all these proposed laws will be enacted and that over half the states still have not responded. Overall, then, it seems likely that the transfer of environmental protection authority from the federal government to the states will lead to less protection.

Environmental protection has surely been affected by the Rehnquist Court, but apparently not because of concerns about or antipathy toward the environment. Rather, decisions on "environmental cases" have been made on the grounds of fundamental political issues such as the separation of powers, protection of private property rights, and federalism. These cases have determined the shape of environmental protection and the shape of a wide range of other fields as well. And what of the future? As Richard Lazarus concludes, "It will be the rare candidate that will have a clear environmental track record from which we can readily predict future votes as a justice in environmental cases."[18] It seems a safe bet, however, that justices who share the views of Scalia and Thomas on rigid separation of powers and strong property rights will provide a stronger majority for decisions that weaken environmental protection. Beyond that predictor, however, all bets are off.

The "Miserly" Approach to Disability Rights

ANDREW J. IMPARATO

In the decades since World War II, disabled Americans have worked to change the public perception of disability from a charity model, where the disabled person is a source of pity evoking paternalism, to a civil rights or social model, where the focus is on removing barriers to participation. Many have also advocated moving away from the medical model, where the disabled person is a patient in need of treatments, more research, and ultimately a "cure." In both the charity and the medical models, disability is viewed as an inherently negative or tragic status and disabled people are often portrayed as helpless victims of fate. In contrast, in the social or civil rights model, disabled people are full citizens seeking self-determination along with economic and political power.

In the civil rights paradigm for disability, the goal is to fix the society, not the disabled person. Many limitations associated with disabling conditions may more accurately be attributed to the interaction between these conditions and the physical and social environment. When the environment is made accessible, disabled people can participate fully notwithstanding their impairments. Supporters of disability rights have emphasized that employers, governments at all levels, and public accommodations should make reasonable adjustments so that disabled people will not be excluded; schools must educate all pupils so that disabled children need not go without schooling, as they once did; and transportation and telecommunications systems should accommodate disabled users so that the infrastructure for commerce and community works for everyone.

Although disability rights advocates achieved important legislative and court victories in the 1970s and 1980s, the civil rights model was not wholeheartedly embraced until Congress enacted the Americans with Disabilities Act (ADA) in 1990.[1] To be sure, signs of the charity model, like Jerry Lewis's annual telethons for the Muscular Dystrophy Association, vex disability rights advocates, and the medical model continues to influence funding for research budgets, most recently concerning efforts to develop genetically engineered humans free of disabling conditions. And yet the ADA has helped refocus Americans on the important goals of equality of opportunity, full participation, independent living, and economic self-sufficiency for the more than 56 million disabled children and adults living in the United States.

Upon signing the ADA into law, President George H. W. Bush remarked, "With today's signing . . . every man, woman and child with a disability can now pass through once-closed doors, into a bright new era of equality, independence and freedom."[2] Unfortunately, since William H. Rehnquist became chief justice of the Supreme Court, the bipartisan congressional and administrative efforts to open those doors have been undermined and sometimes nullified by him and his increasingly activist colleagues. Instead of embracing the civil rights model embodied in the ADA, the Rehnquist Court has repeatedly demonstrated an outdated and offensive paternalism in its approach to disability. To a large extent, Americans with disabilities are still waiting for a landmark Supreme Court decision that truly accelerates their cause in the manner that *Brown v. Board of Education* altered American consciousness around race.

In his concurrence and dissent in an important 1985 case involving a challenge to a zoning ordinance impeding the establishment of a group home for people with cognitive disabilities, Justice Thurgood Marshall discussed the subtleties of analyzing equal protection issues in a disability context.[3] One issue in the case was whether a law that allegedly denies equal protection to people with cognitive disabilities deserved "heightened" scrutiny, like laws challenged by women and racial and ethnic minorities under the Equal Protection Clause of the Fourteenth Amendment. The greater the scrutiny, the greater the chance that the challenged law or activity will be found to violate the Constitution. Discussing how judges determine when a minority is sufficiently discrete and insular to merit a "more searching judicial inquiry into laws adversely affecting it," Justice Marshall noted their ability to apply lessons from history and their own experience:

> Because prejudice spawns prejudice, and stereotypes produce limitations that confirm the stereotype on which they are based, a history of unequal treatment requires sensitivity to the prospect that its vestiges endure. In separating those groups that are discrete and insular from those that are not, as in many important distinctions, "a page of history is worth a volume of logic."[4]

Unfortunately, under the leadership of Chief Justice Rehnquist, the Supreme Court has frequently applied quite faulty logic, demonstrating an appalling insensitivity to the shameful history and ongoing vestiges of disability discrimination in the United States. Its jurisprudence in three critical areas makes this glaringly evident: new constitutional limitations on laws protecting the individual rights of children and adults with disabilities; statutory interpretations dramatically shrinking the protected class under the ADA and other disability rights laws; and a dangerous tendency to defer to bureaucratic prerogatives and "professional" judgments when human rights issues are at stake.

In 1985, the year before Justice Rehnquist was elevated by President Ronald Reagan to serve as chief justice, he joined in Justice Byron White's majority opinion in *Cleburne v. Cleburne Living Center*, holding that the application of a municipal zoning ordinance requiring that a proposed group home for adults with mental retardation had to obtain a special-use permit violated the Equal-Protection Clause of the Fourteenth Amendment.[5] Justice White's opinion (joined also by Justices

Lewis F. Powell, John Paul Stevens, and Sandra Day O'Connor) used an unusually rigorous "rational basis" test to overturn the challenged ordinance's application in that case and held that the Texas municipality at issue had not proffered a rational basis for believing that the proposed group home would pose any special threat to the city's legitimate interests.

Under a traditional "rational basis" test, when a citizen seeks to challenge a law or ordinance under the Equal Protection Clause of the Constitution, he or she must show that the challenged law is not rationally or reasonably related to a legitimate government purpose. If the government can show that the challenged law serves a legitimate policy goal or has a "rational basis," then the law is upheld as a legitimate exercise of the government's power to legislate. Some categories of laws are subjected to more searching review or stricter scrutiny because the constitutional interests at stake require a more substantial showing to justify the challenged unequal treatment. Justice Stevens, joined by Chief Justice Warren Burger, filed a concurring opinion in *Cleburne* asserting that the three standards of equal protection review described in Justice White's opinion more appropriately should be thought of as "a continuum of judgmental responses to differing classifications which have been explained in opinions by terms ranging from 'strict scrutiny' at one extreme to 'rational basis' on the other."[6] Justice Stevens went on to reason that the challenged zoning ordinance was unconstitutional as applied to the group home, noting his unwillingness to believe "that a rational member of this disadvantaged class [people with cognitive disabilities] could ever approve of the discriminatory application of the city's ordinance in this case."[7]

The most cogent and convincing opinion in the *Cleburne* case was filed by Justice Thurgood Marshall, joined by Justices William J. Brennan and Harry A. Blackmun. Justice Marshall, describing his opinion as "concurring in the judgment in part and dissenting in part," argued for an intermediate level of review for equal protection cases involving people with cognitive disabilities similar to the standard the Court had developed for women and for children born out of wedlock. In a passage representing a high-water mark for constitutional jurisprudence in the disability rights arena, Justice Marshall wrote:

For the retarded, just as for Negroes and women, much has changed in recent years, but much remains the same; outdated statutes are still on the books, and irrational fears or ignorance, traceable to the prolonged social and cultural isolation of the retarded, continue to stymie recognition of the dignity and individuality of retarded people. Heightened judicial scrutiny of action appearing to impose unnecessary barriers to the retarded is required in light of increasing recognition that such barriers are inconsistent with evolving principles of equality embedded in the Fourteenth Amendment.[8]

When Congress passed the ADA five years after the *Cleburne* decision, it made explicit findings intended to signify to the federal courts that allegedly discriminatory laws affecting people with disabilities deserved heightened scrutiny under the Constitution. Congress made it clear that it considered people with disabilities to be a "discrete and insular minority" occupying a "position of political powerlessness," that "discrimination against individuals with disabilities continue[s] to be a serious and pervasive social problem," and that people with disabilities have historically been subjected to "purposeful unequal treatment" on the basis of their immutable human characteristics.[9]

In 1993, the Rehnquist Court revisited this issue in an equal protection case challenging the state of Kentucky's procedures for determining when a person with mental retardation may be committed involuntarily to an institution. In *Heller v. Doe*, Justice Anthony Kennedy wrote a majority opinion (joined by Chief Justice Rehnquist and Justices White, Antonin Scalia, and Clarence Thomas) applying a "rational basis" standard and upholding Kentucky's system of involuntary commitment, which made it easier to institutionalize adults with cognitive disabilities than to commit adults with mental illness. Because the former group had not argued for heightened scrutiny in the lower courts, Justice Kennedy wrote that it would be inappropriate to apply a different standard in the Supreme Court. In a separate dissent, Justice Blackmun noted his "continuing adherence to the view that laws that discriminate against individuals with mental retardation, or infringe upon fundamental rights, are subject to heightened scrutiny."[10]

Peculiarly, Justice Blackmun did not cite the congressional findings in the ADA to add weight to his argument.

Justifying a rational basis standard in *Heller*, Justice Kennedy (joined by Justices Rehnquist, White, Scalia, and Thomas) noted that "a classification neither involving fundamental rights nor proceeding along suspect lines is accorded a strong presumption of validity."[11] For the five justices in the *Heller* majority, it appears that the right of an adult with cognitive disabilities to live in a place of his or her choosing was not a "fundamental right." If avoiding involuntary commitment was not a fundamental right for such a person, it would be difficult to discern what would be. Applying the rational basis test, the majority in *Heller* accepted the basis for the challenged distinctions, making it easier to involuntarily lock up Kentucky residents with mental retardation than to involuntarily commit Kentuckians with mental illness.

Justice David Souter, joined (on this issue) by Justices Blackmun, Stevens, and O'Connor, filed a dissent in *Heller* concluding that, even under a rational basis standard, "Kentucky's provision of different procedures for the institutionalization of the mentally retarded and the mentally ill is not supported by any rational justification."[12] Applying a rigorous review reminiscent of the beefed-up rational basis test used by the majority in *Cleburne*, Justice Souter noted that an important "individual liberty" interest was at stake in *Heller* that "encompasses both freedom from restraint and freedom from the stigma that restraint and its justifications impose on an institutionalized person." He concluded that Kentucky should not be permitted under the Equal Protection Clause of the Fourteenth Amendment "to draw a distinction that is difficult to see as resting on anything other than the stereotypical assumption that the retarded are 'perpetual children,' an assumption that has historically been taken to justify the disrespect and 'grotesque mistreatment' to which the retarded have been subjected."[13]

Ironically, whereas the majority in *Heller* went out of its way to avoid deciding the appropriate standard of review for the challenged Kentucky law in that case, in 2001 the Rehnquist Court took pains to announce the appropriateness of a rational basis standard of review for equal protection challenges on the basis of disability. The case, *University of Alabama v. Garrett*, involved allegations of employment discrimination under the ADA by two disabled employees of the state of Alabama.[14]

The real issue in *Garrett* was whether Congress had the authority under Section 5 of the Fourteenth Amendment to abrogate Alabama's Eleventh Amendment immunity to suits for damages by private individuals. Although no state law or regulation was being challenged on constitutional grounds in *Garrett,* and even though Alabama did not even try to argue that the alleged discriminatory treatment of two of its disabled employees was rational, Chief Justice Rehnquist (joined by Justices O'Connor, Scalia, Kennedy, and Thomas) reached the standard of review issue in the context of his discussion of the "limitations that the court's interpretation of the equal protection clause of section § 1 of the Fourteenth Amendment places upon States' treatment of the disabled." Citing and quoting from Justice White's majority opinion in *Cleburne,* he declared that state conduct that discriminates on the basis of disability "incurs only the minimum 'rational-basis' review applicable to general social and economic legislation."

A basic tenet of disability civil rights law that distinguishes it from other civil rights laws is that providing equal opportunity to an employee or customer with a disability sometimes requires the employer or business to treat that employee or customer differently and make a reasonable accommodation or an adjustment—a necessary change from standard operating procedures. For example, an employer may need to purchase a screen reader to enable a blind employee to use his or her computer or a business may need to make an exception to its prohibition on animals in the store for a customer with a service animal. Under the ADA, the failure to make this kind of reasonable accommodation or modification amounts to discrimination.

This important baseline principle of disability discrimination law seems to have been completely missed by the majority in *Garrett.* Chief Justice Rehnquist asserted for the majority in *Garrett*:

> The result of *Cleburne* is that States are not required by the Fourteenth Amendment to make special accommodations for the disabled, so long as their actions toward such individuals are rational. They could quite hard headedly—and perhaps hard-

heartedly—hold to job-qualification requirements which do not make allowance for the disabled. If special accommodations are to be required, they have to come from positive law and not through the Equal Protection Clause.[15]

This analysis completely misses the point that a failure to provide a *reasonable* accommodation is an *irrational* act that results in a denial of equal opportunity for a disabled employee or job applicant. Moving on from its analysis of the constitutional underpinnings of "special accommodations for the disabled," the majority in *Garrett* then struck down those provisions of the ADA that allow individuals with disabilities to bring damage actions against a state when it discriminates in employment on the basis of disability because Congress had failed to document "a pattern of discrimination" in employment by the states that violates the Fourteen Amendment.[16]

In a blistering dissent, Justice Stephen Breyer, joined by Justices Stevens, Souter, and Ruth Bader Ginsburg, offered a detailed review of the legislative findings that would justify a reasonable determination by Congress that there was indeed a widespread problem of unconstitutional disability discrimination in employment by the states in 1990.[17] Breyer strongly took issue with the sleight of hand Chief Justice Rehnquist used to undermine the ADA's constitutionality by applying the rational basis standard of review:

> The problem with the Court's approach is that neither the "burden of proof" that favors States nor any other rule of restraint applicable to *judges* applies to *Congress* when it exercises its § 5 power. "Limitations stemming from the nature of the judicial process . . . have no application to Congress." Rational-basis review—with its presumptions favoring constitutionality—is a "paradigm of *judicial* restraint." And the Congress of the United States is not a lower court. . . .[18]

Justice Breyer is exactly right. The Court failed to recognize that a legislative body is not limited to a record put together by lawyers and a lower court the way the Supreme Court is. Congress can obtain information from all sources, including the victims of discrimination. Congress also reflects public attitudes and beliefs about the nature of disability discrimination and the most appropriate legal remedy for victims. By its indifference toward Congress's superior competence in such matters, the Court, as Breyer said, "improperly invades a power that the Constitution assigns to Congress."

In lamenting the majority's power grab in *Garrett*, Breyer perhaps unintentionally reminds us that the same five activist justices who undermined Congress's constitutional authority in *Garrett* also usurped the role of the electorate and (if necessary) Congress in deciding the outcome of the 2000 presidential election.

As *Garrett* makes clear, the conservative majority on the Rehnquist court has demonstrated a strong unwillingness to use the Equal Protection Clause of the Fourteenth Amendment to safeguard individual rights at the hands of a discriminatory state actor. On the contrary, reinvigorating states' rights sensibilities that the Civil War and the modern civil rights movement apparently have not put to rest, it has gone out of its way to eviscerate whatever protections the Equal Protection Clause might have afforded Americans with disabilities. To be sure, the loss of justices like Marshall, Brennan, and Blackmun dealt a profound blow to anyone who valued the Supreme Court's role as a champion of the civil rights of individuals under the Constitution. Although Justices Stevens and Breyer have supported disability rights more often than not, no justice has emerged as a consistent champion, bringing sensitivity and understanding to the constitutional jurisprudence of disability rights in the manner of a Justice Thurgood Marshall.

The Rehnquist Court also demonstrated breathtaking arrogance when it disregarded congressional intent, unanimous administrative agency interpretations, and the overwhelming majority of federal courts of appeal when it removed civil rights protections from large segments of the ADA's protected class in *Sutton v. United Airlines* (1999) and two related cases.[19] In this *Sutton* trilogy, Justice O'Connor, joined by all but Justices Stevens and Breyer, ruled that individuals with disabilities who can correct their impairments through mitigating measures such as medications and assistive devices do not meet the statutory definition of "individual with a disability" under the ADA. In other words, the ADA no longer protects disabled people who, with treatment and/or assistive devices, are able to function well but nonetheless experience discrimination because of irrational employer behavior. In a case decided early in 2002, the Rehnquist Court further narrowed the scope of the protected class.[20]

Apparently unconcerned that the ADA is a remedial statute that should be "construed broadly to effectuate its purposes," the majority in *Sutton* decided to narrowly limit who gets to bring a claim under the ADA.[21] The ADA defines a disability as a physical or mental impairment that substantially limits one or more major life activities of such individual; a record of such an impairment; or being regarded as having such an impairment.[22] The key issue in the *Sutton* trilogy was straightforward: when a court determines whether an individual has a disability for purposes of the ADA, does it make that assessment based on the individual's natural or "unmitigated" state, or should it take into account how that individual is able to function with the assistance of "mitigating measures" like medication, assistive technology, or prosthetics?

Until the Court's decision in *Sutton*, eight of the nine federal courts of appeal that had addressed the matter, all three executive agencies that had issued regulations or interpretive bulletins under the ADA, and all the key congressional committees that wrote the ADA agreed that a court should determine whether an individual has a disability by assessing the person in his or her unmitigated state.[23] Nevertheless, trying hard to keep the protected class from exceeding the figure of 43 million used in one of Congress's hortatory findings in the ADA, the *Sutton* majority decided to ignore Congress's express instruction that the "purpose of [the ADA is] to provide a clear and comprehensive national mandate for the elimination of discrimination against individuals with disabilities."[24] In her opinion for the majority, Justice O'Connor contrasted the "work disability" approach, which focuses on the individual's reported ability to work, with the "health conditions" approach, which looks at all conditions that impair the health or typical functional abilities of an individual. Then, delving into arcane policy documents to determine the origins of the 43 million figure identified in the ADA's findings, the majority decided incomprehensibly that a slightly smaller figure used in an early version of the ADA "clearly reflects an approach to defining disabilities that is closer to the work disabilities approach than the health conditions approach."[25]

The work disabilities approach is inappropriate in the civil rights context. A good example of a federal disability law that takes a work disabilities approach to determining eligibility is the Social Security Act. To be eligible for disability retirement benefits or Supplemental Security Income benefits under this law, an individual must show an "inability to engage in any substantial gainful activity by reason of any . . . physical or mental impairment which can be expected to result in death or which has lasted or can be expected to last for a continuous period of not less than 12 months."[26] By making an analogy with this work disability definition in the Social Security Act, the *Sutton* majority missed the critical distinction between a narrow statutory definition appropriate for a program providing retirement benefits to support someone who can no longer work and a broad definition appropriate for a civil rights law intended to prohibit acts of disability-related discrimination against people who can work.[27]

As Justice Stevens observes in his *Sutton* dissent, a broad definition of the protected class does not guarantee a job to unqualified job applicants with disabilities.[28] The case simply asked whether people who function well should be able to assert disability discrimination when their condition substantially limits them in the absence of a mitigating measure. Does the ADA let people with correctable conditions "in the door" of civil rights protection? Why not? As Justice Stevens notes, "Inside that door is nothing more than basic protection from irrational and unjustified discrimination because of a characteristic that is beyond a person's control."[29]

Citing the landmark 1987 decision in *School Board of Nassau County v. Arline*, Justice Stevens went on to note that one of the ADA's purposes is to "dismantle employment barriers based on society's accumulated myths and fears."[30] Given this purpose, he pointed out, "It is especially ironic to deny protection for persons with substantially limiting impairments that, when corrected, render them fully able and employable." The majority's decision in *Sutton*, Justice Stevens concluded, "may have the perverse effect of denying coverage for a sizeable portion of the core group of 43 million" people with disabilities that Congress declared its intention to protect.[31] That group includes people with controlled conditions like epilepsy and diabetes, people with prosthetic legs and arms that restore functioning, and people with psychiatric and other health conditions that are well controlled.

This bizarre result was entirely unnecessary. "In order to be faithful to the remedial purposes of the Act," wrote Justice Stevens, "we should give it a generous, rather than a miserly, construction."[32] Sadly, thanks to the Rehnquist Court's "miserly" interpretation of the definition of disability, millions of disabled Americans have been stripped of their civil rights protections.[33]

In January 2002, the Rehnquist Court further narrowed the scope of the ADA's protected class in *Toyota v. Williams*, a case involving an autoworker with carpal tunnel syndrome.[34] The autoworker had successfully argued to the appeals court that her condition met the ADA's definition of disability because it substantially limited her ability to perform manual tasks. In a unanimous decision written by Justice O'Connor, the Rehnquist Court disagreed, holding that to be substantially limited in performing manual tasks, an individual must have an impairment that prevents or severely restricts him or her from doing activities that are of central importance to most people's daily lives.[35] The Court reasoned that Williams had failed to make this showing as a matter of law, in part because of evidence demonstrating that she was able to bathe, brush her teeth, and perform housework notwithstanding her impairments. Questioning the importance of the Equal Employment Opportunity Commission's interpretation of the statute, the Court decided that the statute's reference to "substantially limits" meant "prevents or severely restricts" and its reference to "major" life activities meant activities "of central importance to most people's daily lives." Because Williams was still able to brush her teeth, she failed to demonstrate the kind of impairment that would have invoked the protections of the ADA.[36]

The practical impact of decisions like *Williams* and the *Sutton* trilogy is that disabled plaintiffs find it harder and harder to challenge employment discrimination. Either they lose on the issue of whether they have a disability or the evidence they submit to demonstrate the severity of their impairments is used to question their qualifications for the job. This no-win situation was never intended by Congress, and it leaves millions of disabled Americans without an effective remedy for discrimination.[37]

When Congress enacted the ADA, it found that "historically, society has tended to isolate and segregate individuals with disabilities, and, despite some improvements, such forms of discrimination against individuals with disabilities continue to be a serious and pervasive social problem. . . . Discrimination against individuals with disabilities persists in such critical areas as employment, housing, public accommodations, education, transportation, communication, recreation, institutionalization, health services, voting, and access to public services."[38] Given that much of this discrimination falls within the purview of bureaucracies overseeing programs that serve disabled people, it follows that one good way to address disability discrimination is to challenge discriminatory behavior by those bureaucracies. In two cases where such challenges have been made, the Rehnquist Court has been reluctant to question the judgments of bureaucrats and professionals who make the rules.

In the *Heller* case, a class of plaintiffs with cognitive disabilities sought to challenge Kentucky's system for involuntary commitment, which made it easier to confine these people than to confine adults with mental illness. In defense of their scheme, Kentucky argued that the lower standard of proof followed from the fact that this disability is easier to diagnose than mental illness; that it is easier to determine whether a person with a cognitive disability presents a danger or a threat of danger to self, family, or others than it is to make such a determination for a person with mental illness; and that prevailing methods of treatment for people with disabilities are, as a general rule, less invasive than those for people with mental illness.[39]

Noting that "differences in treatment between the mentally retarded and the mentally ill have long existed in Anglo-American law," and "continu[e] to the present day" in many states, the Court concluded that Kentucky had proffered a rational basis for its challenged commitment standards.[40] The analysis in *Heller* implied that a history of discriminatory treatment that continues to the present can and will be used to justify the continuation of the challenged discriminatory conduct under the Constitution. What are the limits of this bizarre calculation? In *Buck v. Bell* (1927), the Supreme Court held that sterilization of "feeble-minded" individuals was permissible under the Constitution.[41] Should this history be used to justify a state law requiring sterilization of adults with mental retardation in 2002?

As Justice Souter noted in his dissent,

> Surely the Court does not intend to suggest that the irrational and scientifically unsupported beliefs of pre–19th century England can support any distinction in treatment between the mentally ill and the mentally retarded today. At that time, "lunatics" were "[s]een as demonically possessed or the products of parental sin [and] were often punished or left to perish. . . ." The primary purpose of an adjudication of "idiocy" appears to have been to "depriv[e] [an individual] of [his] property and its profits."[42]

Interestingly, Souter disparages the particular history referenced by the majority in *Heller* as "irrational and scientifically unsupported." The notion that reason and science will consistently lead one to the right answer in a disability discrimination case, however, is suspect. As Justice Marshall pointed out in his concurrence and dissent in *Cleburne*, "Fueled by the rising tide of Social Darwinism, the 'science' of eugenics, and the extreme xenophobia of [the late nineteenth and early twentieth centuries], leading medical authorities and others began to portray the 'feeble-minded' as a 'menace to society and civilization' . . . responsible in a large degree for many, if not all, of our social problems."[43]

Making reference to the troubling history of eugenic marriage and sterilization laws, Justice Marshall updated the problem by noting modern laws that exclude individuals with cognitive disabilities from voting. "Courts . . . do not sit or act in a social vacuum. Moral philosophers may debate whether certain inequalities are absolute wrongs, but history makes clear that constitutional principles of equality, like constitutional principles of liberty, property, and due process, evolve over time; what once was a 'natural' and 'self-evident' ordering later comes to be seen as an artificial and invidious constraint on human potential and freedom."[44]

It is precisely this understanding of historical and social context that is missing from the Rehnquist Court's analysis of disability discrimination in cases like *Heller* and *Garrett*. When disability discrimination is alleged, more often than not the Court both sits and acts "in a social vacuum." Rather than recognizing the inherent human right to be free from involuntary confinement, particularly after Congress's findings in the ADA, it has sought refuge in the professional opinions of the state bureaucrats and medical authorities in whose care severely disabled people are often placed.

In 1999, in *Olmstead v. L.C.*, the Supreme Court revisited the issue of institutionalization involved in *Heller*.[45] Two Georgia women with mental disabilities challenged their continued care in a segregated institutional setting. Both plaintiffs were determined by Georgia to be ready for community-based care but had to remain in an institution because of a lack of community-based options. In a plurality opinion, Justice Ginsburg held that the ADA "may require placement of persons with mental disabilities in community settings rather than institutions" when "the State's treatment professionals have determined that community placement is appropriate, the transfer from institutional care to a less restrictive setting is not opposed by the affected individual, and the placement can be reasonably accommodated, taking into account the resources available to the State and the needs of others with mental disabilities."[46] In other words, if you need long-term services and supports, you may have a right to get them in the community, provided you can convince your treating professionals that you are ready to leave the institution and the bureaucracy can accommodate your request within its budgetary limitations.

It is worth noting how the holding in *Olmstead* got watered down as the case made its way through the federal courts. In the district court, Georgia tried to argue that the only reason the plaintiffs were stuck in an institution was inadequate funding, not discrimination, but the court rejected the state's argument, holding that "unnecessary institutional segregation of the disabled constitutes discrimination *per se*, which cannot be justified by a lack of funding." Revisiting the possibility of a cost-based defense by the state, the Eleventh Circuit Court of Appeals decided that such a defense was possible, but that Congress would permit such a defense "only in the most limited of circumstances." A cost-based justification would fail, the Eleventh Circuit reasoned, "unless the State can prove that requiring it to [expend additional funds in order to provide the plaintiffs with integrated services] would be so unreasonable given the demands of the State's mental health budget that it would fundamentally alter the service [the State] provides."[47]

Once *Olmstead* reached the Supreme Court, the state's bureaucratic prerogatives took on greater importance.[48] Although Justice Ginsburg held that "unjustified isolation . . . is properly regarded as discrimination based on disability," she recognized "the State's need to maintain a range of facilities for the care and treatment of persons with diverse mental disabilities, and the State's obligation to administer services with an even hand." Holding that the Eleventh Circuit's remand instruction was "unduly restrictive," she ruled that the lower court must consider "not only the cost of providing community-based care to the litigants, but also the range of services the State provides others with mental disabilities, and the State's obligation to mete out those services equitably."[49]

Throughout her opinion, Justice Ginsburg noted the appropriateness of the reliance by the state on "the reasonable assessments of its own professionals" and the need for the state to have a "comprehensive, effectively working plan for placing qualified persons with mental disabilities in less restrictive settings, and a waiting list that moved at a reasonable pace."[50] In other words, as long as the bureaucracy is functioning properly, the ADA may not require any extraordinary effort on behalf of individuals with disabilities seeking to escape institutional confinement. The approach taken in the lower courts is more consistent with Congress's stated desire to enact a "clear and comprehensive national mandate for the elimination of discrimination against individuals with disabilities."[51]

Not satisfied that the level of deference set out in Justice Ginsburg's opinion was great enough, Justice Kennedy (joined by Justice Breyer)

launched into a laborious discussion of the history of deinstitutional-
ization of people with mental illness and the danger that states may in-
appropriately release people with mental disabilities into substandard
care in the community. "It is of central importance," he opined, "that
courts apply today's decision with great deference to the medical decisions of the responsible, treating physicians and . . . with appropriate
deference to the program funding decisions of state policymakers."[52]
In a dissenting opinion, Justice Thomas (joined by Justices Rehnquist
and Scalia), went even further, saying that "the appropriate course
would be to respect the States' historic role as the dominant authority
responsible for providing services to individuals with disabilities."[53] In
other words, whatever the state decides is good enough.

As the opinions in *Heller* and *Olmstead* demonstrate, when the rights
of disabled individuals to live outside of institutions are at stake, the
Rehnquist Court is reluctant to question the prerogatives of state officials and treating professionals to determine how best to distribute
these freedoms. Its overblown deference to bureaucratic prerogatives
means that disabled people will continue to experience unnecessary
segregation and institutionalization for many years to come.

In 2002, the Supreme Court applied its predisposition to defer to
professionals in two employment cases. The first, *U.S. Airways v. Barnett*,
involved a challenge to an employer's voluntary seniority system that
had resulted in a qualified disabled worker being bumped out of a
job.[54] The majority ruled that the employer's professional obligation to
honor its voluntary seniority system trumps the the disabled employee's
right under the ADA to be reassigned to a vacant position for which he
is qualified. The second case, *Chevron, U.S.A., Inc. v. Echazabal*, was a
challenge to the EEOC's regulation permitting employers to reject a
job applicant who, because of his or her disability, would pose a direct
threat to the employee's own health or safety. The unanimous Court in
Echazabal upheld the challenged regulation, noting in part that an employer's professional obligation to ensure the health and safety of his
workers under the Occupational, Safety, and Health Act was greater
than a disabled employee's right "to operate on equal terms within the
workplace."[55]

Ironically, in a case brought by a disabled golfer seeking access to a
golf cart between shots on the PGA tour, the Rehnquist Court was

much more willing to scrutinize the rationale for the decision to exclude the disabled person.[56] In *PGA Tour, Inc. v. Martin*, Justice Stevens (joined by Justices Rehnquist, O'Connor, Kennedy, Souter, Ginsburg, and Breyer) ruled that an elite golfer with a disability was entitled to a waiver of the rule barring golf carts on the PGA tour. Because the prohibition was designed to highlight the fatigue factor for competitors in a professional tournament, the Court reasoned that the plaintiff, Casey Martin, was entitled to a waiver of the rule given that he had demonstrated in the lower court that he experiences more fatigue even with a golf cart than most players do without. The Court ruled that Martin's opportunity to compete was more important than the administrative burden their holding placed on tour operators. Although Martin's victory was rightly hailed by disability advocates, the unique circumstances of his case will likely limit its impact. And the juxtaposition of the strong holding in *Martin* with the timid analysis in *Olmstead* is troubling. After these two rulings, if you are locked in an institution, the ADA may be little comfort; but, if you are being excluded from an elite sporting event, the ADA may open the doors. Unfortunately, the liberty interests at stake in cases like *Olmstead* and *Heller* and the employment issues in *Garrett*, *Barnett*, and *Echazabal* affect many more Americans than the atypical issues presented in the *Martin* case.

Still reeling from *Garrett* and subsequent losses in the 2001–02 term, disability rights advocates are worried about where the activist Rehnquist Court may strike next. Will they hold Title II of the ADA unconstitutional, thereby gutting what little protection the *Olmstead* decision afforded recipients of state services? In their efforts to rein in congressional authority, will they move on to the Spending Clause, calling into question the constitutionality of decades-old laws like Section 504 of the Rehabilitation Act and the Individuals with Disabilities Education Act?[57] Will they continue to chip away at the scope of the protected class in the ADA, and will we need new laws to redefine that group? Presented a historic opportunity to breathe life into constitutional and statutory protections of the rights of disabled people, the Rehnquist Court has instead harmed the cause of disability rights for generations to come.

Antitrust and Business Power

ELEANOR M. FOX

For most of ninety years, the U.S. antitrust laws stood against private power. Senator John Sherman, father of the Sherman Antitrust Act, spoke of the problems that agitate "the popular mind": "Among them all none is more threatening than the inequality of condition, of wealth, and opportunity that has grown within a single generation out of the concentration of capital into vast combinations."[1] President Woodrow Wilson, in support of the 1914 Clayton Bill, called for a law that "will open the field . . . to scores of men who had been obliged to serve when their abilities entitled them to direct."[2] In 1949, Congressman Emanuel Celler vowed, in support of his bill to strengthen the merger law, to stop the increasing industrial concentration in order to prevent another Hitler from arising.[3]

The first merger challenged under the 1950 merger law came before the Warren Court in 1962, and a unanimous Court applied the law faithfully to its legislative mandate and statutory spirit: Congress sought to prevent the "rising tide of economic concentration" for social and political reasons. "It resolved these competing considerations [pluralism and efficiency] in favor of decentralization."[4]

These statutes have not since been amended by Congress in any significant way. And yet neither Senator Sherman nor Congressman Celler nor Chief Justice Warren would recognize the modern case law of antitrust as having very much affinity to the laws they wrote or applied. As a result of judicial decision making, the U.S. antitrust law is no longer antipower. The law, the jurists say, is proefficiency and proconsumer. In fact, the law is probusiness freedom (it assumes business acts efficiently), subject to a few limiting principles whose purview continually shrinks. The Burger Court set the stage for the U-turn in antitrust; the Rehnquist Court executed the turn.

Since the days of the Warren Court, conservative and libertarian lawyers, economists, and policy makers who identified themselves with a philosophy called the Chicago School sought to take the reins of antitrust. The Chicago School opposes microeconomic intervention by the government. In its strongest form, it presumes that markets nearly always work to keep business responsive to consumers and that government intervention (including antitrust action) nearly always obstructs markets, hurting consumers and impairing the freedom of people in their economic activity. Some Chicago School advocates treat competitor cartels (for example, price-fixing agreements) as an exception that warrants government intervention because cartels are a means to control the market and are inefficient. Others believe that cartels are so fragile in the face of market forces that they will quickly self-destruct. Most Chicago School advocates believe that all people, other than undeserving laggards, are better off with policies that maximize aggregate wealth, and they oppose the use of antitrust laws to achieve a fairer distribution of wealth, a fairer distribution of economic opportunity, or fairer rules of the game; they see no connection between democratic values and market rules that control private power.

These would-be policy makers were not immediately successful. In effect, the Chicago School lay in wait until, first, economic recession and the Nixon era, when the Burger Court put a lid on the expanding proplaintiff antitrust rulings of the 1960s, and, second, the Reagan era, when the Supreme Court, following the lead of Reagan's antitrust chiefs, reformulated the raison d'être of antitrust law. The only reason for antitrust law, they announced, is to remove market obstructions so that business can be more efficient and consumers can get more goods at lower prices, increasing the size of the economic pie. The only proper target of antitrust, they said, is private power that artificially limits the output of goods or services across an entire market; moreover, private power seldom exists unless aided by government.

The Rehnquist Court rhetoric recalls the words, now more than a century old, of the most famous jurist to scorn the Sherman Act, Oliver Wendell Holmes. "State interference is an evil, where it cannot be shown to be a good," he said. "Its cumbrous and expensive machinery ought not to be set in motion unless some clear benefit is to be derived from disturbing the status quo."[5] And he seldom found clear benefit.

Three major antitrust decisions of the Rehnquist Court and the dictum in a dissenting opinion by Justice Antonin Scalia illustrate the enterprise to deflate antitrust.

The first case is *Business Electronics Corporation v. Sharp Electronics Corporation*, a typical example of the use of conservative economic assumptions to change the compass course of U.S. antitrust law.[6] Sharp, a manufacturer of electronic calculators, sold its product through two retailers in the Houston, Texas, area. One of those retailers, Business Electronics, offered the calculators at discount prices; the other retailer, Hartwell, complained to Sharp, which agreed to cut off Business Electronics. Business Electronics sued Sharp and won a jury verdict, on the strength of the case law that proscribed agreements to cut off a discounter in order to eliminate low prices. The Supreme Court reversed this verdict.

As Justice Scalia noted in his opinion in *Sharp*, the case was about a *vertical* restraint. These restraints are in the seller-buyer chain, and usually concern the suppliers' restriction of the freedom of their resellers, such as the freedom to charge low prices. Before *Sharp*, the law contained a strong rule against resale price agreements on grounds that they unduly restrict the freedom of the reseller to make price choices. The freedom to discount and the growth of discounting as a way of business had been shown empirically to lower prices by as much as 20 percent.

Justice Scalia and the Rehnquist Court majority jettisoned the law's preference for freedom of discounting, and reformulated upside down the basis of the rule against vertical price fixing. Scalia not only rejected the terminated discounter's claim but also eradicated the law's protection of the right to discount, undercut the rule against resale price agreements, and trivialized even the concern that such agreements facilitate competitor cartels.

First, the agreement to cut off the discounter concerned only one brand, Sharp calculators; thus it was an "intrabrand" restraint, Scalia said. The antitrust laws do not protect intrabrand competition, he said, but only "interbrand" competition (competition among Sharp and other makers of calculators). "So long as interbrand competition existed, that would provide a 'significant check' on any attempt to exploit intrabrand market power." Second, the Court said (counterhistorically), the support for the rule against vertical price restraints was based on their role in facilitating cartels among producers. That is, if Sharp and its competitors wanted to fix the price of calculators, they might enforce their cartel by agreeing also to require their dealers to charge a specified price. The resale price agreements would reduce the producers' incentive to cheat on their cartel (that is, secretly to charge a lower price to get more business) because the retailer could not in turn charge lower prices to its customers. But, said Justice Scalia, simply disciplining discounters cannot facilitate cartelizing: "Cartels are neither easy to form nor easy to maintain" (a bold statement for a justice to make without evidence). Cartels self-destruct in the face of uncertainty over their terms, and intolerance for discounters fails to supply the price certainty needed to form a cartel.

Moreover, a firm in the position of Sharp may "legitimately" desire a higher price to induce its resellers to provide more service; it may wish to get rid of discounters because of the discounters free ride on the services of full pricers. For example, their customers can get free information from Hartwell and then buy the product from no-frills Business Electronics, undermining Hartwell's incentives to invest in providing service. Therefore, said Scalia, a law against agreements to cut off discounters could "penalize perfectly legitimate conduct." Thus, in *Sharp*, the Supreme Court turned the law's preference for discounting into a preference for producer's freedom to squash discounting.

The second case is *Brooke Group v. Brown & Williamson Tobacco Corporation*.[7] Liggett, predecessor to Brooke Group, had launched a generic (no-frills, no-brand) cigarette, which it offered at a price 30 percent lower than branded cigarettes. This new competition challenged the entrenched four-firm tobacco oligopoly. The smallest of the four firms, Brown & Williamson, had the most to lose and took action. It introduced a directly competing brand and gave discriminatory rebates to those of its large distributors that aggressively fought the war. For eighteen months, Brown & Williamson sold its fighting brand—Black & Whites—to these favored distributors at prices below its marginal cost, incurring a loss of $15 million and inflicting on Liggett a loss of $50 million. Eventually, as expected, Liggett could no longer afford to stay in the war. It was forced to raise its prices high enough to remove the generic threat to the branded oligopoly.

Since, under prior case law, Brown & Williamson's acts appeared to be illegal price discrimination and price predation, Liggett sued. It won a jury verdict. The trial court, however, gave judgment notwithstanding verdict to Brown & Williamson. The Supreme Court affirmed the dismissal of the case on grounds that largely wipe out predatory pricing cases.

Writing for the Court, Justice Anthony Kennedy first commented that price cutting is good. True, to be sure, but not consistent with *Sharp*. "Discouraging a price cut . . . does not constitute sound antitrust policy." The Court argued that the object of predatory pricing is to get rid of the competitor and charge yet higher prices in the future, which assumes recoupment of the investment in price predation, but the cost of predatory pricing is huge and seldom recoupable, argued Kennedy, because the firm loses money on the predatory campaign, and when it tries to recoup by raising prices, new competition swoops in. "Predatory pricing schemes are rarely tried, and even more rarely successful," said Kennedy. Moreover, a failed predatory strategy is entirely good for consumers, who benefit from below-cost prices and never face monopoly prices.

Suggesting that Liggett nonetheless may have regarded Brown &

Williamson's long-enduring below-cost strategy as unfair, the Court said:

> That below-cost pricing may impose painful losses on its target is of no moment to the antitrust laws if competition is not injured. . . .
>
> Even an act of pure malice by one competitor against another does not, without more, state a claim under the federal antitrust laws; those laws do not create a federal law of unfair competition.

Most nations of the world disagree that predation without recoupment is rarely tried and rarely successful. They also disagree that predation is good for competition. They believe that persistent below-marginal-cost pricing, especially as a response to a maverick competitor, deters mavericks and harms competition.

The third case that dramatizes the turn of the Court is *California Dental Association v. Federal Trade Commission*, a case about advertising restraints.[8] Prior to the time of the Rehnquist Court, the law had been harsh on agreements between doctors, dentists, and other professionals that tended to raise prices for their professional services. Since the late 1960s, the Federal Trade Commission and the Department of Justice observed time and again that such professionals, in the name of ethics, enforced gentlemen's agreements not to advertise, solicit, or discount; not to entice away clients; and not to engage in any other commercial practices that threatened to break the pricing structure, thus perpetuating a professional mystique that insulated price gouging.

Three-quarters of California's dentists belonged to the California Dental Association, which had a code of ethics, supported by guidelines. In the name of prohibiting false and misleading advertising, the guidelines forbade simple advertisements such as "10% discount to seniors" or "quality services" at "reasonable prices." The Federal Trade Commission and the appellate court found the guidelines to be anticompetitive by their nature and required the dentists to justify their guidelines as procompetitive or efficient, which they could not do. The Supreme Court reversed this ruling. It said that the likelihood of anticompetitive effects from such advertising bans was not obvious, that the dentists' guidelines might just as well have had net procompetitive effects or no competitive effect at all, and that, without empirical evidence of the likelihood that advertising limitations decreased the quantity of dental services demanded, the government would fail to make its case.

The Court, in an opinion by Justice David Souter, found "puzzling" the appellate court's conclusion that advertising bans, by their nature, are anticompetitive. It said that the appellate court erred because it

> gave no weight to the countervailing, and at least equally plausible, suggestion that restricting difficult-to-verify claims about quality or patient comfort would have a procompetitive effect by preventing misleading or false claims that distort the market. It is, indeed, entirely possible to understand the CDA's restrictions on unverifiable quality and comfort advertising as nothing more than a procompetitive ban on puffery.

This is a very important and dangerous point. The Court appears to have specified the criterion for "harming competition," and it is that which artificially limits market output. Lessening rivalry itself no longer qualifies as anticompetitive. And the Court appears to have placed burdens of proof on plaintiffs and even on the Federal Trade Commission that cannot be met. Predictions from economic theory may not even be enough. Empirical evidence, though unavailable, may be necessary. Moreover, given the indeterminacy of economics, whoever has the burden of proof will lose.

It might be comforting to imagine that the ruling of the *California Dental* case will be confined to professionals. Perhaps the Court would shield professionals from antitrust on the somewhat suspect presumption that we can trust them to do what is best for patients or clients. Perhaps the case will not be the blueprint for steel or software producers. But perhaps it will.

In a fourth opinion, though a dissenting one, Justice Scalia seems to articulate the current Court's philosophy. For some years after Eastman

Kodak entered the market for medical imaging machinery, it encouraged the growth of an entrepreneurial industry to service and repair its
machines and it supplied independent service organizations (ISOs)
with repair parts to facilitate their task. When the business of repairing
and servicing the machines became lucrative, Kodak stopped supply-
ing repair parts to ISOs, required manufacturers of Kodak parts to
boycott them, and raised the price of its own aftermarket service to its
customers. The ISOs sued. Kodak moved to dismiss on grounds that its
conduct was just an intrabrand restraint, it had no power in the imaging machine market, and the imaging machine market was competitive
and therefore could be trusted to punish and thus prevent anticompetitive behavior in the aftermarket. The majority of the Court, in an
opinion by Justice Harry Blackmun, disagreed. Justice Blackmun said
that the case must go to trial because the ISOs had raised material
issues of fact, supported by an economic theory, concerning Kodak's power and exploitation in the aftermarket. Justice Scalia, joined
by Justices Sandra Day O'Connor and Clarence Thomas, dissented.
Kodak's acts, said Scalia, were "potentially procompetitive arrangements." Moreover, the "interbrand market will generally punish intrabrand restraints that consumers do not find in their interest," and
Kodak did not have "the sort of 'monopoly power' sufficient to bring
the sledgehammer of [Section 2 of the Sherman Act] into play."

The Rehnquist Court can indeed be expected to view Section 2 of the
Sherman Act, which prohibits monopolization, as a sledgehammer.
The Court's deep skepticism that private power exists, its belief that
single-firm (noncartel) acts are virtually always procompetitive, and its
belief in the changing, dynamic, and disciplining nature of markets
would lead it almost always to reject a case against a monopolist.

It may have been a blessing to antitrust believers that the Supreme
Court declined to hear a direct appeal from the district court in *United
States and 19 States v. Microsoft*, for there is a significant possibility that
the Supreme Court would have accepted at least one of two arguments
Microsoft made: first, that Microsoft had no monopoly power because
high tech markets are dynamic and fast-moving, and the threat of be-

ing overtaken by outsiders' innovations constrained it always to act like a competitor, and second, that Microsoft, while it may have harmed competitors, never harmed consumers. Output of computer software was always on the increase; competition was not restrained.

Microsoft controls more than 95 percent of operating systems for personal computers. Netscape pioneered the browser and, using the new language, Java, threatened to innovate a software product and platform ("middleware") that would be transportable to any operating system. If successful cross-platform middleware could be launched, applications makers would no longer be enticed into writing their applications for Microsoft; they could profitably write to the middleware, which would function on any operating system. This would break the barriers to entry into the operating system market and dissolve Microsoft's monopoly power.

Microsoft discerned the middleware threat and sprang into action. It designed and carried out a strategy to prevent the Netscape/Java innovation from taking root. Netscape needed access to a critical mass of operating system users, which it would get if users and PC makers could freely choose Netscape's Navigator as their browser for Microsoft's Windows. Microsoft succeeded in closing off all Netscape Navigator's most efficient channels of access to customers. It developed its own browser, the Internet Explorer, which it tied to its operating system, preventing the browser's removal without downgrading other functions. It prevented PC makers from loading Navigator on their PCs along with Windows. It prevented or deterred the major Internet service providers and content providers from including or featuring the Navigator browser. It splintered the Java language, depriving it of its promise to be a cross-platform language that would facilitate the development of middleware.

The Justice Department and states sued and won all aspects of their lawsuit, and the district court entered an order to break Microsoft in two. Microsoft appealed, and the Justice Department sought to channel the appeal directly to the Supreme Court, which declined to hear the case. The appeal was heard by the D.C. Circuit Court of Appeals.

On the appeal, Microsoft's principal ammunition was political philosophy; it tried to set the stage by selling a perspective. The perspective was forcefully presented on the Microsoft Web site as well as in its legal briefs: antitrust intervention into new-economy markets tramples on property rights and personal freedoms, harms innovation and progress, and sets back American competitiveness in the world economy. New-economy markets are different, Microsoft argued. The competition is *for* the market, not *in* the market. The incumbent, having provisionally won, can never rest on its laurels. It must be paranoid to survive. It must always compete hard or it will be instantaneously dislodged. Microsoft articulated this argument in its brief on appeal:

> Dramatic improvements in microprocessors regularly alter the entire competitive landscape of the industry. . . . As Intel chairman Dr. Andrew Grove described in his book, *Only the Paranoid Survive: How to Exploit the Crisis Points That Challenge Every Company*, such technological advances—known as "inflection points" or "paradigm shifts"—can quickly diminish the value of (or eliminate altogether) entire categories of products, making the computer industry inherently unpredictable. . . . Hence, the greatest competitive threat to a leading product frequently comes not from another product within the same category, "but rather a technological advance that renders the boundaries defining the category obsolete."[9]

If accepted the only-the-paranoid-survive theory had three devastating implications for the government's case. First, the trial judge, Thomas Penfield Jackson, would have misdefined the market. The antitrust market had to include all sources of pressure on Microsoft—thus, UNIX, LINUX, Apple, hand-held computers, portal Web sites, and middleware. Second, Judge Jackson would have wrongly held that Microsoft had monopoly power. It had to act like a competitor to survive. And, finally, Judge Jackson would have wrongly held that Microsoft's acts caused harm to competition and consumers. So important is it for a high-tech firm to be free to compete in the gale-tossed world, and so harmful is it to mistake a procompetitive for an anticompetitive act (the theory goes), that courts must be demanding in their requirement of

proof that the challenged acts were anticompetitive and harmed consumers. The only theory of harm to consumers depended on proof
that Microsoft's strategies actually held at bay competitive technologies
that would have overtaken Microsoft in its operating system competition. The government had failed to prove that such technologies (that
is, the middleware of Netscape and Java) actually would have materi-
alized and taken root but for Microsoft's acts. Thus, there was no proof
of causation. Had any one of these three points prevailed, Microsoft
would have won its case. None did.

A major question was whether the government had to prove that
Microsoft's exclusionary acts in fact increased Microsoft's power over
operating systems. There was no proof that it did. Netscape's threat to
innovate middleware and break the back of Microsoft's operating system monopoly may have been only a phantom. The court of appeals
resolved this issue—as to whether the government must prove actual
harm to competition—against Microsoft. It held that the court could
presume that Microsoft's acts caused antitrust harm as long as the anticompetitive conduct "reasonably appeared [at the time of the acts]
capable of making a significant contribution to . . . maintaining monopoly power. . . . We may infer causation when exclusionary conduct
is aimed at producers of nascent competitive technologies." A more
demanding rule "would only encourage monopolists to take more and
earlier anticompetitive action. . . . Suffice it to say that it would be
inimical to the purpose of the Sherman Act to allow monopolists free
rein to squash nascent, albeit unproven, competitors at will—particularly in industries marked by rapid technological advance and frequent
paradigm shifts."[10]

The Court thus took a pragmatic and progressive stand. It upheld
the monopoly maintenance charges while it reversed other claims and
remanded the issue of the appropriate remedy. Had it accepted Microsoft's invitation to abstain from intervention in e-markets, or even to
demand proof that Microsoft's illegal acts actually suppressed the
quantity of computer operating software on the market (output limitation), the plaintiffs would have lost. The whole brilliantly won government victory would have been undone, and Microsoft, and the next
Microsofts, would have been given license to be predatory. Judgment

for Microsoft would have been the death of the law against monopolization.

If the Supreme Court had taken the case on direct appeal, bypassing the appellate court, there is reason to believe that a majority of the justices—attracted to Microsoft's theme song, "Only the Paranoid Survive"—would have joined Justice Scalia in seeing Microsoft as a vigorous competitor, in puzzling over how competition could have been harmed in the face of increasing software sales, and in avoiding at all costs "the sledgehammer" of Section 2.

Even now, the victory for the government against Microsoft may be squandered. The Department of Justice in the George W. Bush administration has agreed with Microsoft to settle for little more than a Band-Aid, and a Band-Aid of doubtful adhesion, given the difficulties of enforcing the final decree. Microsoft has accepted the proposal; nine plaintiff states oppose the Microsoft–federal government agreement. The judge—newly assigned because Judge Jackson compromised his impartiality by giving interviews to the press—must determine whether the agreed settlement is in the public interest. But whatever the specific result in *Microsoft*, the language of the appellate court will stand as precedent. It should have value in reining in future predatory monopolists, even if *United States v. Microsoft* should take its place as one of the Pyrrhic victories of antitrust.

In 1976, Ralph Nader, Mark Green, and Joel Seligman wrote *The Taming of the Giant Corporation*. The title itself suggested the powerful image of the antitrust laws as enacted by Congress and as interpreted by the Supreme Court. In this dawn of the twenty-first century, a counterimage has emerged in the federal agencies and the Supreme Court. It may be called *The Unleashing of the Giant Corporation*. The image-makers argue that business freedom, even for the largest firms, will increase efficiency and bolster American competitiveness in the world. They equate liberalization with freedom from government regulation. Globalization reinforces the laissez-faire stance of twenty-first century U.S. antitrust law.

Business power may outstrip, perhaps already has outstripped, the power of governments. Business firms and networks rise above and spread beyond national borders. National law and its guardians (for example, the Supreme Court) are seriously challenged to contain private power in global markets. Meanwhile, the problem of private power, even more modestly located, is eluding the Rehnquist Court.

No Business like No Business

LAWRENCE E. MITCHELL

Analyzing the Supreme Court's jurisprudence of securities regulation is a bit like studying a dog's tail. Partly for policy reasons and partly by default, the main source of law dealing with the organization, finance, and governance of American corporations is state law, not federal law, and the Supreme Court therefore has little to say about these matters. It's well known that the law of the state of incorporation governs any company's internal relations and that Delaware is the state of incorporation for almost half of all publicly traded companies (which are, for the most part, the companies governed by the securities laws). This has made Delaware the Supreme Court of corporate law and a powerful influence on the majority of the other states.

Federal securities law is, in a real sense, largely external to these workings, as it regulates the selling and buying of securities and the conduct of brokers and dealers in the market. In that way, it is external to the corporation much as antitrust law or labor law might be. But unlike these and other areas of external regulation, it has significant intersections with state law, through its rules prohibiting fraud and its disclosure and reporting requirements regulating the conduct of corporations; here it often touches up against, if it does not intersect or parallel, state law. As a result, the Supreme Court can't help some degree of involvement in matters that we would consider to be corporate governance. At various times in the history of securities law the Court has been more or less willing to attempt to impose some federal uniformity over the behavior of public corporations to depose the rule of one of our smallest states. During the Rehnquist years, in contrast, the Court has significantly pulled back from securities protections, deregulating public corporations and clearing the path for Delaware to maintain its supreme rule. At the same time, the Court has been ever more willing to diminish the external protections for investors in public markets that the securities laws were designed to provide. The importance of this trend can hardly be overstated. A (very) brief history of securities law will help place this Court's work in context.

Much of the work immediately following the enactment of the securities laws involved cleaning up the mess from the stock market crash of 1929 and rectifying the abuses that led to it. Before too long, however, prosperity and economic stability began to return, and enforcement was steady if uninteresting. The securities laws were used to regulate markets, while corporate governance was left to the states. By the mid-1960s it had become apparent that the dominant force in corporate law, the state of Delaware, had pretty much abrogated any responsibility to enforce the fiduciary obligations that officers and directors had to stockholders, an observation documented by William Cary in a famous 1974 *Yale Law Journal* article.[1] Agree with its policy conclusions or not, Cary's article highlighted an oddity of our federal system: the regulation of major multistate and multinational corporations had been left by Congress to the states in which they were incorporated, and tiny Delaware, seizing an opportunity in the early part of the twentieth century, had become home to a disproportionate number of giant corporations and therefore, by default, the arbiter of United States corporate law.[2] As Cary pointed out, the revenues from the chartering business and all that went with it (including the guaranteed employment of Wilmington lawyers as local counsel for big-city corporate firms) gave the Delaware courts every incentive to keep corporate managements happy, and they did so by regularly and consistently (while not quite invariably) limiting managerial obligations.[3]

Cary had an opportunity to attempt to rectify what he saw as the illegitimate federalization of Delaware law. As chairman of the Securities and Exchange Commission in the Kennedy administration, he embarked on an enforcement program designed to use the securities laws (principally their disclosure and antifraud provisions) to place meaningful obligations on directors and officers. This effort was picked up by the Second Circuit Court of Appeals in New York (which, until the maturity of Silicon Valley and the consequent increasing involvement of the Ninth Circuit in securities matters, was considered the Supreme Court of securities law) and by the Supreme Court itself, and in a series of decisions beginning in the mid-1960s and continuing to 1975, the disclosure and fiduciary-like protections of the federal securities laws became a powerful tool to keep managerial misconduct in check.

The brakes were put on by the Supreme Court in 1975, which in respect to securities law can be seen as the real beginning of the Rehnquist Court. The opening salvos of the battle took place principally between Justices Lewis Powell (a former corporate lawyer), for restricting the reach of the securities laws, and Harry Blackmun, for continuing the expansion. And they fought on a battlefield of policy. Broadly stated, Powell's approach to securities jurisprudence was to require some form of serious misconduct on the part of defendant corporations, or their officers or directors, before holding them liable to plaintiffs. He did so by introducing the technique of narrow statutory interpretation, first announced in a 1975 concurrence to a rare opinion by Rehnquist (whose presence in securities matters is almost always as a voter rather than a writer), in a sentence that has become the rallying cry in virtually all the Rehnquist Court's securities opinions: "The starting point in every case involving construction of a statute is the language itself."[4] Blackmun, in contrast and taking his cue from the remedial and market-protective purposes of the laws, was more concerned with the effect on the markets of managerial mistakes, even if the level of misconduct fell short of fraud and even if the statute required an expansive reading to reach the result.

Statutory interpretation may have been the methodology of these opinions, but reading them makes clear that the Supreme Courts that decided these cases understood the policy implications of their actions in terms of the legislature's goals and their effects upon the market and were, appropriately for the Supreme Court, driven by them. Of course it's no surprise that the Supreme Court should be driven by policy; after all, while it decides cases, it does so on the matrix of the larger purposes for which our laws are enacted. This is true even of relatively strict constructionists on the Court, who have a legitimate argument that lawmaking (at least nonconstitutional, regulatory-type lawmaking) ought to be left to Congress. But the Rehnquist Court has gone beyond this, discarding any pretense of finding intent in favor of tortured statutory readings. Not surprisingly, the opinions often make for very bad, or at least confusing, policy.

A case in point is a decision that actually tightens regulation, this one in the area of insider trading. Despite the good outcome, it's fair to say that *United States v. O'Hagan* is one of the most confusing of the Rehnquist Court opinions.[5] I like the decision as a policy matter because I believe in an expansive reading of the securities laws to aim at untoward market effects; I dislike the opinion as both a jurisprudential and a policy matter because it makes no sense either as an opinion protecting markets from unfair trading advantage or as an opinion tying securities violations to relevant illegal conduct. It is a halfway measure resulting from precisely the interpretive problems I'm describing.

The facts in the case are simple. O'Hagan was a partner at Dorsey & Whitney, the firm that represented Grand Metropolitan in its bid to acquire Pillsbury. Although O'Hagan didn't work on the deal, he bought call options on Pillsbury stock as well as stock itself. (A call option is the right to buy stock from the seller of the option at a preset price.) His firm later withdrew from the representation, and O'Hagan sold his stock and options at a profit of more than $4 million. He was convicted by a jury for criminal insider trading, a conviction overturned by the Eighth Circuit Court of Appeals. The Supreme Court reversed the Eighth Circuit and remanded the case for its reconsideration, after which the conviction was affirmed.

The legal issue wasn't too complicated, but it was one with which the Court had struggled on and off for seventeen years, namely whether the insider trading laws developed under the statute and its regulations ought to be interpreted to include what has become known as the misappropriation theory of insider trading. Very briefly, insider trading law traditionally covered the trading activity of those whom the word "insider" would, in common parlance, seem to cover, officers and directors of the company in whose stock they traded. The idea was that such people, because they owe a fiduciary obligation to their corporations' stockholders (which includes the obligation not to profit personally by using corporate assets), were prohibited from using corporate information (a corporate asset) that was not publicly available ("inside information") to trade against their corporations' stockholders (that is, to buy or sell stock in trades with the corporations' stockholders). This is straightforward, and while it required a few judicial twists and turns in light of the breadth and brevity of the statute, it indisputably comports with Congress's intent to prevent fraud and ensure fair markets. Until the 1980s, insider trading wasn't perceived as a serious problem, in part perhaps because insiders had relatively few opportunities to make profits that justified the risk; after all, big price-moving corporate information is not an everyday occurrence. What changed in the 1980s was the explosion of corporate takeovers at substantial premia over stock prices. This was the kind of information that could dramatically alter a stock's price on a given day. The takeover boom provided tempting illicit opportunities that some insiders found impossible to resist, and when these temptations ran into the political ambitions of the United States attorney for the Southern District of New York, Rudolph Giuliani, a number of high-profile prosecutions and convictions resulted.

The problem was that traditional insider trading law didn't always seem to get the bad guys. In the hostile-takeover case, the only traditional insiders were the officers and directors of the unwitting target company, who presumably had no advance notice of the takeover before the rest of the market and therefore no opportunity to profit from the information. But a lot of other people were involved in takeovers, including insiders of the hostile bidder, as well as all the retainers— lawyers, investment bankers, financial printers, and the like. These were the people who knew about the bids in advance of the market, and among these groups emerged a class of people who bought stock in the target companies before takeover bids were announced. Having had no prior relation with the companies, they were not insiders.

Although there was academic debate over whether insider trading was, as an aggregate matter, economically efficient and whether it ought to be permitted, there was no debate that the activities of these people brought them substantial profits at the expense of other (if unidentified) traders. And there was little question that the trading public perceived these people as taking advantage of the rest of us. So a doctrine developed, initially in the Second Circuit, holding that these "tippees" or "outsiders" or "temporary insiders" could be liable for insider trading if they breached a fiduciary duty to someone—usually the bidding company—in using its inside information for their advantage. But the area of criminal liability remained open.

And thus came O'Hagan. He was not an insider of Pillsbury. And while technically he was not an insider of Grand Met either, his firm was a temporary insider or an outsider with fiduciary obligations in its representation of the hostile bidder. O'Hagan, as a partner of the firm, was bound by the fiduciary duty owed by Dorsey & Whitney as Grand Met's agent and lawyer not to use its property for his own purposes, as well as by his fiduciary duty to his partners. Thus, he was in the sight lines of the misappropriation theory.

So far this makes sense. There is some legitimate argument against the misappropriation theory based in the ambiguous language of the statute, but the interesting point for our purpose is the way the Court rationalized the adoption of the misappropriation theory in criminal insider trading cases and, perhaps even more significantly, the parameters they imposed on the theory. For this is where legal technique blinks business sense.

The misappropriation theory comes in two flavors. The first, articulated by Chief Justice Burger, concurring in a 1980 insider trading decision, held that anyone who *stole* inside information was prohibited from using it to trade (unless he first disclosed the information publicly, which of course would defeat the purpose). Burger's theory made good business and legal sense; the offense was the distorting effect that the insider trading had on the market, the unfairness of its tilting the playing field in favor of people in privileged positions, exactly the kind of problem the securities laws were aimed at.

The variant adopted by the current Supreme Court differs. It is, like the rest of the Court's opinions, justifiable only as an elevation of interpretive technique over common sense and policy.

The Court's misappropriation theory holds as follows: only a person who breaches a fiduciary duty to the source of inside information in using that information to trade violates the insider trading laws. The doctrine thus exempts from liability other traders who, by virtue of a privileged (but nonfiduciary) position giving them access to nonpublic information, similarly distort the market. Thus O'Hagan, as a temporary insider of Grand Met and as a fiduciary of his partners at Dorsey & Whitney, committed a crime in trading on the information. This would have been covered under Burger's theory as well as the theory the Court chose to adopt, for O'Hagan was in a privileged position and to allow him to use that position would be to create unfairness in the trading market.

But why is it necessary to find that O'Hagan breached a fiduciary duty to anybody? Anyone with a privileged market position could take advantage of those who don't simply by using that position to obtain secret information. To so hold, as Burger would, that such behavior is prohibited has the policy coherence of looking to the effects of privileged trading on the market (and there is no doubt, given the way that markets work, that such privileged trading could well have market effects). One could argue that such a person ought not to be held liable if there was nothing illegal about the way in which the information was obtained, and this, too, would have a certain policy coherence—it would look to the conduct of persons in the market as the determining factor of liability rather than to the effect on the market, thus elevating traditional notions of criminal law over the concept of regulatory crimes. Were the Court to have held this way, it would at least have alerted the trading public to the possibility that sometimes there is structural unfairness in the markets, allowing traders to make their own decisions about whether they want to play the game and perhaps affecting stock prices.

To understand the silliness of the Court's position, look at what it doesn't cover (the Court acknowledges this gap, if not its silliness). If Dorsey & Whitney had given permission to O'Hagan to use the information (perhaps in lieu of a larger partnership draw) and had informed Grand Met of this fact, O'Hagan's trading would not have breached his fiduciary duty and he would thus have been free of criminal liability *even though the effect of his conduct on the market would have been identical.*[6]

Thus, the Court's attempt to create an effect-based jurisprudence fails because of its insistence on misconduct that has nothing to do with the offense. After all, Dorsey & Whitney wasn't harmed (except, perhaps, in its reputation, although one doubts whether people hold the actions of a rogue partner against an entire firm), and Grand Met wasn't harmed either—there was no evidence that as a result of O'Hagan's actions it paid more to acquire Pillsbury than it had been planning to pay. Finally, and most importantly, the harm on which the violation is based—O'Hagan's breach of fiduciary duty to Dorsey & Whitney and Grand Met—has nothing to do with the harm targeted by the antifraud provisions on which insider trading law is based, that is, distortion of the market by fraudulent trading. So why the half-baked result?

The answer lies in the Court's approach to statutory interpretation and its own precedent. The statute requires "manipulation or deception." The Court could have held that trading on information that was not publicly available was intrinsically manipulative, as when an analyst obtains secret information by talking to a corporate employee. But it had precedents that held that manipulation had a limited technical meaning (principally wash sales and similar prearranged false trades) and that deception required breach of a preexisting duty, such as a fiduciary duty. The kind of insider trading we have been considering does not fit within this narrow understanding of manipulation. So it focused on the word "deception," which implicates fraud. Breach of fiduciary duty is considered constructive fraud, so breach of fiduciary duty amounts to "deception" and criminal liability exists. This makes sense in the case of traditional insiders—the people they are hurting are their own stockholders, and the connection between their deceptive conduct and the harm is clear. To sustain this interpretation in the case of a conduct-based jurisprudence makes sense. But the Court stretched the statutory language in attempting to develop an effect-based theory that makes the violation turn on whether the temporary insider (or "outsider," as the Court put it) had the permission of somebody who had no relationship to the relevant market, in this case traders in Pillsbury stock, to distort the market.

The statutory linchpin is the requirement that the manipulation or deception be "in connection with" the purchase or sale of securities. This requirement has been treated very broadly, and the Court continued to stretch it in *O'Hagan*. The most tenuous connection suffices. For example, O'Hagan's breach—the theft of information—is tied to securities fraud because he used it to buy Pillsbury securities. But because those most likely to be harmed by the theft of information, Dorsey & Whitney and Grand Met, were completely unrelated to the persons harmed by O'Hagan's trades, the sellers of call options on Pillsbury stock and Pillsbury stockholders, his theft of information is deemed unrelated to the statute's goal of preventing market distortion and harm to traders.[7] If the Court had understood its own implicit concern with market effect and simply acknowledged that the policy of the statute was to establish an even playing field, it could have concluded that the use of privilege to obtain, and trade on, information not available to others distorted that playing field and thus was manipulative. This would have corrected the market distortions with which the insider trading rules are concerned. Conversely, the Court could have held that such behavior was neither manipulative nor deceptive with respect to securities markets and therefore was no violation. The halfway measure which Justice Clarence Thomas in dissent rightly called "incoherent," simply confuses the law in the name of the statute and leads to a result where market protection is as much a function of the accident of circumstances as it is anything else.

O'Hagan may be tortured and silly, but at least it has the excuse of arising from prior and long-standing interpretations of an admittedly broad and arguably uncertain statute. Justice Anthony Kennedy's opinion in *Gustafson v. Alloyd* has no similar excuse and presents itself as sheer nonsense.[8] The issue was the much more technical one of whether a prospectus issued in connection with the private offering of securities was a "prospectus" within the meaning of the 1933 Securities Act. That act provides a long series of definitions intended to apply throughout unless otherwise indicated. One of those definitions, appearing in Section 2(10), is of a prospectus, which is said to be "any prospectus, notice, circular, advertisement, letter, or communication, written or by radio or television, which offers any security for sale or confirms the sale of any security."[9] A definition of prospectus is important because it goes directly to the heart of the act, Section 5, which prohibits the offering or sale of any security without an effective registration statement filed with the SEC unless another provision of the act exempts it (there is a statutorily interpreted exemption for so-called private placements, the type of sale at issue in *Gustafson*). And there are very detailed requirements for the form and content of prospectuses to be filed with the SEC. There is also, as a matter of practice, a similarly stylized approach to information distributed in connection with private placements, including the type and form of information contained in a private contract for the sale of stock in an entire company, the issue in *Gustafson*. Practicing lawyers, keenly aware of the legal proscriptions on incomplete or misleading information, as well as of their own potential liability, take as much care with these private documents as they do with public registration statements.

It is almost painfully obvious that the purpose of the statute is to prevent the use of unregulated types of information in connection with the offering and sale of securities, and the securities bar has always been mindful of this in drafting the documents used for that purpose. Not only "prospectuses" (an obviously generic term as it appears in the definition of "prospectus" itself) but advertisements, letters, and even sales confirmations come within the sweep of the definition. Thus, when the issue arose in the case of whether a stock purchase agreement containing allegedly material misinformation was a "prospectus," the answer should have been obvious. The contract was, after all, a "writing" that "offers any security for sale or confirms the sale of any security." And it would be difficult to find many securities lawyers who disagree with that proposition.

Not so the Court. Justice Kennedy, avoiding the definitional section (which corporate practitioners understand provides a substantial part of the action in any corporate document) until he had established his conclusion, began in the middle of the statute with Section 10, which provides that a prospectus is required to contain the information provided in the registration statement, from which he concluded that because there is no registration statement for privately issued securities, no document containing information relating to those securities can be a prospectus.

Now wait. The 1933 Securities Act deals with registration requirements but also provides exemptions from registration (both explicitly
and by judicial interpretation). And there is absolutely nothing in the
definition, Section 2(10), that limits the term "prospectus" to registered
securities. Nor is there anything in Section 12(2), which protects
against negligently misleading statements. In fact, one could argue
that, given the nature of business, this protection is even more necessary in the case of private sales because of the lack of public information, the absence of analysts following the stock and investment
bankers underwriting it, and the likely inability of a purchaser to get
the information unless the seller provides it. These realities, however,
didn't bother the Court. Instead, Justice Kennedy reached his conclusion despite the commonsensical reading that prospectuses for registered offerings are required to contain the information provided in
the registration statement whereas prospectuses for private offerings
had no particular form but, whatever the form, were required to be
negligence-free. In the guise of providing a statutory interpretation, he
simply wrote the definition of a prospectus out of the statute.

Why did the Court reach this conclusion? Had any of the justices
practiced securities law, the correct answer to the problem would have
been obvious. But it is clear that the Court did not understand the way
securities practice is done or what the legitimate concerns of buyers
and sellers are. Kennedy notes, in an attempt at policy defense, "It is
understandable that Congress would provide buyers with a right to rescind . . . [with respect to] a document prepared with care, following
well-established procedures relating to investigations with due diligence. . . . It is not plausible to infer that Congress created this extensive liability for every casual communication between buyer and seller
in the secondary market."

What is plausible, indeed almost certainly correct, is that Congress
attempted to *eliminate* the use of casual communications in the purchase and sale of securities and to promote a great deal of care precisely to preclude the use of misinformation. And the quoted sentence
reveals a stunning ignorance of actual practice—any first-year associate in a law firm could have told Kennedy that virtually the same due
diligence done in every public offering is regularly performed in all pri-

vate offerings, including those of all the stock of a business, if for no other reason than to protect the lawyers themselves from liability.

Instead of following common sense, as to policy and practice, the Court was driven by Kennedy's insistence on a statutory interpretation that preserved "a symmetrical and coherent regulatory scheme in which the operative words have a consistent meaning throughout."[10] But the preservation of a coherent *regulatory* scheme does not necessarily depend on symmetry, no matter how much a sense of statutory elegance might demand it. The world, and certainly the world of business, does not operate with such artifice. Kennedy approaches the problem as if he were a general contractor hell-bent on building a Georgian mansion from a set of Frank Gehry blueprints. Or a physicist manipulating results to avoid experimental protocols, in this case the definitional section designed to infuse the statute with meaning. The order he attempts to enforce upon the form of the statute has nothing to do with the practical realities underlying the regulatory scheme.[11]

Another significant opinion, this one written, surprisingly, by Justice Blackmun—joined by Rehnquist, White, and Marshall, with a partial concurrence by Scalia and dissents by Stevens (joined by Souter), O'Connor (joined by Kennedy), and Kennedy (joined by O'Connor)—suggests, if nothing else, that bad jurisprudence makes strange bedfellows. The case is the 1991 *Lampf, Pleva, et al. v. Gilbertson,* and the issue was the appropriate statute of limitations to apply.[12] Since the 1934 Securities Act did not provide for an express private cause of action but rather one had been implied by the courts, there clearly was no express statute of limitations that went with it. The traditional procedure when a federal statute does not have an express statute of limitations is to borrow the most analogous state statute of limitations. In rejecting this rule and instead creating a federal statute of limitations from the corners of the 1934 act, the Court admitted it was taking an unusual step, especially in light of the fact that Congress was aware of the general rule and presumably expected that it would be applied in cases like this. Since, however, the 1934 act does contain express causes of action with their own statutes of limitations, the Court chose to look within the statute in the interests of creating a more consistent statutory approach.

Of course, as Emerson said, "a foolish consistency is the hobgoblin of little minds." For the sake of consistency, the Court created a statute of limitations for this antifraud provision that runs one year from the discovery of the fraud but with an absolute three-year limit of repose. In other words, if the fraud is not discovered within three years, the plaintiff is out of luck.

The Court's reasoning is tortuous, but its general direction is apparent. It is intriguing to note, however, that in the interests of consistency, perhaps the most plaintiff-friendly securities justice on the Court created a rule that, as Justice Kennedy wrote, "conflicts with traditional limitations periods for fraud-based actions, frustrates the usefulness of Section 10(b) in protecting defrauded investors, and imposes severe practical limitations on a federal implied cause of action that has become an essential component of the protection the law gives to investors who have been injured by unlawful practices."

Why? Because the essence of fraud is concealment. It is entirely possible for far longer than three years to pass before the discovery of a fraud. Indeed, in the Enron case, assuming that fraudulent nondisclosure is found to exist, it is probable that at least some of that fraud occurred outside the three-year limitations period. In fact, although Enron was only a pipeline company at the time of the opinion, the impact of the holding on that case is echoed in Justice Kennedy's remark: "Ponzi schemes, for example, can maintain the illusion of a profit-making enterprise for years, and sophisticated investors might not be able to discover the fraud until long after its perpetration." Using a technical approach rather than a realistic approach to statutory interpretation, the Court again forecloses the possibility of remedies for a large class of investors.

The Rehnquist Court's poor record in interpreting securities law is again evident in the 1994 opinion in *Central Bank of Denver v. First Interstate Bank of Denver.*[13] Justice Kennedy, joined by Rehnquist, O'Connor, Scalia, and Thomas, held that Section 10(b) did not impose civil liability on those who aided and abetted violations of the statute. Invoking the talismanic phrase "the starting point in every case involving con-

struction of a statute is the language itself," Kennedy concluded that
since the language of this admittedly broad and ambiguous statute
didn't expressly provide for aiding and abetting liability, the game was
over and such liability didn't exist. He did go on to address arguments
plaintiffs had made but concluded again with the assertion that the
statutory language was enough.

The logic is ridiculous. While it's true that the statute is the starting
point, the Court has always recognized (as the lower courts generally
have as well) that Section 10(b) is more in the nature of an antifraud
principle than an outcome determinative rule. The Court virtually ignores the development of aiding and abetting liability in common law
and insists on an explicit statutory source. It does recognize the existence of one in a 1909 act of Congress providing for aiding and abetting liability for all federal crimes, which of course would pick up
criminal violations of Section 10(b), but dismisses without any policy
justification other than a felt need to protect potential defendants the
possibility that the principle logically could extend to civil actions as
well. The Court's main concern is that extending aiding and abetting
liability to civil actions under Section 10(b) would reach people who
had not engaged in the conduct prohibited by Section 10(b), without
recognizing that aiding and abetting liability exists *precisely* to extend liability to people who didn't commit the primary violation but provided
significant help to others in committing the prohibited act. The Court
fails to acknowledge that Section 10(b) violations frequently involve the
knowing and essential input of people—accountants, lawyers, investment bankers, and, in this case, indenture trustees—other than the primary violators. Thus, the case significantly limits the efficacy of the
statute in prohibiting fraud.

I've saved the best for last, an opinion by a justice I generally ad-
mire, David Souter. The case is *Virginia Bankshares v. Sandberg*, and it involved a suit by stockholders of First American Bank of Virginia who
were frozen out in a merger of the bank with Virginia Bankshares,
which owned 85 percent of the bank's stock.[14] The stockholders complained that the proxy statement sent out by First American was materially misleading because in it the directors said that the stockholders
would be receiving a "high price" for their stock, a statement a jury

found to be untrue. Misleading proxy statements are prohibited by Section 14(a) of the 1934 Securities Act and the rules the SEC has adopted to implement it. First American and its directors were found liable, a judgment affirmed by the Fourth Circuit. The Supreme Court reversed, with the relevant portion of the opinion joined by Rehnquist, White, O'Connor, and Scalia and dissented from by Blackmun and Stevens (with Marshall and Kennedy joining in various aspects of the dissent).

The legal problem arose because Virginia law did not require that the directors send out a proxy statement in this sort of merger. As a result, the Court concluded that the misleading proxy statement could not have "caused" the merger to occur. Of course, in one sense, even had the proxy statement been legally required, it could not have caused the merger since Virginia Bankshares owned well more than enough stock to approve the merger without a single vote of minority stockholders. But twenty-one years earlier, Justice John Marshall Harlan, Jr., writing for the Court in *Mills v. Electric Auto-Lite Company*, concluded that since the purpose of the proxy rules was to prevent misleading information in proxy statements, and even a proxy statement in the case of a controlled corporation could have adverse effects upon plaintiffs (and, I note, on the market prices of the subsidiary's stock prior to the merger), such statements were indeed causative in a legal sense if the proxy statement was an "essential link in the accomplishment of the transaction."[15] Because the minority's votes were not legally required in this case, the Court held that the proxy statement could not be seen as an essential link in the transaction. Thus a narrow notion of tortlike proximate causation was imported into a remedial statutory scheme clearly designed to protect stockholders in a complex market in which proximate cause is almost always difficult to prove.

The Court overlooked some significant practical aspects of the deal. In the first place, a major reason for the proxy solicitation was that First American and Virginia Bankshares had a director in common and disinterested stockholder ratification was necessary to insulate the transaction from invalidation on conflict-of-interest grounds. The Court declined to decide this argument because it appeared that the merger didn't preclude stockholder pursuit of the state remedy, thus making the argument irrelevant, even though First American's board of directors evidently thought it materially important enough to incur the time and cost of issuing a proxy statement. And even though the proxy statement wasn't legally required, this doesn't alter the fact that the directors actually issued it. Once a misleading proxy statement asking for stockholder approval of the merger had been issued, the damage was done.

This fact was clearly recognized by Stevens, Blackmun, and Marshall in a dissent written by Justice Kennedy in which they noted that, regardless of the state legal requirement, the "real question ought to be whether an injury was shown by the effect the nondisclosure had on the entire merger process, including the period before votes are cast." This showed some understanding of business and market behavior. The dissent recognized that the directors could stop the merger if it was too unpopular with minority stockholders. The "including" phrase showed an appreciation of the effect that proxy misstatements could have on the trading price of First American stocks prior to the merger, harming traders relying on that information. Finally, it acknowledged the practical lack of protection for minority stockholders if thousands of them were required to prove how they would have voted if the information had been accurate. "Those who lack the strength to vote down a proposal have all the more need of disclosure," the dissent noted, demonstrating a clear understanding of the practical realities of being a minority stockholder and the securities law policy of protecting precisely those people. By contrast, the majority rested the bulk of its opinion on the fact that the cause of action under Section 14(a) was implied by the courts rather than being explicit in the statute, and thus as a matter of statutory interpretation limited (although as a matter of statutory interpretation it should also be noted that the statute and rule are very broadly worded and prohibit the use of misleading statements in any proxy statement involving registered securities—and it is clear that First American's shares were registered securities).

The dissent was refreshing in its common sense, but the opinion occurred rather early in the Rehnquist Court, when Blackmun and Marshall could lend weight to Stevens's business understanding. The Court as constituted in 2002 has only the greatly outnumbered Stevens to keep it honest, with the voice of common sense and business sense buried in a battle over statutory interpretation techniques.

There have been some advances in the Court's use of the protective aspects of the securities law but, with the exception of *O'Hagan*, these mostly occurred in the early years of the Rehnquist Court, when Blackmun and Marshall were prominent voices. The clear trend in recent years has been to cut back these protections wherever possible, a trend justified by a dogmatic reliance on statutory language without much regard to the purposes of the statutes or the way they function in the real world of securities trading. It seems obvious that the Court's general purpose is to limit severely the scope of the securities laws, but the justices seem to do so without any real appreciation of the effects on market efficiency. After all, one of the preconditions of an efficient market is an honest market. Moreover, their use of highly artificial and often illogical statutory technique constitutes its own form of deception: if the Court intends to cut back on the securities laws for some policy reason, it ought to be frank and tell us—and tell us why. One suspects that a major reason the Court hasn't done this is that the justices themselves don't quite know why, other than perhaps a knee-jerk attempt to provide benefits to business, benefits that are questionable in a market stripped of investor protections. If the trend continues, not only will the Court leave the markets in a less regulated and therefore riskier condition but it will likely complete the process of leaving virtually all important business policy to the state of Delaware.

Notes

TOM WICKER: *Foreword: Reflections of a Court Watcher*

1. *Worcester v. State of Georgia*, 31 U.S. 515 (1832).
2. 347 U.S. 483 (1954).
3. *Bush v. Gore*, 531 U.S. 98 (2000).
4. *Marbury v. Madison*, 5 U.S. (1 Cranch) 137 (1803).
5. *Dred Scott v. Sandford*, 60 U.S. 393 (1857).
6. 163 U.S. 537 (1896).
7. 343 U.S. 579 (1952).

HERMAN SCHWARTZ: *Introduction*

1. *Bush v. Gore*, 531 U.S. 98 (2000).
2. Ford Fessenden and John M. Broder, "Examining the Vote: The Overview; Study of Disputed Florida Ballots Finds Justices Did Not Cast the Deciding Vote," *New York Times*, Nov. 12, 2001, p. A1.
3. On the military tribunals, see Herman Schwartz, "These Secret Tribunals Ignore Due Process and Treat Suspects As If They Are Presumed Guilty before Trial," *Insight on the News*, Jan. 28, 2002, p. 43, and "Tribunal Injustice," *The Nation*, Jan. 21, 2002.
4. *Near v. Minnesota*, 283 U.S. 697 (1931); *Cantwell v. Connecticut*, 310 U.S. 296 (1940).
5. *Brown v. Board of Education*, 347 U.S. 483 (1954).
6. *Callins v. Collins*, 510 U.S. 1141, 1145 (1994) (Blackmun, J., dissenting).
7. 384 U.S. 436 (1966).
8. 410 U.S. 113 (1973).

9. *Planned Parenthood of Southeastern Pennsylvania v. Casey*, 505 U.S. 833 (1992).

10. *Romer v. Evans*, 517 U.S. 620 (1996); *Boy Scouts v. Dale*, 530 U.S. 640 (2000); *Hurley v. Irish-American Gay, Lesbian, and Bisexual Group of Boston*, 515 U.S. 557 (1995).

11. Craig A. Stern, "Judging the Judges: The First Two Years of the Reagan Bench," *Benchmark* 1 (July–Oct. 1984): 3.

JOHN P. MacKENZIE: *Equal Protection for One Lucky Guy*

1. *Bush v. Gore*, 531 U.S. 98 (2000).

2. *Korematsu v. United States*, 323 U.S. 214 (1944).

3. *Dred Scott v. Sandford*, 60 U.S. 393 (1857); *Plessy v. Ferguson*, 163 U.S. 537 (1896).

4. *Bush v. Palm Beach County Canvassing Board*, 531 U.S. 70 (2000).

5. See *Gore v. Harris*, 772 So. 2d 1243, 1252 (Fla. 2000).

6. See *Bush v. Gore*, 531 U.S. 1046 (2000) (Scalia, J., concurring).

7. *Palm Beach County Canvassing Board. v. Harris*, 772 So. 2d 1292 (Fla. 2000).

8. *Planned Parenthood of Southeastern Pennsylvania v. Casey*, 505 U.S. 833, 854 (1992).

9. *United States v. Virginia*, 518 U.S. 515, 596 (1996) (Scalia, J., dissenting).

10. 406 U.S. 205 (1972).

11. See *Anastasoff v. United States*, 223 F., 3d 898 (8th Cir. 2000).

WILLIAM L. TAYLOR: *Racial Equality: The World According to Rehnquist*

1. 347 U.S. 483 (1954).

2. *Griggs v. Duke Power Company*, 401 U.S. 424 (1971).

3. *San Antonio Independent School District v. Rodriguez*, 411 U.S. 1 (1973); *Milliken v. Bradley*, 418 U.S. 717 (1974).

4. *Washington v. Davis*, 426 U.S. 229 (1976); *Arlington Heights v. Metropolitan Housing Development Corporation*, 429 U.S. 252 (1977); *Mobile v. Bolden*, 446 U.S. 55 (1980).

5. 418 U.S. at 814.

6. See Richard Kluger, *Simple Justice: The History of* Brown v. Board of Education *and Black America's Struggle for Equality* (New York, 1975), pp. 605–09. While Rehnquist claimed during his 1971 confirmation hearings that the memo was prepared to reflect Jackson's views rather than his own, Kluger's review of the circumstances provides strong evidence that this is simply not so.

7. *Washington Post*, July 25, 1986.

8. David Shapiro, "Mr. Justice Rehnquist: A Preliminary View," *Harvard Law Review* 90 (1976): 293, 298.

9. *Keyes v. School District No. 1 of Denver*, 413 U.S. 189 (1973).

10. 422 U.S. 406, 420 (1977).

11. *Dayton II*, 443 U.S. 526 (1979).

12. 490 U.S. 642 (1989).

13. *McDonnell Douglas v. Green*, 411 U.S. 792 (1973).

14. 490 U.S. at 659–60.
15. 491 U.S. 164 (1989).
16. See William Taylor, "The Civil Rights Act of 1991," *Touro Law Review* 9 (1992): 157.
17. *Regents of the University of California v. Bakke*, 483 U.S. 265 (1978).
18. *Adarand Contractors v. Pena*, 515 U.S. 200 (1995).
19. *Hopwood v. Texas*, 78 F. 3d 932, *certiorari denied*, 116 Sup. Ct. 2581 (1996).
20. *Cooper v. Aaron*, 358 U.S. 1 (1958).
21. Another example of Rehnquist's prestidigitation came in *Dayton I* when he held that rescision by a school board of a voluntary desegregation policy was not a violation of the Fourteenth Amendment if the policy had not been implemented. The fact that the policy was rescinded after a successful campaign laced with racial rhetoric to replace the board members who voted for the original policy was deemed irrelevant because it was not "state action."
22. *Mobile v. Bolden*, 446 U.S. 55 (1980).
23. 509 U.S. 630 (1993).
24. *Swann v. Charlotte-Mecklenburg Board of Education*, 402 U.S. 1 (1971).
25. *Milliken v. Bradley*, 433 U.S. 288 (1977).
26. *Oklahoma City Board of Education v. Dowell*, 498 U.S. 237 (1991); *Freeman v. Pitts*, 503 U.S. 467 (1992); *Missouri v. Jenkins*, 515 U.S. 70 (1995).
27. 529 U.S. 598 (2000).
28. 528 U.S. 62 (2000).
29. *Board of Trustees of the University of Alabama v. Garrett*, 531 U.S. 356 (2001).
30. *Alexander v. Sandoval*, 532 U.S. 275 (2001).
31. The more conventional constitutional analysis was provided in the accompanying District of Columbia case, *Bolling v. Sharpe*, 347 U.S. 497 (1954).
32. 115 Sup. Ct. 1275 (2002).
33. 457 U.S. 202 (1982).
34. *Griggs v. Duke Power Company*, 401 U.S. 424, 432 (1971).

CHARLES J. OGLETREE, JR.: *The Rehnquist Revolution in Criminal Procedure*

1. See Herbert L. Packer, "Two Models of the Criminal Process," *University of Pennsylvania Law Review* 113 (1964): 1.
2. For probable cause, see *Illinois v. Gates*, 462 U.S. 213 (1983); for reasonable suspicion, see *United States v. Sokolow*, 490 U.S. 1 (1989).
3. 384 U.S. 436 (1966); 377 U.S. 201 (1964); 367 U.S. 643 (1961).
4. Stanley H. Friedelbaum, *The Rehnquist Court: In Pursuit of Judicial Conservatism* (Westport, 1994), p. 129.
5. 392 U.S. 1 (1968).
6. 491 U.S. 617 (1989).
7. See *Robbins v. California*, 453 U.S. 420, 437 (1981) (Rehnquist, J., dissenting), over-

ruled by *United States v. Ross*, 456 U.S. 798 (1982). See also *Arkansas v. Sanders*, 442 U.S. 753 (1979) (Blackmun, J., and Rehnquist, J., dissenting), modified by *United States v. Ross*, 456 U.S. 798 (1982).

8. See *Katz v. United States*, 389 U.S. 347 (1967).

9. *United States v. Chadwick*, 433 U.S. 1, 19 (1977), abrogated by *California v. Acevedo*, 500 U.S. 565 (1991).

10. 440 U.S. 648, 664–67 (1979) (Rehnquist, J., dissenting).

11. See *Steagald v. United States*, 451 U.S. 204, 223–31 (1981) (Rehnquist, J., dissenting); *Ybarra v. Illinois*, 440 U.S. 85, 98–110 (1979) (Rehnquist, J., dissenting).

12. 442 U.S. 200, 222–23 (1979) (Rehnquist, J., dissenting).

13. 438 U.S. 154, 182 (1978) (Rehnquist, J., dissenting).

14. *Florida v. Jimeno*, 500 U.S. 248, 252 (1991).

15. 500 U.S. 565 (1991).

16. 450 U.S. 288 (1981). As an associate justice, Rehnquist also supported the restriction of double-jeopardy protections, which prevent individuals being tried twice for the same offense. See *Crist v. Bretz*, 437 U.S. 28, 40–53 (1978) (Powell, J., dissenting).

17. 426 U.S. 610, 620–34 (1976).

18. 479 U.S. 157, 170 (1986).

19. "As the Court today acknowledges, since *Miranda* we have explicitly, and repeatedly, interpreted that decision as having announced, not the circumstances in which custodial interrogation runs afoul of the Fifth or Fourteenth Amendment, but rather only 'prophylactic' rules that go beyond the right against compelled self-incrimination" 530 U.S. 428, 450 (2000) (Scalia, J., dissenting).

20. For a critique of Chief Justice Rehnquist's harmless-error analysis, see Charles J. Ogletree, Jr., "The Supreme Court, Comment: *Arizona v. Fulminante*: The Harm of Applying Harmless Error to Coerced Confessions," *Harvard Law Review* 105 (1991): 152.

21. For the death penalty as violating the Eighth Amendment, see 428 U.S. 325, 337–63 (1976) (White, J., dissenting).

22. See *Coker v. Georgia*, 433 U.S. 584, 604–22 (1977) (Burger, C. J., dissenting); *Enmund v. Florida*, 458 U.S. 782, 801–31 (1982) (O'Connor, J., dissenting); *Ford v. Wainwright*, 477 U.S. 399, 431–35 (1986) (Rehnquist, J., dissenting).

23. 433 U.S. 72 (1977).

24. 489 U.S. 288 (1989).

25. *Id.* at 334–45 (Brennan, J., dissenting).

26. James S. Liebman, "More Than 'Slightly Retro': The Rehnquist Court's Rout of Habeas Corpus Jurisdiction in *Teague v. Lane*," *New York University Review of Law and Social Change* 18 (1991): 540–41.

27. Staci Rosche, "How Conservative Is the Rehnquist Court? Three Issues, One Answer," *Fordham Law Review* 65 (1997): 2719.

28. Christopher E. Smith, "Criminal Justice and the U.S. Supreme Court's 1999–2000 Term," *North Dakota Law Review* 77 (2001): 25.

29. 517 U.S. 806 (1996).
30. 528 U.S. 119 (2000).
31. See David A. Harris, "Driving While Black: Racial Profiling on Our Nation's Highways," *American Civil Liberties Union Special Report*, June 1999, http://www.aclu.org/profiling/report/index.html.
32. See Edward Walsh, "The Racial Issue Looming in the Rear-View Mirror; Activists Seek Data on Police 'Profiling,' " *Washington Post*, May 19, 1999, p. A3.
33. Nat Hentoff, "Forgetting the Fourth Amendment in Philadelphia," *Washington Post*, Apr. 16, 1988, p. A25.
34. Diana Jean Schemo, "Singling Out Blacks Where Few Are to Be Found," *New York Times*, Oct. 20, 1992, p. B1.
35. Jim McGee, "In Federal Law Enforcement 'All the Walls Are Down'; Personnel from Assorted Agencies Work Together at FBI Headquarters," *Washington Post*, Oct. 14, 2001, p. A16.
36. For a further discussion of racial profiling, see Charles J. Ogletree, Jr., "Fighting a Just War without an Unjust Loss of Freedom," *Africana.com*, Oct. 11, 2001.

WILLIAM E. HELLERSTEIN: *No Rights of Prisoners*

1. In *Cooper v. Pate*, 378 U.S. 546 (1964) (per curiam), the Court ruled that a prisoner's claim that he had been punished for exercising his religious beliefs could not be dismissed outright. In *Lee v. Washington*, 390 U.S. 333 (per curiam), the Court prohibited the racial segregation of prisoners. In *Johnson v. Avery*, 393 U.S. 483 (1969), the Court ruled that a regulation that prohibited inmates from assisting other inmates in the preparation of habeas corpus petitions was an unconstitutional interference with access to the courts.
2. *Holt v. Sarver*, 309 F. Supp. 367 (E.D. Ark. 1970).
3. *Cruz v. Beto*, 405 U.S. 319 (1972); *Procunier v. Martinez*, 416 U.S. 396 (1974); *Wolff v. McDonnell*, 418 U.S. 539 (1974); *Estelle v. Gamble*, 429 U.S. 97 (1976).
4. Public Law 104–134, 110 Stat. 1321.
5. 482 U.S. 78 (1987).
6. *Korematsu v. United States*, 323 U.S. 214, 246 (1944).
7. 490 U.S. 401 (1989).
8. 121 Sup. Ct. 1475 (2001).
9. 405 U.S. 319 (1972).
10. 482 U.S. 342 (1987).
11. *Young v. Lane*, 922 F. 2d 370 (7th Cir. 1991); *Friend v. Kolodzieczak*, 923 F. 2d 126 (9th Cir. 1991); *Kahey v. Jones*, 836 F. 2d 948 (5th Cir. 1988); *Fromer v. Scully*, 874 F. 2d 69 (2d Cir. 1989); and *Pollock v. Marshall*, 845 F. 2d 656 (6th Cir.), certiorari denied, 488 U.S. 987 (1988).
12. For severity of deprivation, see *Morrisey v. Brewer*, 408 U.S. 471 (1972).
13. 418 U.S. 539 (1974).
14. 515 U.S. 472 (1995).

15. *Johnson v. Avery*, 393 U.S. 483 (1969); *Bounds v. Smith*, 430 U.S. 817 (1977).
16. 518 U.S. 343 (1996).
17. 429 U.S. 97 (1976).
18. 437 U.S. 678 (1978).
19. 501 U.S. 294 (1991).
20. 511 U.S. 294 (1994).
21. 503 U.S. 1 (1992).
22. 509 U.S. 25 (1993).
23. 532 U.S. 731 (2001).
24. *Miranda v. United States*, 384 U.S. 436 (1966); *Dickerson v. United States*, 530 U.S. 428 (2000).

STEPHEN BRIGHT: *Capital Punishment: Accelerating the Dance with Death*

1. *Callins v. Collins*, 510 U.S. 1141 (1994) (Blackmun, J., dissenting from denial of certiorari).
2. *Furman v. Georgia*, 408 U.S. 238 (1972).
3. *Woodson v. North Carolina*, 428 U.S. 280 (1976); *Roberts v. Louisiana*, 428 U.S. 325 (1976).
4. *Coleman v. Balkcom*, 451 U.S. 949 (1981) (Rehnquist, J., dissenting from denial of certiorari).
5. *Coleman v. Thompson*, 501 U.S. 722, 758–59 (1991) (Blackmun, J., dissenting).
6. "Justice O'Connor Expresses New Doubts about Fairness of Capital Punishment," *Baltimore Sun*, July 4, 2001, p. A3.
7. "Florida Lets Speed Govern Executions," *Chicago Tribune*, Feb. 28, 2000, p. N1.
8. 501 U.S. 722, 758 (Blackmun, J., dissenting).
9. *Teague v. Lane*, 489 U.S. 288 (1989); *Brecht v. Abrahamson*, 507 U.S. 619 (1993).
10. *Strickler v. Greene*, 527 U.S. 263 (1999); *Sawyer v. Whitley*, 505 U.S. 333 (1992).
11. *Jacobs v. Scott*, 513 U.S. 1067 (1995).
12. See, e.g., *Schlup v. Delo*, 513 U.S. 298 (1995); *Kyles v. Whitley*, 514 U.S. 419 (1995).
13. Stuart Eskenazi, "Strong Convictions," *Houston Press*, Nov. 18, 1998.
14. "Oklahoma Governor Commutes Death Case; Texas Bill Boosts Defense for the Poor," *Chicago Tribune*, Apr. 11, 2001, p. N8.
15. *Riles v. McCotter*, 799 F. 2d 947, 955 (5th Cir. 1986) (Rubin, J., concurring).
16. *Strickland v. Washington*, 466 U.S. 668 (1984).
17. Remarks of Justice Thurgood Marshall at the Second Circuit Judicial Conference (Sept. 1988), reprinted in 125 F.R.D. 201, 202–03 (1988).
18. "Justice O'Connor Expresses New Doubts about Fairness of Capital Punishment," *op. cit.*
19. *Williams (Terry) v. Taylor*, 529 U.S. 362 (2000).
20. *Gideon v. Wainwright*, 372 U.S. 335 (1963); *Douglas v. California*, 372 U.S. 353 (1963).
21. *Murray v. Giarratano*, 492 U.S. 1 (1989).

22. *McCleskey v. Kemp*, 481 U.S. 279 (1987).
23. *Andrews v. Shulsen*, 485 U.S. 919 (1988).
24. *Perry v. Lynaugh*, 492 U.S. 302 (1989); *Atkins v. Virginia*, 122 Sup. Ct. 2242 (2002).
25. *Stanford v. Kentucky*, 492 U.S. 361 (1989).
26. *McCleskey v. Kemp*, 481 U.S. 279, 344 (1987) (Brennan, J., dissenting).

NORMAN REDLICH: *The Religion Clauses: A Study in Confusion*

1. *Everson v. Board of Education*, 330 U.S. 1 (1947).
 2. *Engel v. Vitale*, 370 U.S. 421 (1962).
 3. 403 U.S. 602 (1971).
 4. 433 U.S. 229 (1977).
 5. *Witters v. Washington Department of Services for the Blind*, 474 U.S. 481 (1986); *Zobrest v. Catalina Foothills School District*, 509 U.S. 1 (1993).
 6. *Agostini v. Felton*, 521 U.S. 203 (1997); *Aguilar v. Felton*, 473 U.S. 402 (1985).
 7. 530 U.S. 793 (2000).
 8. 374 U.S. 203 (1963).
 9. 472 U.S. 38 (1985).
10. 482 U.S. 578 (1987).
11. 505 U.S. 577 (1992).
12. 530 U.S. 290 (2000).
13. 250 F. 3d 1330 (11th Cir. 2001), certiorari denied, 122 Sup. Ct. 579 (2001).
14. 454 U.S. 263 (1981).
15. 515 U.S. 819 (1995).
16. 533 U.S. 98 (2001).
17. 494 U.S. 872 (1990).
18. 508 U.S. 520 (1993).
19. 521 U.S. 507 (1997).
20. 449 U.S. 39 (1980).
21. 465 U.S. 668 (1984).
22. 492 U.S. 573 (1989).
23. *Zelman v. Simmons-Harris*, 122 Sup. Ct. 2460 (2002).

JAMIN B. RASKIN: *The First Amendment: The High Ground and the Low Road*

1. *Hustler v. Falwell*, 485 U.S. 46 (1988); *Texas v. Johnson*, 491 U.S. 397 (1989); *Rosenberger v. Rector and Visitors of the University of Virginia* 515 U.S. 819 (1995).
 2. 521 U.S. 844 (1997), invalidating as both vague and overboard the Communications Decency Act, which criminalized knowing transmission on the Internet of indecent messages to minors and knowing display of patently offensive messages accessible to minors, 122 Sup. Ct. 1389 (2002). A similar opinion was *Sable Communications of California, Inc. v. FCC*, 492 U.S. 115 (1989), striking down congressional restrictions on interstate "dial-a-porn" messages.

3. *New York Times v. Sullivan*, 376 U.S. 254 (1964), holds that public figures may recover in state libel actions only if they can show "actual malice" by defendants, meaning knowledge or reckless disregard of the falsity of alleged defamatory statements. *Cohen v. California*, 403 U.S. 15 (1971), invalidates the criminal conviction of a young man who wore "Fuck the Draft" on his jacket into a courtroom, finding that "one man's vulgarity is another's lyric" and political "cacophony" is a sign of "strength." *Brandenburg v. Ohio*, 395 U.S. 444 (1969), holds that advocacy of the use of illegal force is constitutionally protected "except where such advocacy is directed to inciting or producing imminent lawless action and is likely to incite or produce such action."

4. 505 U.S. 377 (1992).

5. *Buckley v. Valeo*, 424 U.S. 1 (1976).

6. See, e.g., *Schenck v. Pro-Choice Network*, 117 Sup. Ct. 855, 867 (1997), in which Chief Justice Rehnquist upheld an injunctive-fixed buffer zone outside abortion clinics but struck down a "floating" fifteen-foot buffer zone, stating that "speech in public areas is at its most protected on public sidewalks."

7. 530 U.S. 640 (2000).

8. 515 U.S. 557 (1995).

9. Texas law made it a crime to "deface, damage or otherwise physically mistreat" the American flag "in a way that the actor knows will seriously offend one or more persons likely to observe or discover his action," 491 U.S. 397, 435 (1989).

10. 319 U.S. 624 (1943).

11. 485 U.S. 48, 46–48 (1988).

12. *Id.* at 55.

13. 454 U.S. 263 (1981).

14. 523 U.S. 666 (1998). Jamin B. Raskin filed an amicus brief in this case on behalf of Perot '96, Ross Perot's 1996 presidential campaign organization.

15. *Arkansas Educational Television Commission v. Forbes*, 93 F. 3d 497 (8th Cir. 1996).

16. 523 U.S. 666, 680 (1993).

17. 93 F. 3d at 497.

18. *Timmons v. Twin Cities Area New Party*, 520 U.S. 351, 356 (1997).

19. 73 F. 3d 196, 198 (8th Cir., 1997).

20. 505 U.S. 222 (1992).

21. *Hazelwood School District v. Kuhlmeier, Tinker v. Des Moines School District*, 484 U.S. 260 (1988); 393 U.S. 503 (1969).

22. 478 U.S. 675 (1986).

23. 500 U.S. 173 (1991).

24. 500 U.S. at 210 (Blackmun, J., and Marshall, J., dissenting).

25. 530 U.S. 703 (2000); Colorado Revised Statutes, sec. 18–9–122(3) (2000).

26. 524 U.S. 569 (1998), quoting 20 U.S.C. sec. 954(d)(1).

27. *Id.* at 581.

28. *Id.* at 590, 591 (Scalia, J., and Thomas, J., concurring).

29. 531 U.S. 533 (2001).

CHAI FELDBLUM: *Gay Rights*

1. 478 U.S. 186 (1986).
2. *Boy Scouts of America v. Dale*, 530 U.S. 640 (2000).
3. *Griswold v. Connecticut*, 381 U.S. 479 (1965).
4. *Hardwick*, 478 U.S. at 206, quoting *Wisconsin v. Yoder*, 406 U.S. 205, 223–24 (1972).
5. *Hurley v. Irish-American Gay, Lesbian, and Bisexual Group of Boston*, 515 U.S. 557 (1995).
6. *Id.* at 574.
7. *Inside-OUT: A Report on the Experiences of Lesbians, Gays and Bisexuals in America and the Public's Views on Issues and Policies Related to Sexual Orientation.* Kaiser Family Foundation Pub. 3193, available at http://www.kff.org.
8. *Romer v. Evans*, 517 U.S. 620, 632 (1996).
9. *Id.* at 644 (Scalia, J., dissenting).
10. *Equality Foundation of Greater Cincinnati, Inc. v. City of Cincinnati*, 54 F. 3d 261 (6th Cir. 1995).
11. 525 U.S. 943 (1998). *Equality Foundation of Greater Cincinnati, Inc. v. City of Cincinnati*, 128 F. 3d 289 (6th Cir. 1997), certiorari denied, 525 U.S. 943 (1998).
12. *Baker v. State of Vermont*, 744 A. 2d 864 (Sup. Ct. Vt. 1999).

SUSAN ESTRICH: *The Politics of Abortion*

1. 410 U.S. 113 (1973).
2. 492 U.S. 490 (1989).
3. 505 U.S. 833 (1992).
4. *Stenberg v. Carhart*, 530 U.S. 914 (2000).

HERMAN SCHWARTZ: *The States' Rights Assault on Federal Authority*

1. *Hammer v. Dagenhart*, 247 U.S. 251 (1918); *Bailey v. Drexel Furniture Company*, 259 U.S. 20 (1922).
2. *United States v. Butler*, 297 U.S. 1 (1936); *Carter v. Carter Coal Company*, 298 U.S. 238 (1936).
3. *Wickard v. Filburn*, 317 U.S. 111 (1942).
4. George Lardner, Jr., and Saundra Saperstein, "A Chief Justice–Designate with Big Ambitions Even as a Boy, Rehnquist Hoped to Change the Government," *Washington Post*, July 6, 1986, p. 8, available at 1986 WC 2035528. See also Richard Kluger, *Simple Justice: The History of* Brown v. Board of Education *and Black America's Struggle for Equality* (New York, 1975), pp. 605–09.
5. *National League of Cities v. Usery*, 426 U.S. 833 (1976).
6. *Garcia v. San Antonio Metropolitan Transit Authority*, 469 U.S. 528 (1985).
7. 415 U.S. 651 (1974).
8. *Atascadero State Hospital v. Scanlon*, 473 U.S. 234 (1985).
9. 505 U.S. 144 (1992).

10. *Printz v. United States*, 521 U.S. 898 (1997).

11. 514 U.S. 549 (1995).

12. Congress promptly amended the law to reflect the fact that most guns move in interstate commerce, and the amended law has not been challenged. See Seth P. Waxman, "Symposium: Shifting the Balance of Power? The Supreme Court, Federalism and State Sovereign Immunity." Foreword: "Does the Solicitor General Matter?" *Stanford Law Review* 53 (2001): 1125.

13. *United States v. Morrison*, 529 U.S. 598 (2000).

14. *Seminole Tribe of Florida v. Florida*, 517 U.S. 44 (1996); *Alden v. Maine*, 527 U.S. 706 (1999); *College Savings Bank v. Florida*, 527 U.S. 666 (1999).

15. *Seminole Tribe*, 517 U.S. at 57.

16. *Ex parte Young*, 209 U.S. 123 (1908).

17. *Seminole Tribe*, 517 U.S. at 76.

18. *Westside Mothers v. Haveman*, 133 F. Supp. 2d 549 (E.D. Mich. 2001), *reversed*, 289 F. 3d 852 (6th Cir. 2002); *Joseph A. ex rel Wolfe v. Ingram*, 262 F. 3d 1113 (10th Cir. 2001).

19. 2002 U.S. Lexis 3794 (May 28, 2002).

20. *Employment Division v. Smith*, 494 U.S. 872 (1990) *City of Boerne v. Flores*, 521 U.S. 507 (1997).

21. *Kimel v. Florida Board of Regents*, 528 U.S. 62 (2000); *Morrison*, 529 U.S. at 620; *Board of Trustees v. Garrett*, 531 U.S. 356 (2001).

22. *U.S. Term Limits, Inc. v. Thornton*, 514 U.S. 779 (1995); *Reno v. Condon*, 528 U.S. 141 (2000).

23. *Gregory v. Ashcroft*, 501 U.S. 452, 458, 1991.

24. *Id.* at 501 U.S. at 456.

25. Edward L. Rubin, "Puppy Federalism and the Blessings of America," *Annals*, March 2001, p. 37. See also Herman Schwartz, "The Supreme Court's Federalism: Fig Leaf for Conservatives," *Annals*, March 2001, p. 119.

26. Harold Hyman, *A More Perfect Union: The Impact of the Civil War and Reconstruction on the Constitution* (New York, 1973), p. 12, n. 18. See, e.g., *Slochower v. Board of Education*, 350 U.S. 551 (1956); *Stuyvesant Town Corporation v. United States*, 346 U.S. 864 (1953).

27. Stephen Labaton, "States Seek to Counter U.S. Deregulation," *New York Times*, Jan. 13, 2002, sect. 1, p. 22.

28. "State Legislators Mix Public and Private Business," *New York Times*, May 21, 2001, p. A26.

29. Sheryll D. Cashin, "Federalism, Welfare Reform and the Minority Poor: Accounting for the Tyranny of State Majorities," *Columbia Law Review* 99 (1999): 552–53, n. 6.

30. Editorial, "Turning Away the Needy," *New York Times*, July 31, 2000, p. A18.

31. Nina Bernstein, "Bingo, Blood and Burial Plots in the Quest for Food Stamps," *New York Times*, Aug. 13, 2000, p. A1.

32. Despite the urgency of the terrorism threat, in October and November 2001, Attorney General John Ashcroft decided, despite strongly supported legislation in Oregon, California, and elsewhere, to go after doctors who assist terminally ill pa-

tients to die or who prescribe marijuana for medical reasons. See Sam Howe Verhovek, "U.S. Acts to Stop Assisted Suicides," *New York Times*, Nov. 7, 2001, p. A1.

33. *Westside Mothers*, 133 F. Supp. 2d at 562; *Joseph A.*, 262 F. 3d at 1123.

34. For example, even in the immediate aftermath of the World Trade Center tragedy, conservative Republicans in the House of Representatives and President Bush opposed federalizing airport security because it would create a federal entity, despite the obvious and continuing failures of private security arrangements. See Lizette Alvarez, "A Nation Challenged: Airport Security; Bush Seeking House Allies on Airport Security Plan," *New York Times*, Nov. 1, 2001, p. B1.

DAVID C. VLADECK and ALAN B. MORRISON: *The Roles, Rights, and Responsibilities of the Executive Branch*

1. *Department of Justice v. Reporters Committee for Freedom of the Press*, 489 U.S. 749 (1989).
2. *Department of State v. Ray*, 502 U.S. 164 (1991).
3. *Department of the Interior v. Klamath Water Users Protective Association*, 532 U.S. 1 (2001).
4. *Lujan v. National Wildlife Federation*, 497 U.S. 871 (1990); *Lujan v. Defenders of Wildlife*, 504 U.S. 555 (1992).
5. *Steel Company v. Citizens for a Better Environment*, 523 U.S. 83 (1998).
6. *Friends of the Earth, Inc. v. Laidlaw Environmental Services (TOC), Inc.*, 528 U.S. 167 (2000).
7. *Ohio Forestry Association, Inc. v. Sierra Club*, 523 U.S. 726 (1998).
8. *Chevron, U.S.A., Inc. v. Natural Resources Defense Council, Inc.*, 467 U.S. 837 (1984).
9. See *United States v. Mead Corporation*, 533 U.S. 218, 231, at nn. 12 and 13 and accompanying text (2001).
10. *Christensen v. Harris County*, 529 U.S. 576 (2000).
11. 533 U.S. 218.
12. *FDA v. Brown & Williamson Tobacco Corporation*, 529 U.S. 120 (2000).
13. *Whitman v. American Trucking Associations*, 531 U.S. 457 (2001).
14. *INS v. Chadha*, 462 U.S. 919 (1983); *Bowsher v. Synar*, 478 U.S. 714 (1986).
15. *Morrison v. Olson*, 487 U.S. 654 (1988). The "Morrison" in this case was Alexia Morrison, independent counsel, not Alan B. Morrison, coauthor of this chapter.
16. *Raines v. Byrd*, 521 U.S. 811 (1997).
17. *Clinton v. City of New York*, 524 U.S. 417 (1998).
18. *Lorillard Tobacco Company v. Reilly*, 532 U.S. 956 (2001).
19. *Buckman Company v. Plaintiffs' Legal Committee*, 531 U.S. 341 (2001).
20. *Geier v. American Honda Motor Corporation*, 529 U.S. 861 (2000).

JAMES SALZMAN: *Environmental Law*

1. Richard J. Lazarus, "Restoring What's Environmental about Environmental Law in the Supreme Court," *UCLA Law Review* 47 (2000): 737.
2. Edwin Kneedler, "It's Not about the Environment Anymore," *Environmental Forum* 17 (2000): 46.

3. 405 U.S. 727 (1972).

4. *Lujan v. National Wildlife Federation*, 497 U.S. 871 (1990); *Lujan v. Defenders of Wildlife*, 504 U.S. 555 (1992).

5. 523 U.S. 83 (1998).

6. 528 U.S. 167 (2000).

7. *Id*. at 204–05, 209.

8. 505 U.S. 1003 (1992). See also *Palazzolo v. Rhode Island*, 533 U.S. 606 (2001) (holding that "post-enactment purchasers," those who acquire title after the effective date of a state-imposed land-use restriction, may still recover under *Lucas*).

9. 514 U.S. 549 (1995).

10. 529 U.S. 598 (2000).

11. *Id*. at 599.

12. Michael J. Gerhardt, "Federal Environmental Regulation in a Post-*Lopez* World: Some Questions and Answers," *Environmental Law Reporter* 30 (2000): 10980.

13. In dissenting from the denial of certiorari, Justice Thomas wrote that "the Corps' basis for jurisdiction rests entirely on the actual or potential presence of migratory birds on petitioner's land. In light of *Lopez*, I have serious doubts about the propriety of the Corps' assertion of jurisdiction over petitioner's land in this case" (*Cargill, Inc. v. United States*, 516 U.S. 955, 958 [1995]).

14. 531 U.S. 159 (2001).

15. 474 U.S. 121 (1985).

16. 531 U.S. 159, 160–61 (2001).

17. *Id*. at 172–73.

18. Lazarus, "Restoring What's Environmental," p. 764, n. 1.

ANDREW J. IMPARATO: *The "Miserly" Approach to Disability Rights*

1. 42 U.S.C. Sect. 12101(a)(8).

2. *Equality of Opportunity: The Making of the Americans with Disabilities Act* (Washington, D.C.: National Council on Disability, 1997), appendix G.

3. *Cleburne v. Cleburne Living Center*, 473 U.S. 432 (1985).

4. *Id*. at 473, quoting *New York Trust Company v. Eisner*, 256 U.S. 345, 349 (1921) (Holmes, J.).

5. *Id*.

6. *Id*. at 451 (Stevens, J., concurring).

7. *Id*. at 455.

8. *Id*. at 467.

9. 42 U.S.C. Sect. 12101(a)(7), (a)(2), (a)(7).

10. *Heller v. Doe*, 509 U.S. 312, 335 (1993) (Blackmun J., dissenting). Internal citations omitted.

11. *Id*. at 319, citing *FCC v. Beach Communications, Inc.*, 508 U.S. 307, 314–15 (1993).

12. *Id*. at 335 (Souter, J., dissenting).

13. *Id*. at 348.

14. *Board of Trustees of University of Alabama v. Garrett*, 121 Sup. Ct. 955 (2001). Patricia

Garrett, a nurse who was treated for breast cancer, alleged that she was demoted by the University of Alabama Hospital in Birmingham because of her cancer. The other employee whose suit was consolidated with Garrett's, Milton Ash, was a security officer with the Alabama Department of Youth Services. Ash, who had chronic asthma, challenged his employer's denial of a request to modify his duties to minimize his exposure to carbon monoxide and cigarette smoke. Ash also challenged his employer's denial of a reassignment to a daytime shift to accommodate his sleep apnea. Alabama successfully moved for summary judgment in both cases in the trial court on the ground that the ADA exceeded Congress's authority to abrogate the state's Eleventh Amendment immunity to these types of suits. See 989 F. Supp. 1409, 1410 (N.D. Ala. 1998). After the cases were consolidated on appeal, the Eleventh Circuit Court of Appeals reversed, holding that the ADA validly abrogates the state's Eleventh Amendment immunity. See 193 F. 3d 1426, 1433 (C.A. 11 1998).

15. *Id.* at 964.

16. *Id.* at 967–68.

17. See, e.g., *id.* at 972 (Breyer, J., dissenting).

18. *Id.* at 972–73. Emphasis in original.

19. *Sutton v. United Airlines*, 527 U.S. 471 (1999). See also *Murphy v. United Parcel Service, Inc.*, 527 U.S. 516 (1999), and *Albertson's, Inc. v. Kirkingburg*, 527 U.S. 555 (1999). *Sutton* involved twin sisters with severe myopia fully correctable with eyeglasses who challenged their rejection for positions as commercial airline pilots. *Murphy* involved a UPS mechanic with high blood pressure that was responsive to medication. *Kirkingburg* involved a truck driver with monocular vision. In both *Murphy* and *Kirkingburg*, plaintiffs challenged their terminations by alleging discrimination on the basis of disability.

20. *Toyota v. Williams*, 534 U.S. 184 (2002).

21. *Tcherepnin v. Knight*, 389 U.S. 332, 336 (1967), quoted by Justice Stevens in his dissenting opinion in *Sutton*, 527 U.S. at 504. The narrow approach adopted in the *Sutton* trilogy can be contrasted with a broader approach applied in a 1998 case called *Bragdon v. Abbott*, 524 U.S. 624. In that case, with Justice Kennedy writing for the majority, the Court ruled that a dental patient with asymptomatic HIV infection was covered by the ADA because she was limited in the major life activity of reproduction. Deferring to the opinions of the administrative enforcement agencies and court interpretations of similar language defining disability under the Rehabilitation Act, the *Bragdon* Court reasoned that Congress clearly intended that asymptomatic HIV-positive individuals be covered by the ADA. Just one year after *Bragdon*, the Court felt free to disregard similar interpretations and precedents that would have weighed in support of the plaintiffs in the *Sutton* trilogy. See *Chevron, U.S.A., Inc. v. Echazabal*, 536 U.S. 122 Sup. Ct. 2045 (June 10, 2002) (discussed below).

22. 42 U.S.C. Sect. 12102(2).

23. See *Sutton*, 527 U.S. at 495–96 (Stevens, J., dissenting).

24. 42 U.S.C. Sect. 12101(b)(1).

25. *Sutton*, 527 U.S. at 485.

26. 42 U.S.C. Sect. 423(d)(1)(A).

27. See *Cleveland v. Policy Management Systems Corporation*, 526 U.S. 795 at 801 (Breyer, J., noting for a unanimous Court that the "Social Security Act and the ADA both help individuals with disabilities, but in different ways").

28. See *Sutton*, 527 U.S. at 503–04.

29. *Id.* at 504. The equal opportunity "door" can be contrasted with other "doors" of eligibility that enable a severely disabled young person to retire at age eighteen (the Social Security Act) or enable a person to park in a specially designated space for people with mobility impairments. In the former case, there is no down side to opening the door wide. In the latter case, there are good reasons carefully to limit who gets in the door.

30. *Id.* at 509–10, citing 480 U.S. 273 (1987), involving a teacher with tuberculosis who challenged discriminatory termination.

31. *Id.* at 510, 512.

32. *Id.* at 495.

33. For an analysis of lower court decisions in the aftermath of *Sutton*, see Chai Feldblum, "Honey, They Shrunk Our Law: Ways the Courts Have Systematically Denied the Civil Rights of Persons Intended to Be Protected by the ADA," covering cases through the year 2000, available at www.aapd-dc.org.

34. 534 U.S. 184 (2002).

35. *Id.*, slip op. at 13.

36. *Id.*, slip op. at 9–17.

37. In a newspaper article published shortly after the decision, Congressman Steny Hoyer, who managed passage of the bill in the House, criticized the decision for misconstruing what Congress had actually intended: "43 million people . . . seemed like a lot and we thought that showed we intended the law to be broad rather than narrow" ("Not Exactly What We Intended, Justice O'Connor," *Washington Post*, Jan. 20, 2002, pp. B1, B5.)

38. 42 U.S.C. Sect. 12101(a)(2), (a)(3).

39. *Heller*, 509 U.S. at 321–26.

40. *Id.* at 326, 327. "At English common law there was a 'marked distinction' in the treatment accorded 'idiots' (the mentally retarded) and 'lunatics' (the mentally ill)," the Court observed, citing F. Pollock and F. Maitland, *The History of English Law* (Boston, 1909), vol. 1, p. 481.

41. 274 U.S. 200, 207 (1927) (Holmes, J.).

42. *Heller*, 509 U.S. at 346, n. 6 (Souter, J., dissenting, citing S. Herr, *Rights and Advocacy for Retarded People* [Lexington, MA, 1983], p. 9.)

43. *Cleburne*, 473 U.S. at 461–62.

44. *Id.* at 464, 466, comparing *Plessy v. Ferguson*, 163 U.S. 537 (1896), with *Brown v. Board of Education*, 347 U.S. 483 (1954).

45. 527 U.S. 581 (1999).

46. *Id.* at 587.

47. *Id.* at 594; 595, citing 138 F. 3d at 902; 595, citing 138 F. 3d at 905.

48. Only Justice Stevens, filing a separate concurrence, supported the analysis of the Eleventh Circuit, 527 U.S. at 607–08.
49. *Id.* at 597.
50. *Id.* at 602, 605–06.
51. 42 U.S.C. Sect. 12101(b)(1).
52. 527 U.S. at 608–10 (Kennedy, J., concurring).
53. *Id.* at 625 (Thomas, J., dissenting).
54. 122 Sup. Ct. 1516 (2002).
55. 122 Sup. Ct. 2045 (2002).
56. *PGA Tour, Inc. v. Martin,* 121 Sup. Ct. 1879 (2001), allowing Casey Martin to use a golf cart would not fundamentally alter the tournament.
57. For a harbinger of narrow interpretations of Congress's powers under the Spending Clause, see *Barnes v. Gorman,* 536 U.S. 122 Sup. Ct. 2097 (June 17, 2002) (punitive damages not available to injured parties suing under Title II of the ADA and Sect. 504 of the Rehabilitation Act.)

ELEANOR M. FOX: *Antitrust and Business Power*

1. *Congressional Record* 2460 (1890).
2. *Address by the President on Trusts and Monopolies before the Joint Session of Congress (Jan. 20, 1914),* 63d Cong., 2d sess. 1914, H. Doc. 625, 5.
3. 95 *Congressional Record* 11486 (1949).
4. *Brown Shoe Company v. United States,* 370 U.S. 294 (1962).
5. Oliver Wendell Holmes, *The Common Law* (1881), p. 96. The Sherman Act itself he famously called "economic humbug."
6. 485 U.S. 717 (1988).
7. 509 U.S. 209 (1993).
8. 526 U.S. 756 (1999).
9. Brief of Microsoft Corporation on appeal to D.C. Circuit, Nov. 27, 2000, at 16.
10. *United States v. Microsoft Corporation,* 253 F. 3d 34 (D.C. Cir.), certiorari denied, 122 Sup. Ct. 350 (2001).

LAWRENCE E. MITCHELL: *No Business like No Business*

1. William L. Cary, Federalism and Corporate Law: Reflections Upon Delaware 83 Yale L. J. 663 (1974). That abrogation was again affirmed in an article by three sitting Delaware judges, reported in *The New York Times* on June 15, 2001, in which they suggested that managers should be more free to manage than they are, an argument that would, from a doctrinal perspective, diminish fiduciary obligations. I actually agree with this conclusion, although with a different implementation that retains supporting duties. See Lawrence E. Mitchell, *Corporate Irresponsibility: America's Newest Export* (New Haven, 2002).
2. Delaware's primacy is aided by a rule of law known as the internal affairs doctrine, which holds that the law of the state of incorporation governs the relation-

ships among directors, officers, and stockholders, no matter where the corporation actually does its business and no matter where the case is adjudicated. Thus a corporation incorporated in Delaware with offices and facilities in New York, Tennessee, Texas, California, Illinois, London, Hong Kong, and Singapore will be governed by Delaware law, no matter which court (at least in the United States) hears the case and even though it does no business in Delaware.

3. The debate over Cary's views is principally about whether these limitations have been economically efficient and therefore presumably beneficial. Nobody seriously disputes the proposition that the duties of directors and officers in Delaware corporations are far from rigorous.

4. *Blue Chip Stamps v. Manor Drug Stores*, 421 U.S. 723 (1975). In light of what I shall have to say about the Rehnquist Court I do want to make it clear that for Powell, who understood perfectly well what he was doing as a policy matter, the statutory language was indeed the starting point and not, as it is for the current Court, the whole point.

5. 521 U.S. 642 (1997).

6. It's not clear from the opinion whether Grand Met could have overridden this permission by objecting—it seems that O'Hagan's primary breach was to Dorsey & Whitney. At the very least, Grand Met could have fired the firm and sought an injunction against O'Hagan's using the information.

7. Justice Thomas's dissent (joined by Rehnquist), in one of the few bright lights (from a policy perspective) of this Court's securities jurisprudence, understands the way the Court's stretch of the "in connection with" requirement creates an incoherent result.

8. 513 U.S. 561 (1995).

9. The statute has been renumbered since this decision. I adhere to the numbering in use at the time of the case.

10. Underlying this approach is also the Court's desire to cut back dramatically on the scope of the securities laws. Even when it doesn't succeed (see *O'Hagan*), there nonetheless seems to be a Court-side insistence on technical manipulation, despite the fact that the opinions are also laden with policy talk with respect to the effect of the interpretation at issue. The policy talk is almost always dicta, as any law student can see, and, as in *Gustafson*, frequently devoid of any meaningful understanding of markets or business. The real action lies within the statute.

11. Justice Thomas completely eschews policy or any mention of the practices and operations of the secondary markets in a dissenting opinion that never for a moment strays beyond the techniques of statutory interpretation, making it no better in terms of business policy even though reaching what I believe to be the right result.

12. 501 U.S. 350 (1991).

13. 511 U.S. 164 (1994).

14. 501 U.S. 1083 (1991).

15. 396 U.S. 375 (1970). *Mills* was arguably distinguishable from *Virginia Bankshares* in that in the former case, the controlling stockholder held over a majority of the stock but two-thirds of the stockholders were required to approve the merger, a fact that required that at least some of the minority votes be counted.

Contributors

STEPHEN BRIGHT has been the Director of the Southern Center for Human Rights in Atlanta since 1982, and teaches courses on the death penalty and criminal law at the Harvard and Yale Law Schools.

SUSAN ESTRICH was the first woman president of the Harvard Law Review and the first woman to run a Presidential campaign. Formerly a tenured professor of law at Harvard, she is currently the Robert Kingsley Professor of Law and Political Science at the University of Southern California, a commentator for Fox News, and the author of five books, including *Sex & Power* (2000). She graduated from Wellesley College and Harvard Law School.

CHAI FELDBLUM teaches at the Georgetown University Law Center. A former law clerk to Justice Harry Blackmun, she has been legal counsel to the National Gay and Lesbian Task Force and President of the Disability Rights Counsel.

ELEANOR M. FOX is the Walter J. Derenberg Professor of Trade Regulation at New York University School of Law, where she teaches and writes on antitrust law, European Union law, and issues of globalization.

WILLIAM E. HELLERSTEIN is a professor of law at Brooklyn Law School and director of the Brooklyn Law School Second Look Program Clinic. He teaches constitutional law, criminal procedure, and civil rights law. He was the attorney-in-charge of the Criminal Appeals Bureau of the New York Legal Aid Society for seventeen years and is a former staff attorney with the United States Commission on Civil Rights. He has written and lectured extensively on the rights of criminal defendants and the rights of prisoners.

ANDREW J. IMPARATO is the president and chief executive officer of the American Association of People with Disabilities (AAPD), a national membership organization based in Washington, D.C. AAPD advocates for public policies that promote the goals of the Americans with Disabilities Act. Prior to joining AAPD, Imparato worked as an attorney with the National Council on Disability, the U.S. Equal Employment Opportunity Commission, the U.S. Senate Subcommittee on Disability Policy, and the Disability Law Center in Boston, Massachusetts. He acknowledges the assistance of Jacqueline Okun, American University Law School, Class of 2002, and Adam Jed, Yale University, Class of 2002.

JOHN P. MACKENZIE covered the Supreme Court for *The Washington Post* from 1965 to 1977 and wrote editorials for *The New York Times* from 1977 to 1997. He is the author of *The Appearance of Justice* (1974).

LAWRENCE E. MITCHELL is John Theodore Fey Research Professor of Law at The George Washington University, where he is also Founding Director of the Sloan Program for the Study of Business in Society and the International Institute for Corporate Governance and Accountability. He is the author of numerous scholarly articles on corporate governance and responsibility, a casebook on corporate finance, and *Stacked Deck: A Story of Selfishness in America* (1998) and *Corporate Irresponsibility: America's Newest Export* (2001).

ALAN B. MORRISON founded the Public Citizen Litigation Group with Ralph Nader in 1972. In addition to the more than forty cases that he and his colleagues have argued in the Supreme Court (winning more than 60 percent), they also run a project in which they help several dozen lawyers each year, most with limited Supreme Court experience, brief and argue their cases. Mr. Morrison is currently teaching at Stanford Law School, and in the past has taught at Harvard, New York University, Tulane University, and University of Hawaii Law Schools.

CHARLES J. OGLETREE, JR., is the Jesse Climenko Professor of Law at Harvard Law School, where he has taught for the past eighteen years. Professor Ogletree has appeared as the moderator of many public television programs and as a commentator on national television and public radio information shows. He is the author and co-author of numerous articles and books on a wide variety of issues concerning the criminal justice system.

JAMIN B. RASKIN is a professor of constitutional law at American University's Washington College of Law and founder of its Marshall-Brennan Fellowship Program, which sends law students into public high schools to teach a course in constitutional literacy. He is the author of *We the Students* (2000) and the forthcoming, *Overruling Democracy: The Supreme Court Versus the American People* (Routledge 2003). Raskin is a former assistant attorney general of Massachusetts and has written widely about the First Amendment.

NORMAN REDLICH is dean emeritus and Judge Edward Weinfeld Professor of Law Emeritus at New York University Law School. He is chair of the American Jewish Congress's Governing Council, co-chair of the American Jewish Congress's Commission on Law and Social Action, and in 2002 he received the Lifetime Achievement Award from the Lawyers' Committee for Civil Rights Under Law. Dean Redlich acknowledges the assistance of Chi T. Steve Kwok, class of 2002, Yale Law School.

JAMES SALZMAN is a professor of law at American University's Washington College of Law. He has lectured on environmental law and policy in the Americas, Europe, Asia, Australia, and Africa and has served as a visiting professor at Harvard and Stanford Law Schools.

HERMAN SCHWARTZ is a professor of law at American University's Washington College of Law. He is a civil rights and civil liberties activist who has written extensively on constitutional law and human rights in the United States and abroad, and has served in both federal and state government. His books include *Packing the Courts: The Conservative Campaign to Rewrite the Constitution* (1988) and *The Struggle for Constitutional Justice in Post-Communist Europe* (2000) and he is the editor of *The Burger Years: Rights and Wrongs of the Supreme Court, 1969–1986* (1987). He lives in Washington, D.C.

WILLIAM L. TAYLOR is a Washington, D.C., lawyer who has been a civil rights advocate for more than four decades. He was a staff lawyer for Thurgood Marshall at the NAACP Legal Defense Fund in the 1950s and general counsel and staff director for the U.S. Commission on Civil Rights in the 1960s. He is an adjunct professor at the Georgetown Law School and is president of the Leadership Conference Education Fund. He has filed briefs in the Supreme Court in the Warren, Burger, and Rehnquist eras.

DAVID C. VLADECK teaches at Georgetown University Law Center. He is counsel to Public Citizen Litigation Group, where he, and his coauthor Alan B. Morrison, litigated a number of the constitutional and administrative law cases discussed in their chapter.

TOM WICKER is a former columnist for *The New York Times* and is the author of many essays and more than 15 books, including *Dwight D. Eisenhower* (2002) and *JFK and LBJ: The Influence of Personality upon Politics* (1991). He has received numerous awards for journalism and literature, and holds several honorary degrees.

Index